Civil
Service
Reform
in
Brazil: *Principles versus Practice*

LATIN AMERICAN MONOGRAPHS, No. 13
INSTITUTE OF LATIN AMERICAN STUDIES
THE UNIVERSITY OF TEXAS

Civil Service Reform in Brazil

Principles versus Practice

by LAWRENCE S. GRAHAM

Published for the Institute of Latin American Studies by the

UNIVERSITY OF TEXAS PRESS

AUSTIN

Library of Congress Catalog Card No. 68-63543

Copyright © 1968 by Lawrence S. Graham

ISBN 978-0-292-76896-3

www.utpress.utexas.edu/index.php/rp-form

First paperback printing, 2014

For Jane

ACKNOWLEDGMENTS

For assistance in the preparation of this book I am indebted to Professor Gladys M. Kammerer, who devoted many hours to reading and commenting on the original dissertation, and to Professors Harry Kantor and Harry W. Hutchinson, all of the University of Florida. I would also like to thank a number of people in Rio de Janeiro: Professor Diogo Lordello de Mello, director of research at the Fundação Getúlio Vargas, and Professors Edward J. Jones, Jr., Ivan L. Richardson, and David Mars, who were members of the University of Southern California/AID mission in public administration at the Fundação Getúlio Vargas during the period research was conducted in Brazil (1964–1965). My gratitude is likewise extended to Arminda de Campos and Gil Vicente Soares, students in the Brazilian School of Public Administration (EBAP), and Gary Mounce, a graduate student at The University of Texas, who served as research assistants. For the mechanics of preparing this manuscript I want to acknowledge the assistance of Mrs. Margaret McGrade, Mrs. Barbara Persenaire, and Mrs. Kay Hancock. Finally I would like to express my appreciation to the Department of Health, Education, and Welfare for a grant received under the National Defense Education Act, which made field work possible, and to The University of Texas Research Institute for a grant to cover preparation of the book manuscript.

L.S.G.

Austin, Texas

CONTENTS

LIST OF TABLES

**Civil
Service
Reform
in
Brazil:** *Principles versus Practice*

Introduction

Recently a trend has developed within public administration to establish a comparative basis for generalization within the discipline and to place the field of comparative administration within the wider context of comparative political studies. This is, in part, a reflection of a significant movement within the social sciences as a whole which looks toward an integrative approach to man and the environment in which he lives. For some time students of public administration have shown a growing awareness of the inadequacy of traditional approaches and have expressed a need to reach into political science and the other social sciences for new tools and concepts.

The traditional approach has been judged inadequate for several reasons. For the most part public administration, as the discipline has developed in the United States, has been too culture-bound by American values and standards, in particular, and Western European ones, in general. Legalism and formalism have characterized traditional studies, to the neglect of the informal and of the overall political, social, economic, and cultural context. The approach has been descriptive and prescriptive rather than analytic and comparative and has failed to provide useful classifications and indicators. Previous categories have been inadequate—almost totally normative and confusing —and few, if any, concepts or techniques for determining similarities or differences among administrative systems have been produced. Consequently, empirical studies, when they have appeared, have usually focused attention on the unique and thus have been incapable of generalization.

Brazil is an important chapter in the history of attempts to reform administrative systems outside the United States and Western Europe through the use of traditional concepts and techniques. This experience in administration is of value not only for Brazil's sister republics in the Caribbean and in Central and South America, but also for other countries where similar developmental problems and dynamic change have awakened interest in civil service reform.

For some thirty-five years Brazilian leaders in the public administration field have been trying to initiate fundamental change in their nation's administrative system by imposing concepts and techniques borrowed from American experience. They have attempted to create a "modern" public personnel system which will replace favoritism and patronage with rational recruitment practices and they have devoted considerable time and effort toward putting into practice ideas and techniques borrowed from the economy and efficiency movement in the United States. But, today, a look at the functional side of the Brazilian system shows that, in spite of many institutional changes and much civil service legislation, very little has been accomplished in the way of economy and efficiency, the two guiding lights of the administrative reform movement.

Why has it been so difficult to attain these objectives? Are these goals valid in the Brazilian context? Have they helped Brazil move toward the broader goal of becoming a "modern" nation-state? These questions necessarily lead into the political arena. Hence, it is relevant to ask: Has the Brazilian political structure changed in the last thirty-five years? If so, what effects have these changes had on the federal civil service? Are Brazilian patronage problems unique? Does comparative analysis enhance our understanding of the difficulties of civil service reform in Brazil? These are basic questions which must be answered in order to come to grips with the gap between the principles preached and the practices observed in Brazilian administration.

In answering these questions, it is assumed that the separation of politics and administration is impossible in the Brazilian setting. It is further assumed that conflicting value systems must be considered in order to understand political conflict, whether within the context of an administrative system or not. This especially applies to the attempts at administrative reform since 1936. Whether one examines the creation of an agency of general administration to oversee the administrative system—the Administrative Department of the Public Service (Departamento Administrativo do Serviço Público—DASP) —or the efforts to institute merit system practices, one is certain to encounter a mixture of traditional Brazilian values with values coming from American administrative reform experience and from the Weberian approach to bureaucracy.

The purpose of this study is to analyze the Brazilian experience with reform of its federal civil service and to demonstrate the interrelationships between the ideas and concepts on which the reform movement has been based and the political context within which the federal civil service has operated. Such an approach involves three levels of analysis. First, values existing in Brazilian society at large will be defined in order to establish the values on which Brazil's political institutions are based and to single out those values which have been inherent in the administrative reform movement. Secondly, material substantially confined to the Brazilian experience will be considered. In this respect, it is a study of the unique, for the basic data have been gathered within a single country. This material, however, gains significance only if placed in a larger context. Thus, the final level entails both intra- and cross-cultural comparisons.

While earlier experience in Brazilian public administration is relevant and an historical perspective is essential to an understanding of the changing character of the civil service, emphasis will fall on the years between 1945 and 1964. This era was selected because it offers a view of the interaction between administration and politics within the context of an open system of government and it marks a particularly crucial phase in the course of Brazilian political development, a phase with a definite beginning and end. Since April, 1964, the country has returned to a closed system of government in which troublesome political forces have been excluded from politics, a congress subservient to the executive has been insured, and the development of mass-based politics has been halted.

CHAPTER I

The Conceptual Framework

Before data relevant to the Brazilian reform experience can be applied to the broad questions raised in the Introduction, further consideration of the questions themselves, in terms of relationships between key factors, is required. These relationships will be established through a series of primary and secondary propositions stating hypothetical relationships between two or more variables. The propositions, which ultimately will be evaluated to judge whether they can be supported by empirical evidence, serve as a guide for the ordering of acquired data.

To begin with, three independent variables, or factors, were selected to discover their possible relationship with a dependent variable (the object of this study): the behavior of the Brazilian federal civil service system. These variables are: (1) the political understructure on which the civil service is based; (2) the use of the norms governing administrative behavior which conflict with the demands of the social and political systems; and (3) the application of the techniques of scientific management without adequate attention to the functional requirements of the existing administrative system and without sufficient consideration for the human elements concerned.

Stated as a central hypothesis, these variables are contained in the following proposition: The attempt to reform the Brazilian federal civil service through the use of American-style public personnel policies has led to the creation of an administrative system, characterized by a high degree of formalism, in which there is considerable discrepancy between norms and reality. This formalism is a consequence of the political understructure on which the civil service is based, of the use of norms governing administrative behavior which conflict with the demands of the social and political systems, and of the application of the techniques of scientific management without adequate attention to the functional requirements of the existing administrative system and without sufficient consideration for the human elements concerned. An important additional variable (considered an intervening variable because it affects the relationship between the independent variables and the object of the study) is the size of the civilian bureaucracy.

The discrepancy between norms and reality exists at several levels and cannot be reduced to a simple dichotomy. First, a substantial gap is found between the formal administrative apparatus, as expressed in legal norms and laws, and the way the human elements involved behave. On the one hand, a value commitment to a merit system and to a neutral civil service is contained in the movement for administrative reform and subsequent legislation; on the other hand, the continuance of a functioning patronage system undercuts the legal requirements imposed. The degree of this divergence between formal institutions and human behavior, however, depends on whether the comparison of administrative performance is among federal agencies and ministries; between federal, state, and local institutions; or according to regions of the country. Thus one cannot correctly refer only to the contrast between the traditional administrative systems operating in Brazil and the objectives of modernizing them, for variations in political and administrative development differ greatly from one extreme of the country to the other and the institution of patronage operates in many ways.

The scope of this study is limited to the federal civil service. By and large, contrasts existing among the state administrative systems are excluded, although one probably can observe a developmental continuum in action at the state level, extending from the administrative system functioning in São Paulo to the traditional administrative systems operating in the Northeast. Brazilian bureaucracy, at both the national and regional levels, is large and complex and has not yet been adequately analyzed. For this reason, it is difficult at this stage to create a proper image of the total administrative system or systems in operation in Brazil; yet such an attempt must be made if change in contemporary administrative practices is to be introduced and made to function. Probably much of the difficulty in creating a centralized, effective, coordinated national administrative system is due precisely to this absence of an understanding of the way in which Brazilian administration has operated in its sociopolitical context. In this respect, Brazilian administration reflects the pluralistic, overlapping, and heterogeneous character of Brazilian social and political institutions. This is particularly true of developments between 1945 and 1964, when, as the bureaucracy continued to grow in size and complexity, the federal administrative structure became diffuse and uncontrollable through the decentralization of politics; the emergence of multiple, competing parties of a factional character, divided internally along regional lines; and the increase in demands for services from the central government as the Brazilian economy reached the take-off stage.[1] The major characteristic of this period is the failure to develop an open administrative system responsive and responsible to the political system.

The following more careful examination of the three independent variables previously set forth is the source of a series of secondary propositions. Of the three independent variables, the first is by far the most complex and the most important in understanding Brazilian reform experience since it directs attention to the political system within which public administration functions. From this variable—the nature of the political understructure—three sets of propositions can be developed.

The first set is based on this initial proposition: In instituting any program of administrative reform in a transitional society, the presence of a strong central government which insures political stability is more important than the style of government, i.e., whether it is a dictatorship or a democracy.[2] This statement, in turn, leads to two additional propositions. First, the success in instituting merit system practices under the first Vargas government is to be explained in part by the presence of a strong central government committed to the reform of the federal civil service, initially through the Federal Civil Service Council and later through the DASP. (In looking at the events since 1945 it is important to remember that merit system practices in the federal civil service as a whole were first instituted during the ambiguous phase of semidictatorship prevailing before the establishment of the Estado Novo.) The second subproposition states that the post-1945 problems of both expanding and defending a rationalized public personnel system are explained in part by the excessive decentralization of authority (formal power) and control (informal

---

[1] The concept "take-off stage" is based on W. W. Rostow, *The Stages of Economic Growth: A Non-Communist Manifesto*. Rostow states, "It is possible to identify all societies, in their economic dimensions, as lying within one of five categories: the traditional society, the preconditions for take-off, the take-off, the drive to maturity, and the age of high mass-consumption" (p. 4). According to his framework, Brazil has entered the take-off stage of economic growth (p. 127).

[2] This variable is based on Arthur S. Banks and Robert B. Textor, *A Cross-Polity Survey*, p. 112.

power)[3] and by the multiplicity of competing groups in a society undergoing fundamental change, where there is a lack of consensus on the means for resolving conflict and on the basic goals of the state. Since 1945, then, the civil service system has been based on political understructure entirely different from that of the preceding period —an understructure characterized by many regionally oriented, competing parties and by little development of national party responsibility.

The second set of propositions, explaining the nature of the political understructure, centers around the following statement: Any program of basic reform in a traditional administrative system is certain to create opposition. The way this opposition is expressed depends on the interrelation between the degree of centralization within the bureaucracy and the style of politics (the degree to which there exists an open or closed political system). This distinction does not, however, imply a dichotomization of two polar styles of politics, but rather a continuum along which various political styles can be located. The degree of participation in the political process is the criterion used here for locating political styles.

It is also hypothesized that in a centralized system of administration opposition to reform is more difficult to express because of the existence of a more effective control system capable of overriding traditional patterns and values. This control is more "effective" because major policy decisions can be made only at the top of the hierarchical structure. In contrast, in a decentralized system of administration it is easier to express opposition to reform because of the existence of numerous semi-independent administrative hierarchies, each with considerable authority for making decisions over policy and with insufficient central control over traditional patterns and values. Under a dictatorship—a closed system of government—the artificial no-conflict status of politics forces opposition to administrative reform to be internalized within both the administrative system and the external political system. In a transitional society such internalization is almost certain to result in the confusing of basic issues and problems and in the blurring of lines between traditional, elitist-oriented groups, who oppose change; liberal groups, who oppose dictatorship and desire political democracy; and revolutionary groups, who oppose the continuation of a capitalistic system and are committed to egalitarian values. However, within the framework of an open, competitive

[3] This distinction between formal and informal power is based on Fred W. Riggs, *Administration in Developing Countries: The Theory of Prismatic Society*, p. 209.

style of politics following immediately after a period of dictatorship, it becomes easier not only to isolate the forces opposed to administrative reform, but also to understand the desire of these various groups to emasculate such an organization as DASP and to undercut public personnel reforms.

It is further hypothesized that this reaction to administrative reform during the Vargas era is related to fear of the bureaucracy as a control instrument in a no-party, authoritarian system, a fear resulting from experience with such control. An important motivation of the political parties since 1945 has been their desire to make the bureaucracy responsible to the external political system. This factor is crucial to an understanding of the subsequent struggle between the legislative and executive branches over the control of patronage. In this context, spoils system practices theoretically take on a functional character and are only dysfunctional if we look at the socioeconomic pressures generated by industrialization and urbanization and the subsequent need for expanded and highly specialized public services.

The final set of propositions related to the first independent variable concern the role of DASP as an agent of the executive.[4] It is hypothesized that the close association of DASP and of the whole administrative reform movement with the Vargas dictatorship was inimical to the goals and objectives of administrative reform after 1945. Because reform was administered from the top down and was not based upon any popular movement outside the government, the entire program came to rely exclusively on the executive for its success. Consequently, once executive support in Brazil was no longer forthcoming and a preference was shown for spoils system practices, a strong reaction to administrative reform set in. This experience is the reverse of the movement for civil service reform in the United States, which began in the latter half of the nineteenth century and was based on pressures from many different quarters for an end to widespread corruption in government. That movement was but a part of a more general one to reform and to moralize the whole political process, as well as to readjust basic imbalances that had developed in the political system.[5]

[4] The importance of this element is discussed by Gilbert B. Siegel in "The Vicissitudes of Governmental Reform in Brazil: A Study of the DASP" (unpublished Ph.D. dissertation) and in "The DASP: A Study in the Deterioration of an Organization Power Base" in Robert T. Daland (ed.), *Perspectives of Brazilian Public Administration*, Vol. I, esp. p. 34.

[5] For a discussion of the American administrative reform see Dwight Waldo, *The Administrative State: A Study of the Political Theory of American Public Ad-*

From the second independent variable—the use of new norms and principles governing administrative behavior—two propositions have been developed. First, the gap between the formal requirements of the merit system and the realities of current public personnel practices is explained to a considerable extent by the irrelevance of these concepts to the functioning of the bureaucratic system. Secondly, the imposition of these newer norms and principles upon traditional values has led to conflict within the administrative system as a whole. Consequently, different individuals within the bureaucracy react in different ways. Some are committed to the new value orientation, others are committed to the traditional value orientation, and still others to both. Thus, a substantial body of intermediate or transitional individuals is attracted both to the older set of norms and principles and to the newer ones. Riggs calls these individuals "polynormative" or "normless."[6] Such a value conflict within the individual leads to his supporting the merit system verbally, while in practice he depends upon a particular person to obtain government employment for him extralegally.[7]

To test the validity of the central hypothesis and the propositions built around it, the models Riggs and Diamant have offered for the study of comparative administration will be utilized to isolate meaningful patterns in the interaction of politics and administration in Brazil.[8]

In constructing a model for the analysis of administrative systems in "developing" areas, Riggs postulates that all existing administrative systems may be evaluated by establishing what he terms a developmental continuum. At one extreme he places a "fused" model in which all structures are highly diffuse and undifferentiated. This model can be used for the analysis of administration in static agrarian societies. At the other end he places a model in which all structures are highly specific and specialized. This "diffracted" model can be used for the analysis of administration in modern industrial societies, such as those in North America and Western Europe. Between these two extremes Riggs inserts what he calls a "prismatic" model for the analysis of administration in countries attempting to break the hold

ministration, and Leonard D. White, *The Republican Era, 1869–1901: A Study in Administrative History.*

[6] Riggs, *Administration in Developing Countries,* pp. 176–177.

[7] Gilbert B. Siegel, "Administration, Values and the Merit System in Brazil," in Daland (ed.), *Perspectives of Brazilian Public Administration,* p. 10.

[8] Riggs, *Administration in Developing Countries;* Alfred Diamant, "Bureaucracy in Developmental Movement Regimes: A Bureaucratic Model for Developing Societies."

of traditional society and to modernize. These are the countries which have been termed "developing" in the framework of Almond and Coleman.[9] Here they will be referred to as "transitional."

In the "prismatic" model, Riggs hypothesizes that the contrasting patterns occurring in the "fused" and "diffracted" models interact and overlap. While agricultural and industrial societies would be concentrated to a fairly high degree around the respective polar extremes of the continuum and would show a relatively homogeneous distribution of traits, a transitional society approaching the "prismatic" model would demonstrate "a wide variation between its still predominantly traditional hinterland and its 'modernized' urbanized centers." Such a society would also show a relatively heterogeneous distribution of traits; that is, it would combine traditional, relatively fused traits with relatively diffracted ones.[10] The extent to which heterogeneity and overlapping patterns occur, is an important factor, for ". . . the more prismatic . . . a society, the greater will be the social gap between its rural and urban sectors. In both fused and diffracted societies the urban-rural discontinuity will not, presumably, be so great."[11]

In terms of public administration, these models reflect three different sets of conditions. In a "diffracted" society, one would encounter "a set of concrete structures or institutions specialized for the performance of administrative functions." In a "fused" society, one would not expect to find "any concrete structures specifically oriented toward administrative functions." In a "prismatic" society, one would encounter "certain administrative structures operating quite specifically and effectively, while in other fields or parts of the society, no such structures [would be] found."[12] As a consequence of this situation and the influence exerted on transitional countries by external models or standards,

. . . it is easier to adopt by fiat or law a formal organizational structure with a manifest administrative function than it is to institutionalize corresponding social behavior. . . . Hence, many formally administrative structures in transitional societies turn out to be mere façades, while the effective administrative work remains a latent function of older, more diffuse institutions.[13]

[9] Gabriel A. Almond and James S. Coleman (eds.), *The Politics of Developing Areas.*
[10] Riggs, *Administration in Developing Countries*, p. 29.
[11] *Ibid.*, pp. 32–33.
[12] *Ibid.*, p. 33.
[13] *Ibid.*, p. 34.

The result is formalism: a situation in which visible forms, such as prescribed rules and laws, neither represent reality nor correspond to human behavior.[14]

Diamant offers an alternative model that complements Riggs's work and can be used to offer another perspective on the Brazilian federal civil service. Since he criticizes Riggs's model for being too abstract and general, his model might be examined to see whether his attempt at building more components into a typology of political styles and economic development is relevant in the Brazilian context and whether it is of assistance in simplifying complex reality. Whereas Riggs visualizes three distinct models on a continuum against which all societies may be evaluated, Diamant conceives of political development as an on-going process in which new goals and demands are met in a flexible manner by a variety of patterns. While Riggs is concerned with the formulation of functional concepts which can be used to define relationships in transitional societies, Diamant focuses his attention on the goals of politics—an element which, he says, is neglected in Riggs's analysis because of his lack of concern with alternative patterns or strategies of development. At this point Diamant's definition of political development is crucial to understanding his approach:

In its most general form . . . political development is a process by which a political system acquires an increased capacity to sustain successfully and continuously new types of organizations. For this process to continue over time a differentiated and centralized polity must come into being which must be able to command resources from and power over wide spheres and regions of the society. In this most general form political development is certainly a multi-normative process, in which a variety of demands and goals are being pursued simultaneously; . . . this ability to process several major demands and goals concurrently marks the "success" or "failure" of modernization.[15]

Since political development, as he conceives of the process, does not require the creation of particular kinds of institutions and it can move forward, stop, or be reversed, the matter of goals in a particular polity is of great importance. Diamant postulates that the two basic political goals of developing societies are nation-building and socio-economic progress. By "nation-building" he means the creation of an integrated political community within fixed geographical boundaries where the nation-state is the dominant political institution.[16]

---

[14] *Ibid.*, p. 15.
[15] Diamant, "Bureaucracy in Developmental Movement Regimes," p. 5.
[16] *Ibid.*, pp. 6, 7, 9, 10.

To this conceptual framework he relates Almond's idea that all political systems must acquire certain capacities to deal with four sets of problems: (1) an integrative capacity, which will provide for the creation of national unity and a centralized bureaucracy; (2) an international accommodative capability, which will provide a mechanism for meeting external pressures and demands; (3) a participation capability, which will lead to the creation of a political culture of civic obligation and of a democratic political structure; and (4) a welfare or distributive capacity, which will provide for widespread dissemination of welfare standards and accommodation between political and social structures. Diamant states that, except for the third element, these sets of problems fit into his conception of political development. Breakdown or failure in a political system, then, stems from the fact that a particular society has had to acquire too many of these capabilities at the same time.[17]

He also postulates that, as a developing society faces the widening range of demands that accompany modernization, an egalitarian mass society emerges which is independent of its democratic or nondemocratic character.[18]

Finally, on the basis of the work done by Banks and Textor, Diamant develops a chart organizing all the polities in existence today into categories based on two variables: (1) political system goals—whether they are postdevelopmental, developmental, or predevelopmental—and (2) political system styles—whether they are a polyarchy, a limited polyarchy, a movement regime, or traditional-autocratic. According to his analysis, Brazil is a limited polyarchy with developmental political system goals. He uses the term "polyarchy" to indicate "that the political regime is broadly representative, that power is not excessively centralized or monopolized, and that alternative policies have a chance to be heard and considered freely."[19] A limited polyarchy is a political system style "where polyarchal features have been restricted or eliminated, or, where there is an appearance of polyarchy, considerable limitations have been placed on it."[20]

Throughout the following chapters these two models for the study of public administration will be referred to constantly as reference points for understanding the behavior of the Brazilian federal civil service. Given the complexity of the subject, subsequent chapters will also focus on one or another of the variables isolated previously and

[17] *Ibid.*, p. 12.
[18] *Ibid.*, p. 15.
[19] *Ibid.*, p. 27.
[20] *Ibid.*

on the propositions built upon them. Chapter II sketches the broad lines of Brazilian political and administrative development. The following two chapters deal with the theoretical framework within which the movement to reform the Brazilian federal civil service has functioned. The subject matter is centered around conceptual developments in Brazilian public administration. Since these concepts have their origin in American public administration, Chapters III and IV approach this material from the perspective of comparative organization theory. Chapter V is designed to complement Chapters III and IV by introducing individual perceptions of the federal civil service, on the basis of interview material. These are images of the civil service which bear a close correlation with the abstract ideas developed in the literature of public administration in Brazil. Chapters VI, VII, VIII, IX, and X are concerned with the political environment in which the national civil service has functioned. In Chapter VI a model is developed for the study of the Brazilian political system, based on various analytic approaches taken by Brazilian authors in explaining their politics. This is followed by an analysis of the political understructure of the Brazilian federal civil service. In Chapters VIII and IX attention is directed to the influence of the newly emergent political parties on the allocation of jobs in the federal civil service. The theme of Chapter X is the gap between the norms imposed in administrative reform and the sociopolitical environment. Central to this topic is the patronage problem in the national administrative system, and comparative material is used to make this analysis more meaningful. In the final chapter conclusions are set forth in terms of the propositions stated at the outset and the central hypothesis is reexamined to determine its validity.

CHAPTER II

The Setting

Considered within the framework of the model and terminology proposed by Diamant, the course of Brazilian political development has been quite uneven. As an independent nation-state, however, Brazil has experienced essentially only a single political system style: limited polyarchy. The one exception to this statement is the Estado Novo, when Getúlio Vargas ruled in a traditional-autocratic political style within the framework of a state theoretically approaching a movement regime.[1] Yet it was precisely during this period that the political system goals changed from predevelopmental to developmental.

Since the arrival of the Portuguese Court in Rio de Janeiro in 1808, the focal point of the Brazilian political system has been the executive —whether an hereditary monarch, a self-appointed guardian, or an elected president. This institutional continuity between past and present is perhaps best captured in the phrase "His Majesty, The President of Brazil."[2] All effective government in Brazil seems to have relied on the presence of a strong executive. This reliance, in turn, may well reflect the prominence of personalism as a central value in Brazilian culture and involve the whole notion of charisma as an essential attribute of leadership.

---

[1] According to Alfred Diamant those political systems which are of a "movement regime" type consist of a revolutionary mass-movement, guided by a centralized elite or vanguard party, with a core ideology and an organizational network extending down to the village level. The category "traditional-autocratic" refers to "those polities whose political style has remained traditional, such as Iran and Nepal, as well as certain modernized polities whose autocracies or militaristic political style closely resembles the traditional autocracies, such as Spain, Portugal, or Paraguay." "Bureaucracy in Developmental Movement Regimes: A Bureaucratic Model for Developing Societies," pp. 27, 29.

[2] Ernest Hambloch, *His Majesty, The President of Brazil: A Study of Constitutional Brazil.*

Related to the importance of the executive as a reference point in Brazilian politics and administration is the theme of centralization of authority (formal power) and control (effective power).[3] Although Riggs speaks of the "disengagement" of authority and control as characteristic of transitional societies,[4] this situation has been present in Brazil from the time the first governor-general was sent out from Lisbon in 1549. By the end of the colonial period, the existing administrative system provided unity for the Brazilian "cultural archipelago,"[5] the diverse regions under the authority of the Portuguese Crown. Nevertheless, many of the regions—especially those directed by their own *audiencias*—were quite successful in escaping central control as exercised by the viceroy. In general, the Brazilian colonies were never subjected to the extremes of monarchical absolutism from which the Spanish colonies in America suffered. Centralization was imposed on Brazil relatively late, and when it did occur, it appeared in a much more moderate form.[6]

Brazilian unity received a substantial boost in 1808, when the Court of Dom João VI, then prince regent, fled from Lisbon to Rio de Janeiro in the face of the Napoleonic invasion of the Iberian peninsula. With Rio now the seat of the Portuguese Empire, Brazil received the impact of four centuries of Portuguese imperial institutions. The bureaucracy played a dominant role among these institutions, for in the course of creating a trade-based empire in the East, Portugal had found it necessary to create a vast administrative apparatus. Many new administrative entities appeared in Rio because of the presence of the Court, and a number of aristocratic public servants, associated with the royal house, descended on the new capital. Their reinforcement of the idea of public positions (*cargos públicos*) as sinecures was the most inauspicious development for the future of Brazilian administration.[7]

Although Rio's status as capital of the Empire was relatively short-lived (the Court returned to Lisbon after the Portuguese Revolution of 1820), the imperial institutional base remained and provided the

[3] Fred W. Riggs, *Administration in Developing Countries: The Theory of Prismatic Society*, p. 209.

[4] *Ibid.*, p. 281.

[5] Clodomir Vianna Moog, *An Interpretation of Brazilian Literature*, pp. 16–17.

[6] Eulália Maria Lahmeyer Lobo, *Processo Administrativo Ibero-Americano: Aspectos Sócio-Econômicos—Período Colonial*, pp. 549, 559. This book offers an excellent comparative administrative history of the Spanish and Portuguese colonial experience in the Western hemisphere.

[7] "O Cargo Público e Seu Caráter Regalista e Patrimonial na Administração Colonial," in João Guilherme de Aragão, *Administração e Cultura*, pp. 163–168.

foundation for the creation of an independent monarchy in 1822, with a member of the House of Bragança on the throne.

With independence the person of the monarch remained the symbol of political legitimacy, but the goals of the administration system changed. Whereas the primary concern of the Portuguese State had been the exercise of fiscal controls of a tributary nature and the maintenance of an overseas empire, the new Brazilian government turned its attention to the objective of national unity.

For the first time a truly national administrative system was created. During this process, however, the gap between formal authority and effective control remained because the impact of the administrative system was, for all practical purposes, still limited to the major cities and its focus was the Court in Rio. In the provinces, clan and oligarchical politics[8] predominated and factional political struggles continued to be couched in local and personal terms. There simply was no need for extensive administrative activities. What demands there were for administrative services came primarily from merchants and those engaged in import-export trade.

Thus, the imperial administration turned its attention more to the larger cities and to the Court than to the countryside; it took care more of external commerce than of internal commerce—of the railroads and the ports which tied the country to the outside world rather than the regional and local communications and supply network. It was mostly an administration that had a regulatory character, with limited financial resources and a small number of employees. Its aristocratic orientation was manifested in the expenses of the Court which reached half or more of all the total expenditures. . . . On the one hand, these were for activities carried on at the service of the Court or for its entertainment. On the other, however, these were service activities for the dominant classes [with a purpose] since the Monarch was interested in attracting to the Court the power [and resources] of the country's rural aristocracy and mercantile bourgeoisie.[9]

In theory the Empire was strictly a unitary state, but, as in the case of other traditional systems, the control over local power structures by the central government, as expressed through the administrative system, was negligible and subject to considerable variation as the effectiveness of the monarchy fluctuated. Given the predomi-

---

[8] This distinction is based on concepts developed by Guerreiro Ramos and discussed in Chapter VI.

[9] Mário Wagner Vieira da Cunha, *O Sistema Administrativo Brasileiro, 1930–1950*, pp. 32–33. (This translation from Portuguese, as well as all subsequent ones, is the author's.)

nance of local loyalties and the problem of internal communications in such a vast territory, the main accomplishment of the Empire was the creation and preservation of union among the Portuguese-speaking provinces and the avoidance of the emergence of a series of independent republics.

Joined with this evolution toward national unity was the transition from a clan to an oligarchical style of politics. Familialistic patterns of politics continued to function, but they were brought into focus around regional centers—particularly with the abdication of Pedro I in 1831, with the establishment of a regency (1831–1840), and with the publication of the law of August 12, 1834. This law brought into force the *Ato Adicional* and, on the basis of Article 71 of the 1824 constitution, provided for changes in provincial government.[10] The *Ato* decentralized a substantial part of the power of the national government and, when put into effect, made it considerably easier for regional interests to organize around provincial capitals. Between 1831 and 1836 the provinces achieved substantial autonomy, only to see it constrained in 1837 by a revival of those interests defending the monarchy.

A crucial element in this competition between the centralizing force of the monarchy and the desire of the provinces for greater autonomy was the transferral of a substantial part of the patronage power away from the executive and its dispersal at the regional level. The Crown, however, did retain the right to name officials to the National Treasury, the Ministry of War and Navy, and the General Post Office, and to select presidents of the provinces, bishops, commanders-superior in the National Guard, members of the higher courts (Relações e Tribunais Superiores), and employees in the schools of medicine and law and in the academies.[11] Even though the authority of the central government was reestablished by the declaration of the majority of Pedro II in 1840, the Crown never regained complete control over the patronage power at the provincial level.

Despite serious obstacles to the creation of a centralized government, the Crown used its appointive powers to help build a body of trained public servants, and isolated attempts were made at the national level to select governmental employees on the basis of capacity. The first recorded instance of a public examination is in 1808, when written and oral tests were announced for the selection of surgeons for the Royal Brigade and the Royal Navy. In general, the Portuguese

10 For the text of the 1824 Constitution and amendments to it see Fernando H. Mendes de Almeida (ed.), *Constituições do Brasil.*
11 Visconde do Uruguay, *Ensaio sôbre o Direito Administrativo,* p. 215.

king, Dom João VI, has been credited with the search for qualified elements for the public service. Similarly, when independence was established and the first constitution was prepared in 1824, an article was included subscribing to the principle that all public positions—whether political, civil, or military—were open to all citizens on the basis of their qualifications. Both Brazilian monarchs, Dom Pedro I and Dom Pedro II, were interested in establishing a competent higher civil service based on educated elements in the upper class, especially within the Public Treasury.[12] But these attempts were made within the context of a state primarily interested in integrating and providing for its elite groups. The obstacles to centralization were such that an independent national civil service did not emerge. Nevertheless, the various emperors—as a moderating power in the midst of factional politics—have usually been credited with the maintenance of high standards in the selection of civil servants, and this has been in contrast with the spoils system practiced at the provincial level.[13]

In 1889, the attempt to create a unitary state ended: Dom Pedro II was deposed, the monarchy abolished, and a federal republic created. Under the Constitution of 1891 the provinces, now named states, exercised almost complete autonomy. Although the political forms changed, the social and economic structure of the country remained much the same. The country retained its agrarian character and its dependence on foreign markets, and little was achieved in the way of establishing an internal network of communications. Instead, each major regional port was tied directly with its overseas market. In terms of Diamant's definition, the First Republic represented a step backward in political development.

Even though the formal structure of the First Republic was based on the imitation of American political institutions, its functioning was totally different. Politics centered around a series of regional political bosses (coronéis), some with more, some with less, power. The preeminent figure in each state was the governor, who shared his power through a system of alliances with local leaders at the municipal level. At the national level, the president's authority (i.e. his formal power) was broad, but his control was limited by the autonomy of the states. As a consequence of this framework of interlocking

---

[12] "O Cargo Público no Século XIX e o Sistema do Mérito," in Aragão, *Administração e Cultura*, pp. 169–173. For a listing of the early attempts at public examinations based on competence, see the articles by Braga, Lopes, and Nascimento Silva listed in Bibliography.

[13] João Camillo de Oliveira Torres, *O Presidencialismo no Brasil*, pp. 113–114.

personal alliances, the president of the Republic was selected according to what is known as "governor politics" (*a política dos governadores*)—and its subsequent corollary, "the politics of coffee with milk" (*a política de café com leite*). This latter phrase refers to the dominant alliance of the period, between the states of São Paulo (the center of Brazil's coffee production) and Minas Gerais (a cattle-raising and milk-producing state). In such a situation, where all states enjoyed considerable autonomy, regional developmental contrasts continued to grow, with obvious consequences for the distribution of power among the various states.

The concept of federalism, based on North American experience and transferred to an agrarian, regionally divided country where personal politics predominated, served merely to undermine the main contribution of the Empire—the establishment of the semblance of national unity in a territory larger than the continental United States and faced with serious problems of communication. The comments of Oliveira Torres add insight to this matter:

> [During the Republic] Brazil was a "cultural archipelago" [where] political power was for all practical purposes concentrated in the hands of the presidents of the states.
> The federal government maintained in fact a consciousness of the bid for unity in our history, but in general it did not possess the means to accomplish this since all [effective] power was handed over to the states.
> A more profound analysis of the general conditions of Brazilian public administration during the republican regime before 1930 reveals this singular fact: the federal government disposed of only two arms to maintain its authority in the whole of Brazilian territory—the Army and the National Telegraph.[14]

This observation is nowhere better borne out than in the case of the Canudos rebellion at the turn of the century, when the federal government was able to halt the primitively armed movement of a religious fanatic in the hinterland of the state of Bahia only after a tremendous expenditure in men, resources, and effort.[15]

As a consequence of the weakness of the central government a highly diffuse network of state administrative systems, at contrasting stages of development, emerged and took priority over an only partially effective federal administration. These regional administrative systems were entirely at the service of the rural patriarchs who con-

[14] João Camillo Oliveira Torres, *A Formação do Federalismo no Brasil*, p. 239.
[15] The classic account of this rebellion is Euclides da Cunha, *Rebellion in the Backlands (Os Sertões)*, trans. Samuel Putnam.

trolled the patronage power. Hence, the only limiting factor on the expansion of public jobs at this level was the financial resources of the individual states. The main interest of the regional political bosses was the provision of public order and the maintenance of as much power as possible within the regional capitals. From this situation stems the emphasis of these political bosses on police services and their unwillingness to allow the degree of municipal authority provided for in the Constitution of 1891.[16]

With the loss of the national focus provided by the Empire only two basic functions remained for the administrative system: the furnishing of employment for marginal members of the upper sector[17] and the supplying of minimal services for the national government and for commercial interests involved in foreign trade. The fact that these functions often could be carried out just as well by state administrations further contributed to the weakening of these newer national administrative organs. Among the service responsibilities left solely to the federal administration was the handling of national finances and the supplying of public services for a rapidly growing federal district. This limited the scope of federal administration substantially to the economic and political center of the country—the Rio de Janeiro–São Paulo–Minas Gerais triangle. Only after 1920 did the federal government begin attempts to establish itself over the order created by the rural patriarchs—in such areas as police matters, education, public health, and communications.[18]

Regardless of this situation, there was apparently a top group of able public functionaries who continued to work in the federal government's major ministries. According to Loewenstein, they were attracted to these positions by relatively good pay and by the considerable prestige the position offered. He accounts for the presence of these officials on the basis of the continuation of an elitist tradition inherited from the Empire and founded on French precedents.[19]

This administrative system was no longer tenable by 1930, a convenient dividing point in the course of Brazilian political development marking the collapse of the political order on which the First Republic was based and the initiation of a new era in Brazilian politics and administration. In October of that year Getúlio Vargas achieved power through revolt, established a provisional government, and, on

[16] Vieira da Cunha, *O Sistema Administrativo Brasileiro*, p. 36.
[17] Richard N. Adams, "Introduction [to Social Organization]," in Dwight B. Heath and Richard N. Adams (eds.), *Contemporary Cultures and Societies of Latin America*, pp. 266–270.
[18] Vieira da Cunha, *O Sistema Administrativo Brasileiro*, pp. 34–35.
[19] Karl Loewenstein, *Brazil under Vargas*, pp. 17–18.

November 11, issued a decree suspending the Constitution of 1891. These events began a movement which led to the concentration of effective power in the hands of the federal executive. This process reached its conclusion with the coup d'etat of November 10, 1937, and the establishment of a unitary state.

The changes instituted in the decree of November 11, 1930, are significant, not so much because they granted Vargas sufficient authority (formal power) to re-create a strong executive, but because he had the necessary control (effective power) to make these changes meaningful. Article 1 granted the president not only discretionary powers of an executive and legislative nature—until a constituent assembly should meet to decide on the country's reorganization—but also the exclusive right to appoint and dismiss public officials. Article 2 dissolved all representative and deliberative assemblies, federal, state, and municipal; Article 4 stated that federal and state constitutions were to remain in force, but subject to modification by governmental decree. Article 5 suspended all constitutional guarantees, as well as the right of the courts to review decrees and acts of the government. Article 11 gave the executive the authority to appoint to each state a federal delegate (*interventor*) with the power to exercise all state legislative and excutive powers and to appoint and dismiss all mayors under his jurisdiction.[20]

In November, 1933, Vargas convoked a constituent assembly, and on July 16, 1934, he promulgated a new constitution. While this constitution restored the federal republic in name and granted increased powers to the federal government, its chief characteristic was "autocratic presidentialism,"[21] an aspect Vargas made operational.

Nevertheless, this period of legal "democracy" and reconstituted federalism was short-lived. On December 18, 1935, the chamber of deputies and the senate passed a constitutional amendment allowing them to grant the president authority to declare a "state of grave internal commotion," under which all constitutional guarantees could be suspended. Through this amendment Vargas was able to exercise almost absolute power. Then, in late 1937, he used it to destroy the state he had created. With presidential elections in the offing, he initiated action by demanding that congress declare the existence of a "state of grave internal commotion." This was followed by a congressional act granting him state-of-war powers for ninety days, as of October 2. Finally, on November 10, he called in the troops, dissolved

[20] *Ibid.*, p. 18.
[21] *Ibid.*, p. 22.

congress, and established a dictatorship under the name of Estado Novo.[22]

Politically, this was a period of great instability: in the face of the collapse of the system built around rurally oriented state oligarchies, Vargas took the initiative and attempted to create a new basis of equilibrium and consensus. Economically and administratively, it was a period of change. Beginning in 1930, when the worldwide depression had meant the loss of the country's foreign markets, the first real push toward industrialization and diversification of the economy was undertaken. Certainly, World War I had given an impetus to economic growth, but it was nothing compared with the changes destined to occur during the 1930's. The increase in the domestic prices of imported goods after 1929 and the growth of real income after 1934 provided a strong incentive for the establishment of new industries. In the process, large amounts of capital were diverted from coffee into industry and trade. Although the agricultural sector of the economy continued to suffer from the fall in world prices throughout these years, the industrial sector had recovered its 1929 level by 1933. By the end of the 1930's, in contrast to what had occurred in many of the largely industrial countries, Brazil had reached a per capita income superior to that of 1929.[23]

In public administration attention was turned toward the reorganization of the older ministries and the creation of new administrative entities. The first ministry to suffer modification was the Ministry of Agriculture, Industry, and Commerce. The responsibilities for industry and commerce were passed on to a new ministry, that of Labor, Industry, and Commerce, created by Decree 19495 of December 17, 1930; then, through Decree 22338 of January 11, 1933, this ministry was itself reorganized. The Ministry of Justice and Interior Affairs was the second ministry to undergo change. Since its creation during the Empire, it had been one of the most important. Several of its previous functions were removed, and these were combined in 1931 to create the Ministry of Education and Health. This same year, the National Coffee Council was formed to deal with the continuing coffee crisis. Finally, in recognition of the need for reorganization in public finance, the structure and methods of work of the Ministry of Finance were ordered updated under Decree 24036 of March 26, 1934.[24]

[22] *Ibid.*, pp. 28–29, 34–37.
[23] Brazilian Embassy, *Survey of the Brazilian Economy, 1959*, pp. 2–3.
[24] Vieira da Cunha, *O Sistema Administrativo Brasileiro*, pp. 49–51, 59.

By mid-1934, this phase of administrative innovation had halted with the promulgation of the new constitution and the return to partisan politics; it was only to be resumed with the declaration of the Estado Novo in 1937.

Yet concern for administrative reform and expanded public service continued to be expressed in the new congress through the leadership of Vargas. An interparliamentary commission of ten members was created under the name of, first, the Mixed Commission on Economic and Financial Reform (Comissão Mista de Reforma Econômico-Financeira) and, later, the Commission for Readjustment and Tributary Reform (Comissão de Readjustamento e Reforma Tributária). Under its auspices, a subcommittee of four men was established to prepare a report on conditions in the federal civil service and to offer proposals for its reorganization.[25] This report contained several suggestions: the creation of two general schedules for the federal civil service, with a division between central and regional administration; the establishment of a uniform classification plan; and the formation of a central personnel agency.[26]

The Nabuco Report, however, was suppressed and a new subcommittee was created to deal with the problems of classification and pay in the federal civil service. From this committee came a report proposing three alternative organization plans: a classification of positions based on performance; a five-step pay plan independent of promotion; and a general readjustment based on the creation of a career system within each ministry—providing for pay according to performance and for advancement according to qualification. Vargas selected the third alternative.[27]

Out of this preparatory work came the Law of Readjustment (Law 284 of October 23, 1936), which established a classification plan, a central personnel agency, and the principle that admission to the career civil service henceforth would occur only through public examination. A fourth aspect, the establishment of efficiency commissions, was a failure from the outset.

In theory the position (*cargo*) was the basic unit of the classification plan, with a logical progression from position to class to career

---

[25] Kleber Nascimento, *Classificação de Cargos no Brasil*, pp. 32–33.

[26] Gilbert Siegel, "The Vicissitudes of Governmental Reform in Brazil: A Study of the DASP," pp. 70–72.

[27] *Ibid.*, pp. 74–76. Siegel does not make it clear who suppressed the Nabuco Report. Most probably it was Vargas, but sufficient information to justify this assertion is not available.

to *quadro*; in practice, however, salary differentiation and the concept of classes became the criteria for classification.[28] Little effort was made to characterize the duties and responsibilities of individual positions because of the lack of administrative technicians trained in these skills. Within the careers, which were, in effect, the basic units in each ministry, advancement was made according to length of service.

Not all positions, however, were placed under careers; some were separated into a special category and called *cargos isolados*—independent positions. Such positions were not subject to the requirement of a public examination and could be filled according to the wishes of the executive. Regardless of this situation, it seems, noncareer civil service positions located at the middle management level were filled by persons who had entered the civil service through examination.[29]

The basic contribution of the classification plan was that, for the first time, it provided a means for systematizing the pay scales and for establishing a semblance of order in the federal civil service. It was to remain the only plan in existence at the federal level until a new classification plan was passed by congress in 1960.

The second aspect of the Law of Readjustment involved the creation of a central personnel agency, modeled after the United States Civil Service Commission. The Federal Civil Service Council (Conselho Federal do Serviço Público Civil) was organized as a collegial body consisting of five members, appointed by the president, who were to possess specialized knowledge of public administration and who were not to be active in partisan politics. The Council's responsibilities included the preparation and administration of federal civil service entrance examinations, the expression of opinion about the removal of public officials, and assistance or advice on plans submitted by the efficiency commissions for the improvement of the public service.[30]

[28] The criterion of salary differentiation was later formalized in the 1939 statute for public functionaries. *"Quadro"* means literally a table or chart; however, it is used here in the sense of a service. Because of this meaning and because the term *serviço* is used with the same connotation in the 1960 classification law, the Portuguese word has been retained.

[29] Ennor de Almeida Carneiro, "Política de Remuneração," *Revista do Serviço Público*, LXVII (April, 1955), 41, 44 [hereafter cited as *RSP*; because *RSP ano* and volume designations have not been used consistently over the years, volume number with date of issue is the best guide for locating the material]; Moacyr Ribeiro Briggs, "Evolução da Administração Pública Federal," *RSP*, III (August, 1938), 16–17; Brazil, Ministro Extraordinário para a Reforma Administrativa, "Normas para Preservação e Revigoramento do Sistema do Mérito," p. 4; Siegel, "The Vicissitudes of Governmental Reform," pp. 77–79, 110–111.

[30] Siegel, *ibid.*, pp. 80–81, 85.

While this law is often referred to as the origin of the Brazilian merit system, it instituted a merit system only in the sense that initial entrance into the federal civil service was to occur through selection on the basis of public examination. This matter is crucial when we reach the period between 1945 and 1964. Despite the widespread belief that the postwar years represented a return to an open spoils system in that they followed a period during which a merit system conducive to a neutral and impartial civil service had been in effect, it must be remembered that a merit system, as the term is understood in the United States and Western Europe, did not make its appearance during the Vargas era.

In this connection it is useful to ask: Who stood to benefit most from the reforms instituted during the late 1930's? Who were in a position to lose most? What effect did these reforms have on political development when open political debate was reinstituted in 1946?

The Estado Novo was essentially a highly centralized administrative, no-party state following the dictates of its absolute ruler under a paper constitution. The governmental system was centralized to a degree hitherto unknown in Brazil. Under an hierarchical arrangement consisting of *interventores* (agents of the executive), State Departments of the Public Service (Departamentos Estaduais do Serviço Público), and the minister of justice, the states became little more than administrative units. In the municipalities, the prefects were given powers which, at the local level, paralleled those of the *interventor*. They were directly responsible to the *interventor* and to the president of the appropriate State Department of the Public Service. Because these state administrative organizations were patterned after the national DASP, they were called *daspinhos*.

According to Loewenstein, these administrative departments were composed of from four to ten members. The smaller states usually had four; the middle-sized states, five; and the key states of Minas Gerais, São Paulo, and Rio Grande do Sul, ten each. They functioned both as the state legislature and as the supervisory body for the *interventor* and the minister of justice (when his actions fell within the area of their jurisdiction). Although the *interventor* was responsible for the study, approval, and declaration of all state laws and decrees, these were valid only when sanctioned by the president of the *daspinho*. If the *daspinho* opposed any act or decree executed by the *interventor*, a two-thirds vote by this body was sufficient to suspend action until a decision was reached by the chief executive. In addition to this control, the state administrative department was responsible for reporting on all appeals against the *interventor*. These appeals were submitted, through the minister of justice, to the president of the Republic.

It is not difficult to understand why, under this combination of circumstances, the president of the state *daspinho* was usually more powerful than the *interventor*. Loewenstein further states that during this era

. . . the Administrative Department [was] a team of hard-hitting, hardworking, thoroughly efficient professional bureaucrats—mostly young lawyers, but also technicians, such as accountants, civil engineers, agricultural experts, statisticians—while in the Interventor's office the efficiency of the staff [was] vitiated by ineradicable patronage.[31]

At the national level, both formal and effective powers were centralized in the office of the chief executive. The principal organization through which this centralization was achieved was the Administrative Department of the Public Service (DASP), established on July 30, 1938, through Decree-Law 579. In the absence of a deliberate assembly, the DASP provided the legislation necessary to bring into effect Article 67 of the new constitution. This article provided for the creation of a general administrative department which would undertake a detailed study of the national administrative system with the intention of instituting changes along the lines of economy and efficiency. It also gave this department responsibility for the annual preparation of the budget and authority to exercise control over its use, with the understanding that guide lines were to be provided by the executive. The decree-law, however, broadened the new department's functions to include the institution of central control over personnel and materiel and the responsibility for rendering assistance to the president of the Republic in reviewing proposed legislation. Thus, from the outset, DASP was designed to function in theory as an organ of general administration similar to that conceived by Willoughby.[32]

Within the area of public personnel administration, the collegial Federal Civil Service Council was replaced and incorporated into the new bureau of general administration, under the control of a single head, the president of DASP. Initially, the new organization func-

---

[31] Loewenstein, *Brazil under Vargas*, pp. 62–68, esp. 64.

[32] Beatriz Marqués de Souza Wahrlich, "An Analysis of DASP: A Contribution to the Study of Comparative Administration" (Unpublished paper), p. 3. See also her reference: William Franklin Willoughby, *Principles of Public Administration, With Special Reference to the National and State Governments of the United States*, pp. 360–361.

tioned as a central personnel agency. Attention was focused on establishing limitations on patronage, instituting competitive entrance examinations, and creating controls to insure the maintenance of these policies. DASP was also granted authority to check on every placement, transfer, promotion, leave, disciplinary measure, and any other minor action that pertained to personnel practices in the ministries. Further, it was given the responsibility for the maintenance of both a pre-service and an in-service training program.[33]

In addition to these controls established over public service personnel, a coordinative apparatus was created under the name of the Council of Administration of Personnel. It was designed to promote better coordination and greater efficiency among those organs concerned with personnel, within both DASP and the ministries. The members of the council were the chiefs or directors of the personnel agencies in the ministries, and, within DASP, the directors of Personnel Orientation and Control, Personnel Research, and Selection and Training.

In theory, DASP was designed to operate as a technical organization. For individual ministerial organs this meant they were responsible to DASP for what were deemed to be technical affairs and to the usual hierarchy of ministerial authority for general administrative patterns. In practice DASP functioned quite differently. Since it came into existence within the context of a dictatorship committed to modernization without the mechanism of a mass-based party, it provided a convenient means for central control over the national administrative system. As an agent of the executive it exercised responsibilities which went beyond purely technical concerns.[34] DASP became a sort of superministry, and it was against this power that hostility developed, both within the administrative system and outside of it. This hostility was increased by Vargas' use of the DASP as a focal point for criticism which might have fallen more directly on his regime.

Although the goal of the administrative reform movement was the introduction of efficiency, economy, and rationality in the federal civil service, within the context of the more general goals of an integrated nation-state and the institution of socioeconomic changes leading to modernization this goal became an instrumental objective. By 1937, these values of efficiency, economy, and rationality had become closely identified with a closed bureaucratic system at the service of a modernizing elite. The crucial point, then, is not so much whether the

[33] *Ibid.*, pp. 10–11.
[34] Siegel, "The Vicissitudes of Governmental Reform," p. 129.

techniques advocated were good or bad inherently as it is the way in which they were employed. After all, since the Vargas government was one in which the administrative structure of the state provided an excellent means for the mobilization and control of energy expended in the political process, these values were certain to be used for the ends of that state. The notion that administration could be separated from the surrounding political environment—particularly when many new developments were taking place in the social, the economic, and the political realms—was used at a later date to give this modernizing elite a means of legitimizing its authority. At the outset, however, there was no doubt that political and administrative matters were inseparable. The higher civil service, in conjunction with the military, was used as an instrument of political integration to overcome a highly divided, dispersed, rurally-dominated social order. During the Estado Novo the Brazilian federal civil service became both an object and an agent of modernization.

An indication of the political goals toward which civil service reform was directed is to be found in an article published by Azevedo Amaral in April, 1938.[35] The idea of the separation of administration from politics, he wrote, might be necessary in a liberal democratic state because of the struggle for power among competing groups, but, within the context of the Estado Novo, such a concept was superfluous:

> An apolitical administration is, in the atmosphere of the Estado Novo, an absurdity which implies making ineffective the very instruments through which the State's objectives ought to be achieved. . . .
> The distinction between politics and administration cannot exist in state organizations. . . . Under a liberal democratic regime the State, in conformity with the fictions created around promiscuous, direct suffrage, was in reality conquered alternately by one or another social group. These groups used the parties as their organs of political expression. Given these conditions, it was actually convenient and at the same time necessary for public employees, in carrying out the responsibilities of their positions, to keep themselves beyond the influence of that which was called politics, although politics was hardly more than a contradicting and anarchical manifestation of the representative currents of special interests. . . . Today this is no longer necessary, for the State and the Nation are identical and there is only one set of politics.[36]

Under these circumstances, Amaral asserted, it was not enough to recruit civil servants possessing "intellectual, cultural, moral, and

---

[35] Azevedo Amaral, "Política e Serviço Público," *RSP*, II (April, 1938), 13–15.
[36] *Ibid.*, p. 14.

technical qualifications." What the government needed was a body of civil servants in harmony with the political goals of the state. Unless the government could obtain a political commitment from its civil servants, he believed, the "efficiency of state power" would be endangered.[37]

During the 1930's, public administration theory as it had developed in the United States and Western Europe had not yet come to terms with these problems of the overall goals of the political system and how administration fitted into the broader social matrix of a given society. Hence, in recognizing the need for administrative reform in the Brazilian civil service simply to get things done, the emphasis was placed on the acquisition of new techniques from abroad. Little, if any, attention was drawn to the importance of the underlying societal norms and the nature of economic and political development in the United States, the principal country from which the technical elite took the principles of scientific management. They accepted and subscribed to the belief that there was in existence a body of techniques of universal validity—independent of the surrounding political and social system. When applied correctly, these techniques would modernize the administrative system and lead the way to the immediate goals of rationality, economy, and efficiency.

In a sense, this emphasis on administrative mechanics is understandable, for the necessity of introducing new skills and techniques in the federal civil service did exist. For example, when the first classification plan was attempted in 1936, Brazilians interested in public administration were quite aware of the lack of technicians properly trained in the collection and analysis of the data required to establish a meaningful system of classification for the federal civil service. The same may be said of other aspects of public administration—organization and methods, budgeting, personnel administration, or whatever. From this awareness stems the interest in sending Brazilians abroad for technical training in public administration, an interest which in the postwar era was further stimulated by the technical assistance program of the United States.

It is questionable, however, whether the Vargas administrative reforms, carried out under the auspices of a cosmopolitan technical elite concentrated primarily within DASP, succeeded in altering the real character of the public service. Of the three basic sources on administrative change in the 1930's—Siegel, Vieira de Cunha, and Loewenstein—only the last provides an insight into the nature of the civil

[37] *Ibid.*, pp. 14–15.

service in that period, and his comments apply essentially to the Estado Novo at the time of its greatest success. Even then, Loewenstein was somewhat skeptical about the success of having imposed rationalized administrative concepts upon a civil service in which positions were often sought by those who wished to combine a maximum of security with a minimum of effort. He pointed out that the civil service was still vastly overstaffed and that the traditional attitude of viewing public employment as a sinecure continued. He also suggested that the technical reforms had served merely to make the system more formalistic when he stated that, although admission to the civil service was subject to the theoretical rule of competitive examination, "university diplomas . . . [were] still considered as official and 'pull' as unofficial equivalents." While merit was the official criterion, many of the main positions in the ministries were filled on the basis of political appointments, and ministers and *interventores* selected for themselves staffs of secretaries and advisers. Finally he saw little change in the origin of public officials. A number of Italian- or German-descended public employees were found at the middle level, but Luso-Brazilians continued to exercise a sort of unofficial monopoly at the higher positions.[38]

Another indication that much of the civil service remained unchanged despite the technical reforms comes from a brief reference by José de Nazaré Teixeira Dias to the problem of supervision. Writing in mid-1942, he pointed to the fact that the institution of examinations for entrance into the lower ranks was serving to increase tension within the public service. He attributed this to the divergence in preparation and training between the new body of individuals selected on the basis of qualification and their supervisors, who lacked the proper preparation for their responsibilities and were not influenced by the new standards.[39] On this basis he called for the focusing of attention on the middle ranks of the career civil service and for the use there of individuals trained in the new techniques. Part of the difficulty, it seems, was the fact that, even though the technical elite was committed to the modernization of the civil service according to concepts imported from the United States, this group was numerically too small and its members were faced with the necessity of retaining many prereform employees to man the ministerial offices.

This situation was strengthened by the continuation of the practice of promotions on the basis of seniority within the career civil service.

[38] Loewenstein, *Brazil under Vargas*, pp. 102, 104–105.
[39] José de Nazaré Teixeira Dias, "A Formação de Supervisores," *RSP*, III (August, 1942), p. 27.

In an article published in February, 1945, at the end of the Vargas regime, Alaim Carneiro spoke of these difficulties. According to his analysis, two basic problems in changing the nature of the civil service lay in the fact that promotions, decided on the basis of years of service, undercut the "merit system" and that the rate of turnover was exceptionally low. He ascribed this latter difficulty in part to the adoption of "efficiency bulletins" (*boletins de eficiência*) and their mechanical use without any relation to what they were designed to accomplish. He claimed that these bulletins adopted a numerical criterion which was based on the search for mathematical precision, one that was incompatible with the need for a subjective judgment. All this, he felt, pointed to the necessity for a new promotions system which was more rational and just and which would exclude promotions on the basis of seniority.[40]

Still another viewpoint on the success, or lack of it, in altering the Brazilian civil service is offered by Urbano C. Berquó. While this article appeared in April, 1938, placing it at the beginning of the dictatorship, it is the only source encountered that dealt with the problem of internal resistance to civil service reforms. It is unique among the materials examined for this period in that it alone raises the question of how one might change human nature so that it will accept rationalizing reforms. He is quite candid in referring to the authoritarian character of the Vargas regime and to the necessity for a loyal civil service committed to its reforms:

Discontentment and incomprehension can create an unfortunate situation. Because of hostility to the new regime or because of a desire to make the systematization of the Union's personnel administration on the basis of professional careers unviable, many servants of the State may be led to act as retarding or upsetting elements for governmental action.

Under the present regime in Brazil it is in no way admissible that a functionary consider himself *neutral* or *indifferent* and, *a fortiori*, that he adopt a hostile attitude toward the path embarked upon by the national government for the treatment and solution of public affairs. The comfortable *laissez-aller* of the era of liberalism—fortunately now dead—does not coincide at all with the responsibility which is involved in the undertaking of any public function, however humble it may be. Within the context of the old meaning of the word *partisan*—which no longer has any reason to exist among us—it is evident that every functionary should be *apolitical*. But, according to the point of view of the *national interest* —which is that of the authoritarian State—there is no doubt that it re-

---

[40] Alaim de Almeida Carneiro, "A Promoção nos Serviços Públicos," *RSP*, I (February, 1945), pp. 40–41.

quires of one a political consciousness in which the higher the position occupied or the more influential it may be, the greater the understanding. ... *Discontentment* and *incomprehension* ... constitute the two fountains from which passive resistance has issued forth; its clearest manifestations are such that even the most unprepared observers do not hesitate in including such resistance within the definition of *sabotage*.[41]

In this passage, Berquó is speaking of opposition within the federal civil service to the carrying out of the reforms instituted by Law 284 (1936) and the Federal Civil Service Council. Later, in the same article, he reduces those opposing the rationalization of the public personnel system to individuals who are either unqualified technically to continue to occupy their positions and feel that their security is threatened or who are opposed to any alteration in the traditional way of doing things and seek protection in excessive amounts of paper work.[42]

Yet another approach in evaluating the success of Vargas in changing the nature of the Brazilian civil service is examination of DASP attempts to institute controls over one of the more powerful traditional ministries. Such an instance is provided by DASP's efforts to take from the Ministry of Finance the power to formulate and administer the budget. In the decree-law establishing DASP, budgetary responsibilities similar to those of the United States Bureau of the Budget were included. The Ministry of Finance, however, put up such strong resistance to this measure that DASP's control remained largely formal. The compromise worked out provided for the formation of a special budget commission within the Ministry of Finance, under the chairmanship of the president of DASP. Although this was to be merely a temporary arrangement until DASP established its own budget division, it continued to function until early 1945, when Decree-Law 7416 (of March 26) created the appropriate Division of the Budget.[43] By this time, however, the Vargas government had begun to deteriorate, and it was not long before the dictator resigned and DASP was faced with a new government hostile to its very existence. With this change in regime in late 1945, what influence DASP had over the budget, with its president as chairman of the budget commission in the Ministry of Finance, disappeared. The Ministry regained its traditional power in full and DASP's Division of the Budget

[41] Urbano C. Berquó, "Eficiência Administrativa e Sabotagem Burocratica," *RSP*, II (April, 1938), pp. 5–6.
[42] *Ibid.*, p. 7.
[43] Wahrlich, "An Analysis of DASP," pp. 1–2, 4–5.

functioned simply as part of a formal budget process unrelated to the real decisions on how the public moneys would be allocated.[44]

Aggravating what appears to have been a gap between the formal controls (the authority structure) and the effective power of DASP over the national administration was Law 284's separation of public employees into two basic classes—public functionaries (*funcionários públicos*) and supplementary personnel (*extranumerários*). The notion of a career civil service existed only in relation to the public functionary, and his rights, privileges, and obligations were codified by the Vargas government in a statute issued by Decree-Law 1712 of October 10, 1939. Of the two groups, the first enjoyed a privileged position in terms of salary, security, and status, but the second was numerically larger and continued to increase in size. Entrance into the former was restricted to selection on the basis of merit, as determined by public examination, while admission to the latter depended on political or personal favoritism. Generally speaking, the *extranumerário* was marginal to the whole process of rationalization carried out under the direction of DASP.[45] Such a statement, however, must be qualified, for, according to Decree-Law 1909 (of December 26, 1939), the requirement of a competitive public examination was extended to *extranumerários mensalistas* (supplementary personnel hired by the month). In addition, access to the career civil service was open to employees in this category by Decree-Law 5175 (of January 7, 1943).

There was, then, a very definite effort to create an elite career service. In this instance, merit as a qualification for entrance was completely separated from any egalitarian values. Because education was a privilege enjoyed by a relatively small percentage of the total population, the requirement of a public examination, based on specific, academic knowledge, had the effect of closing off admission to the career civil service for the less privileged and channeling them into the *extranumerário* category. On the other hand, those individuals with upper-class status but without specialized knowledge could still obtain public employment by occupying positions above or parallel to the career service, granted they had the proper political access. Thus, Riggs's categories for analysis are helpful in understanding interrelations in a transitional society, such as Brazil's. He distinguishes three types of recruitment norms: ascription (selection on the basis of

[44] Siegel, "The Vicissitudes of Governmental Reform," pp. 148–154.
[45] Vieira da Cunha, *O Sistema Administrativo Brasileiro*, pp. 93, 100–101.

kinship and personal ties); achievement (selection on the basis of technical skills and qualification), and attainment (selection on the basis of a combination of the first two types).[46] If the examinations administered are placed in the broader context of Brazilian society, it becomes clear that they functioned according to attainment norms and that recruitment on the basis of ascription was by no means entirely displaced.

These were years of rapid change in Brazilian public administration. Ministerial staffs grew in size and their contacts throughout the country widened; two new ministries appeared; and the DASP apparatus emerged as a sort of superministry designed to coordinate the whole administrative system. Effective coordination, however, was further complicated by the creation of independent agencies and commissions: the *autarquias* (independent or semi-independent governmental entities) and the social security institutes. Both contributed to the expansion of federal services and to an increase in the number of public employees. At the state level, many other new administrative bodies also emerged. By 1945, integration of the public service had become ever more a necessity, but the one organization created for that purpose, the DASP, failed to provide effective coordination, largely because of its desire to maintain as much control as possible in its own hands. Still, this period was the moment of its greatest power, for it enjoyed privileged access to the chief executive and influence upon him.

Vargas was an authoritarian, and his regime was a highly personal one. His government provided a degree of unification hitherto unknown in Brazil; yet it also set the country on the road to industrialization and the creation of a national market. As dictator, Vargas substantially replaced the "old regime" which had existed before 1930 and installed a new governmental apparatus, largely bureaucratic in character, designed to impose modernization on the nation from above. He was also responsible for initiating an almost complete reform and unification of Brazilian civil and criminal law.[47] And, when he saw the order of the New State was beginning to crumble, he established a new party system and began the transition back to an open system of government. Nevertheless, in spite of the fact that tremendous energies had been devoted to the modernization of Brazil

---

[46] Riggs, *Administration in Developing Countries*, pp. 128, 135, 167.

[47] Loewenstein, *Brazil under Vargas*, pp. 86–89, 103, 107, 110, 112. See the Criminal Procedural Code, Decree-Law 3680, October 3, 1941; Decree-Law 2627, September 26, 1940; and the Civil Procedure Code, Decree-law 2965, January 16, 1941.

in economics, administration, and law, traditional sociopolitical forces showed surprising vitality. For, with the opening up of the political process in 1945, they regrouped themselves within the framework of the new party system and reemerged as a major political element which had to be contended with.

This experience with administrative reform in Brazil is parallel in certain respects with the attempts of Peter the Great to change the character of the Russian civil service. Certainly, such a comparison is risky in that basic differences are involved—the most obvious, for Brazil, being the lack of both an authoritarian tradition and the historic drive to unite an empire of diverse peoples and nations. But some similarities that synthesize administrative trends in Brazil are worth noting here, regardless of the fact that distinct periods of time and different cultures are involved. While the technical elite in the Vargas era tried to use North American administrative organization and practices as a model for modernization, Peter the Great turned to the most rationalized administrative system of his day—the Swedish—and attempted to impose it upon the Russian system. In both instances, one of the major factors resulting in failure to obtain the desired change was that the men called upon to serve the state were essentially the same men who had held office before the reforms were imposed. Their values and behavior remained much the same despite the forcible introduction of new techniques and ways of doing things. Given the elite character of these societies and the lack of any system of mass education from which new individuals might be drawn, it was impossible simply to dismiss the mass of older public functionaries and replace them with others. The really basic changes needed in the functioning of the civil service could not be effected without relating them to the broader problems of these societies. Just as in the era of Peter the Great, so in the Vargas period tremendous energies were devoted to modernization, but a traditional society and a traditional bureaucracy largely frustrated its designs. Likewise, the two chiefs of state were much more successful in the economic than in the political-administrative sphere. Finally, both reforming elites in the civil service identified their own authority with that of the executive and found themselves largely isolated from the social forces emerging in their respective countries.[48]

---

[48] For a more detailed treatment of the administrative reforms of Peter the Great, see Merle Fainsod, "Bureaucracy and Modernization: The Russian and Soviet Case" in Joseph La Palombara (ed.), *Bureaucracy and Political Development.*

CHAPTER III

The Theoretical Foundations of the Reform Movement

The ideas and personalities that have had a major influence on the civil service reform movement are the theme of this chapter and the two following ones. This will lead to a consideration of what was isolated as the third independent variable: the application of the techniques of scientific management without adequate attention to the functional requirements of the existing administrative system and without sufficient consideration for the human elements. In many respects the administrative concepts imported from abroad and the individuals identified with them have set the scene and conditioned the solutions offered to specific problems in the public personnel field. Once the theoretical foundation of the civil service reform movement has been established, the civil service and its political environment can be considered.

Because Brazilian administrative theory since the late 1930's has developed almost exclusively from a North American basis, an analysis of public administration in the United States will first be presented. The purpose here is to capture the highlights of American organization theory as it has evolved in the postwar years and to illuminate the variety of approaches that can be utilized through models for studying organizations.[1] Once this has been accomplished, the path organization theory has pursued in Brazil will be examined, and its similarities and contrasts with organization theory in the United States will be pointed out.

Organization theory as it first developed in the United States is characterized by a "machine model" approach to the study of administration. It is task-oriented and substantially excludes human behav-

---

[1] This approach to the analysis of public administration is based on the analytic framework developed by Gladys M. Kammerer.

ior from the study of administration. A basic assumption is the passivity of human interests. The human instrument in this context becomes little more than a communications network, a problem-solving mechanism into which problems are fed and from which expected answers result.

This mode of analysis emerged originally out of Taylorism, with its search for "the one best way" in the development of administrative techniques and with its orientation toward economy and efficiency as the goals of the organization. Taylor was essentially responsible for the rearrangement of procedures to increase efficiency and economy and to eliminate all unnecessary steps in a capitalist, industrial setup. Out of his initial work as an engineer in industry came the school of scientific management.

Until the 1930's, scientific management, with its locus substantially confined to business administration, concentrated its efforts at the workshop level. Time and motion studies, based on the idea of reducing tasks to their simplest elements and speeding up production, were initiated. These, in turn, led to a modification of the machine model approach to account for the element of human fatigue and to allow for a physiological approach by management to worker production.

Despite this close association with business administration, administrative management theory as a field in itself got under way during the course of World War I. At the government level, the ideas of economy and efficiency were first applied through the Bureau of Efficiency, an organization created by Congress during the war years. This bureau raised the whole question of position classification according to individual duties and responsibilities. Then, with the Position Classification Act of 1923, this school of thought was able to introduce the principle of equal pay for equal work into the federal civil service. Although economy and efficiency were major objectives, they were related to a general reform movement, one aspect of which was the moralization of American administrative practices through the removal of favoritism and corruption and through the institution of a merit system.

In the 1930's, the scientific management school entered a new phase of development, one which was to carry it to its highest level of conceptualization.[2] Attention began to shift from the workshop level,

[2] Examples of this school are: John M. Gaus, "A Theory of Organization in Public Administration," in Gaus, Leonard D. White, and Marshall E. Dimock (eds.), *The Frontiers of Public Administration*; Comstock Glaser, *Administrative Procedure: A Practical Handbook for the Administrative Analyst*; Luther Gulick and Lyndall Urwick, *Papers on the Science of Administration*; and Lyndall Urwick, "Public Administration and Business Management," *Public Administration*

the focus of Taylorism, to the top of the administrative hierarchy, where organizational charts entered into vogue and where the manipulation of subordinate administrative units was emphasized. The crucial characteristic of this new development was the objective of creating a rational, ordered administrative structure in which the administrator could get things done. The key word became "coordination"—coordination to achieve the same goals of economy and efficiency. Out of this concern with coordination within the organization came a series of concepts which took on the attributes of universally applicable rules. These included such ideas as the span of control, the unity of command, the homogeneity of work, the dichotomy of staff and line, the principle of generalist administrators, and the idea that specialists should be "on tap, but not on top." Such principles were based on the idea that since all organizations were hierarchical in character, the basic problem was how to organize all of the functions and responsibilities of the organization under the executive at the top. In this context, attention was given to Continental administrative writers such as Fayol, and Gulick was able to develop his POSDCORB concept. This catchword summarized the responsibilities of the administrator: planning, organization, staffing, directing, coordinating, reporting, and budgeting.[3]

The scientific management school, with its concern for utilitarian principles of action, consciously attempted to assume away the problem of values; yet unconsciously it imposed its own values, for it emphasized how one could and should be able to get things done with a minimum of expense and a maximum of efficiency. In this creation of a "science of administration" it was believed that not only were values unrelated to objective facts, but also that they should and could be separated. Likewise, it was postulated that administration must be separated from the conflicts which take place in the political arena. Thus, the question of who should rule was fairly obvious: generalist administrators—for they would constitute an educated ruling class. At the national level, this meant the President as the head of the bureaucracy, but a bureaucracy selected on democratic bases. The ideal was the British administrative class, and the goal was the creation of

Review, XVII (Spring, 1957), 77–82. Critiques of the scientific management school are found in: Robert T. Golembiewski, *Behavior and Organization: O & M and the Small Group*; James G. March and Herbert A. Simon, *Organizations*; and Dwight Waldo, *The Administrative State: A Study of the Political Theory of American Public Administration*.

[3] Luther Gulick, "Notes on the Theory of Organization," in Gulick and Urwick, *Papers on the Science of Administration*, p. 13.

an aristocracy of talent. The legislative branch in such a situation was downgraded and the notion of a strict separation of powers was rigidly maintained. But the problem of who would determine the ends of the State and the goals and values of public administration remained unresolved. The scientific management school, regardless of its belief that it was objective and scientific in its procedures, was thus highly prescriptive. These weaknesses were transferred *in toto* to Brazil.

Once it became obvious, as in the reorganization of the Patent Office, that neither the scientific principles of administration nor the integration and coordination concerns of administrative management theorists was particularly applicable to real-life situations, modifications in administrative management theory began to occur. Two men who have made a significant contribution in this respect are Chester I. Barnard and Marshall E. Dimock.[4]

Recognizing the deficiencies of the machine model approach to administration, Barnard added two elements to traditional administrative theory: the importance of the individual, especially the executive, in an organizational context and the notion of equilibrium and disequilibrium in the organization. Both these aspects are related to his attempt to lessen the authority and control aspects of hierarchical organization. This was to be achieved by creating conditions conducive to greater cooperation between management and the workers, with an eye toward increasing productivity.

Barnard's concept of the executive is a persuader who seeks to win his employees over to his point of view. One of the techniques designed to achieve this end, and thus to bring about equilibrium in the organization, is the attempt to increase individual participation in decision-making. Two premises are involved: the idea that an organization is faced primarily with a problem-solving task and the notion that significant changes in human behavior can be brought about rapidly only if the persons expected to change are brought into the decision-making process. However, since the executive is responsible for structuring the situation to his or the management's advantage, this becomes but another manipulatory approach to human behavior.

Thus Barnard did not challenge the goals of the scientific management school. His solutions remain prescriptive, not empirical, in character. They are designed simply to make the traditional framework of administrative theory more operational. Even though he stresses coordination and the importance of influencing the behavior of the

[4] See Barnard, *The Functions of the Executive*, and Dimock, *The Executive in Action*.

members of the organization, he does not get into the entire problem of behavior. He is primarily concerned with vertical relationships; horizontal relationships enter in only as a means of expediting the vertical. This allows for the maintenance of the traditional goals of economy and efficiency. The properly functioning organization, he maintains, is "productive"; it is not wasteful of human energy and it is always in equilibrium.

Dimock is responsible for upsetting the idea that an organization is a "closed" system. Certain external factors, he points out, must be taken into account because of the influence they exert on the internal structure of the organization. In this respect he challenges one of the major tenets of the traditional school: the principle of uniformity. His approach, in contrast, emphasizes one's adjustment to the specific situation with which he comes into contact. In spite of this emphasis on the particular, however, he still subscribes to a rational, step-by-step approach to public administration. For him administration is a clear-cut, simple process if correctly approached.

In view of the inadequacies of traditional theory, he sought to establish a new set of organization principles on the basis of his personal experience. These include: (1) the establishment of a clear flow of communications; (2) the adaptation of structure to the peculiar requirements of a given situation so that there may be complete coincidence between function and vehicle; (3) the provision of an organizational structure adaptable to changing conditions; (4) the maintenance of organizational analysis as the continuous responsibility of the executive, rather than its periodic pursuit by the expert; (5) the establishment of a groove; and (6) an awareness of the gap between theory and reality. Although his approach was pragmatic in character, he too did not seek to change the goals of traditional public administration.

The first real departures from traditional organization theory are found in the human relations school, in which an interest in the individual within the large group replaces concern with the task. Whereas the goals of economy and efficiency remain constant, a real attempt is made to explain the nature of conflict within the organization.

The distinctive character of this school of thought is based on the Hawthorne experiments and the writings of F. J. Roethlisberger and W. J. Dickson.[5] The purpose of these experiments originally was to get at the physical factors influencing production. It was not long, how-

[5] Roethlisberger and Dickson, *Management and the Worker: An Account of a Research Program Conducted by the Western Electric Company, Hawthorne Works, Chicago.*

ever, before the researchers involved had decided that the crucial factor was not physiological, but rather a matter of group identification. This led, in turn, to an examination of external environmental influences on the individual worker. Another significant discovery was that steps that were rational to management would often be interpreted nonrationally by the workers. Also, it was observed that there were informal patterns of behavior within the organization that revolved around the cohesion of workers. In many cases this led to a divergence between the informal and the formal organization, between the natural group leader and the supervisor. In such situations it was noted that one's social relationships within a group might well be stronger than a particular economic incentive.

Nevertheless, in the human relations school the individual remained as much a passive instrument of the organization—although the focus now came to rest on the large group—as in the machine model of traditional administration. Similarly, the search for means to maintain equilibrium in the organization, begun by those in the transitional phase, continued, although the techniques advocated had changed. Further, the question of goal formation was never touched. The basic contribution of this school, then, lies in the attention it has drawn to the dysfunctional side of organizational behavior.

The decision-making model represents an even more fundamental departure from traditional public administration in that, while it is task-oriented, the emphasis moves away from concern with structure and with the adaptation of the individual to a particular set of circumstances, deemed proper and best, to a preoccupation with problem-solving in the organization as the essential process. At its basis is a focus on the decision as a fundamental unit for administrative analysis. Within the confines of this model there are two entirely different conceptualizations: the abstract and the concrete.

Herbert A. Simon is primarily concerned with administration as a series of rational decisions. He departs from the assumption that human behavior in the organization is, if not wholly rational, at least in substantial part intended to be so. He limits the purpose of administrative theory to the establishment of a boundary between the rational and the nonrational aspects of human behavior, for, according to his concept, administrative theory is responsible for developing a "theory of intended and bounded rationality." Proceeding from this foundation, he constructs a model of administrative man as opposed to economic man. While economic man theoretically "maximizes" by selecting the best alternatives from among those available to him, administrative man "satisfices" by looking for a course of action satisfactory or "good enough." Simon uses the term "satisfice" to indicate the selection of the best course of action from among those alternatives immediately available. Economic man may well deal with the real world in all its complexities, but administrative man, because of the boundary separating him from the outside world, recognizes that his world is a drastically simplified model of the real one. Since administrative man "satisfices" rather than "maximizes," he can make his choices without first examining all possible alternatives. By treating the world as rather "empty" and ignoring the "interrelatedness of all things," administrative man can "make his decisions with relatively simple rules of thumb that do not make impossible demands on his capacity for thought."[6]

The problem with this highly theoretical model is that it does not recognize the series of nonrational factors that enters into administrative behavior and that cannot be properly excluded if the administrative process is to be understood. (It is precisely to the nonrational factors in administration that many of the other models direct their attention.) Furthermore, by concentrating at the operational level, Simon avoids the whole problem of the changing goals of the organization which occur over a time span. After all, what is rational may well vary from one period to another, according to what the goals of the organization are. Finally, this model tends to be static.

In contrast to Simon's abstract model is the concrete case study approach to administration, exemplified by the work of Harold Stein[7] and the Inter-University Case Program. Its distinctive contribution has been to get politics back into the study of administration. By focusing on specific decision-making issues in real life situations it has developed an awareness of the environment surrounding administration; it has directed attention to the rational and nonrational aspects of human behavior in organization; and it has dealt with the problems created by conflicting goals and values.

But this analytic model is not without its problems. Although one of the goals of this model has been to build a body of knowledge from which generalizations about the administrative process can be reached, one of the most vexing problems has been how to impose

    [6] Herbert A. Simon, *Administrative Behavior: A Study of Decision-making Processes in Administrative Organization*, pp. xvi, xxiii–xxvi. For further developments in his conceptual model, see *Models of Man, Social and Rational: Mathematical Essays on Rational Human Behavior in a Social Setting* and "The Decision-making Schema: A Reply," in *Public Administrative Review*, XVIII (Winter, 1958), 60–62.
    [7] Stein, *Public Administration and Policy Development: A Case Book*.

standards of relevance so that comparability can be achieved on a case-to-case basis. As the Inter-University Case Program has evolved, its cases have been essentially studies of the unique. Thus, while this method of analysis has helped to illuminate the internal process of public administration in relation to its external political goals and environment, it has failed to contribute to the development of any general theory about decision-making precisely because of the unique and unrelated character of its cases. Furthermore, there is the problem of where the cut-off falls in these materials, for in reality these cases reach no final resolution. They are but a part of the on-going administrative process.

These deficiencies in the case study approach have been largely overcome more recently in the model that Aaron Wildavsky has developed for the analysis of the politics of the budgetary process. Wildavsky directs his attention to the overall decision-making process in a specific area. In doing so he avoids the uniqueness of the case study method, although he uses the method to collect data and on this basis seeks to generalize about the budgetary process. He likewise makes Simon's concept of "satisficing" operational by demonstrating that it is an important element in administrative behavior in budgetary matters. His concern is essentially with the individual units in the decision-making process and with the strategies and techniques they use to get public funds or to limit expenditures. This process is preeminently political. The merits of this approach are best summarized in his definition of budgeting. It is "concerned with the translation of financial resources into human purposes." It is

. . . an incremental process, proceeding from a historical basis, guided by accepted notions of fair shares, in which decisions are fragmented, made in sequence by specialized bodies, and coordinated through repeated attacks on problems and through multiple feed-back mechanisms.[8]

For Wildavsky, budgeting is an on-going process which is to be better understood by relating it to its political environment and by seeking to comprehend it through analysis of the process over an extended time span. This concept broadens the whole basis of the decision-making model and opens it up to new possibilities by combining the abstract and the concrete into an effective synthesis.

In contrast to the three previous models, the bureaucracy model concentrates on the organization per se or the large group in an organizational setting. Within this conceptual framework the move-

[8] Aaron Wildavsky, *The Politics of the Budgetary Process*, pp. 1, 62.

ment has been from a concern with the formalistic aspects of bureaucracy to one in which the researcher directs his attention toward human elements in a bureaucratic context.[9]

The point of departure for this analytic approach is the Weberian notion of bureaucracy. As an ideal-type construct, it is designed to offer a prototype for modern society. The following elements may be observed as being characteristic: rationality, impersonality, hierarchy of authority, formality, a rational set of rules, the importance of position, legitimacy, trained personnel, a career service, a monistic set of relationships, and the bureaucratization of society. Among these, the matter of legitimacy is of key importance, for, according to Weber, it is by reason of this legitimacy, granted by a formal act of law, that a bureaucracy has authority over its members. It also makes possible the creation of a rational set of rules, and these provide an operational basis for the entire organization and make necessary the maintenance of written records. This development of a set of rules and a written record, in turn, provides impersonality once it is assumed that the behavior of the administrator is neutral and impartial. This situation also necessitates the existence of trained personnel having the capacity to carry out specific duties. Since continuity is a major aspect of a functioning bureaucracy, this means that a career service, with systematic methods of recruitment and internal mobility based entirely on competency, is essential. Likewise, status is attached to the position and is not related to the individual personality; once an individual leaves a position, he leaves his previous status behind. Another aspect of the individual bureaucrat's position is the notion of a fixed salary established according to function and responsibility. Since a rational organization consisting of a monistic set of relationships is assumed, it is important that the hierarchy of authority be maintained and that each individual bureaucrat demonstrate a sense of obligation to the position above and responsibility to those below him. What emerges, then, is the image of a highly structured impersonal organization based on a set of authoritative relationships. While the internal objectives of the organization are economy, efficiency, and rationality, the whole matter of goals is left to be determined externally.

Those who have followed the bureaucratic model in analyzing organizations have attempted to perfect it by making it more dynamic,

---

[9] The discussion of this model is based on the following sources: Peter B. Blau, *The Dynamics of Bureaucracy: A Study of Inter-personal Relations in Two Governmental Agencies*; Robert K. Merton *et al.* (eds.), *Reader in Bureaucracy*; and W. Lloyd Warner *et al.*, *The American Federal Executive*.

by enabling it to deal with conflict, and by directing attention to the informal aspects of bureaucratic behavior. This involves breaking with a machine model approach to human behavior. The basic premise from which these writers operate is that each organization has a life of its own and can be examined as a living entity.

Concentration on the functions and dysfunctions of the organization is one way of getting at its dynamics and dealing with the fact that the Weberian assumption of the predictability of performance and the elimination of friction is not valid. The major interest here is in understanding the continual flux of an organization and the adaptations or the adjustments it continually undergoes. There is also an awareness of the variety of bureaucratic forms and the need to arrive at a set of common characteristics which can be interrelated with specific bureaucratic structures at particular points in time.

Another approach within this model is concerned with the fact that it cannot be assumed, as it is in the Weberian model, that people will do as they are told and that impersonality can be absolutely achieved. In this respect, attention is devoted to human behavior within a bureaucratic setting in other than neutral and impartial terms. After all, administrators, it is recognized, have individual values and are influenced by them. This leads to a consideration of the informal aspects of authority and the whole matter of the development of organizational loyalties and commitment to a specific set of goals. Nothing insures that the individuals in the organization will automatically develop a loyalty to the organization and a firm commitment to its goals. The problem of organization here becomes interwoven with that of recruitment and training.

In a third approach the organization is envisioned as a social system operating in a particular social setting and influenced by forms tangential to its rationally ordered structure and stated goals. This approach attacks the view of the organization as a self-contained unit constituting a closed system. Organization dynamics, according to this viewpoint, are a consequence of the process of continual adjustment and accommodation to a changing environment. A second aspect entering into the analysis of the dynamic and changing character of an organization is the informal internal structure that develops independently and interacts with the formal one. Attention is thus directed to the internal relevance of organization behavior and to understanding the external and internal forces which mold and change an organization's character.

The most recent development within the bureaucratic model has been the application of mass survey techniques to understand, in global terms, the characteristics of the American federal civil service. In this case, through an exhaustive examination of the backgrounds of civil servants, the degree of representativeness of the bureaucratic system in relation to its social environment is established. Through interviewing, character types of the civil servant are established. The focus here is on the bureaucracy essentially as a large group, analyzed according to various social criteria (for example, family, marital status, sex, geographical distribution, education, and previous employment experience). What emerges is an image of a bureaucracy, based not so much on an ideal-type construct as on a model constructed from the use of statistically relevant data.[10]

Like the bureaucratic model, the compliance structure model begins with an interest in the large organization as the fundamental unit of analysis. It differs in that, whereas the former directs its attention to the behavior of the organization, the latter concentrates on the behavior of the people involved as crucial to understanding how an organization functions. Writers who follow this approach challenge the coercive character of authority as it is found in the Weberian model and emphasize the importance of compliance on the part of subordinates. Within this model, several different paths are followed in analyzing compliance patterns and the nature of authority in the organization, but all begin with a recognition of the conflict potential in any organization and approach it on the basis of conflicting orientations among superiors and subordinates. The compliance structure within any organization, then, revolves around the fact that two parties are involved: one who exercises power and one who responds to it either in the direction of alienation or of commitment. Similarly, all recognize the necessity of developing some means for handling the interrelationship between organizational and individual values and goals to reduce conflict and to maintain an effective organization.

The particular way in which conflict is handled by the different writers who follow this analytic approach varies considerably. Selznick, in this particular case, focuses his attention on the "cooptation" process, that is, the way new elements are absorbed formally or informally into "the leadership- or policy-determining structure of an organization" when external threats to its stability or existence arise.

---

[10] Examples of these four approaches, in their respective order, are: Alvin W. Gouldner, "On Weber's Analysis of Bureaucratic Rules," in Merton *et al.* (eds.), *Reader in Bureaucracy*; Blau, *The Dynamics of Bureaucracy*, Chapter I; Philip Selznick, "A Theory of Organizational Commitments," in *Reader in Bureaucracy*; Warner *et al.*, *The American Federal Executive.*

The significance of cooptation lies not only in the fact that it may change or broaden the nature of leadership but also in its influence on the character and the role of the organization.[11] Presthus is oriented toward the people in the organization—their roles, how they conceive of themselves, and their personality types—while Thompson is interested in the problem created by conflict between those in specialist and hierarchial roles.[12] Hower and Orth limit their discussion to the conflict between scientists and management in industrial research organizations which arises as a consequence of two very different value orientations. They stress the need of management for a human relations skill and the necessity of open communications within the organization.[13] In contrast, Blau and Etzioni provide a much wider orientation: the former focuses on effective authority as dependent on the willingness of subordinates to comply with directives by a superior, while the latter, distinguishing between three types of power and three types of involvement in organizations, states that to maintain an effective organization there must be congruence between its goal and its compliance structure.[14] The three kinds of involvement Etzioni singles out are coercive, remunerative, and normative, while the three kinds of power are alienative, calculative, and moral. From this syndrome, three congruent types appear: the coercive organization, the utilitarian organization, and the normative organization.

In the rationalized systems model attention shifts away from the compliance structure and is directed toward the formal organization as a patterned set of interacting and interdependent variables, isolated from the external social system. Action within the organization is explained in terms of input-output, feedback relationships. Using the business firm as his prototype and taking concepts from sociology, Argyris constructs a highly rationalized model around two sets of variables: the formal organization and the individual.[15] He bases his construct on an image of human beings as need-fulfilling, goal-achieving entities and of formal organizations as complex patterns of interdependent variables. An essential element in the model is the assump-

[11] Philip Selznick, *TVA and the Grassroots: A Study in the Sociology of Formal Organization*, pp. 13, 15.

[12] Robert Presthus, *The Organizational Society: An Analysis and a Theory*, and Victor A. Thompson, *Modern Organization*.

[13] Ralph H. Hower and Charles D. Orth, *Managers and Scientists: Some Human Problems in Industrial Research Organization*.

[14] Peter M. Blau, "Critical Remarks on Weber's Theory of Authority," *American Political Science Review*, LVII (June, 1963), pp. 305–317; Amitai Etzioni, *A Comparative Analysis of Complex Organizations*.

[15] Chris Argyris, "Understanding Human Behavior in Organizations: One Viewpoint," in Mason Haire (ed.), *Modern Organization Theory: A Symposium*.

tion that all human beings are incomplete by themselves and, as such, they achieve wholeness only through interaction with others. Organization, Argyris claims, is a strategy; it is a human strategy designed to achieve certain objectives. Assuming the existence of a relatively mature individual and a formal organization that maximizes the principles of scientific management, he has as his primary objective the study of the impact of the formal organization on the individual. To achieve this goal, he conceives of a genetic model which, once completed, will also provide dynamic explanations of organized behavior.

The social systems models go one step beyond Argyris' highly rationalized model. Whereas he visualizes the organization as a closed system, these models conceive of formal organizations as open systems in that they interact with a larger social system. The crucial variable introduced here that is missing from so much other administrative analysis is the environment within which the organization operates.

The first of these constructs, the structural-functional model, is based on Parsonian analysis. According to Talcott Parsons, the distinguishing characteristic of an organization, as opposed to other social systems, is the primacy of its orientation to the attainment of a specific goal. He defines an organization as "a system which, as the attainment of its goal, 'produces' an identifiable something which can be utilized in some way by another system, an input."[16] The structure of an organization, he says, may be considered from two points of view: the cultural-institutional and the group or role. His emphasis, however, is upon the former.

In analysis of the structure of any social system, Parsons states that the major point of reference is its value patterns. These define the system's basic orientation in terms of the situation in which it operates and serve as a guide for the activities of those participating. Viewed as a system, these value patterns must necessarily function as a subsystem of a higher order and interact with it.

Since organizations may be classified according to the type of goal or function around which they are organized, the value system can be used to provide a basis for classification. Parsons, however, uses this concept in yet another way—as one of the major components of a social system. In this respect the value system is but one of four analytic categories. The others are the adaptive mechanisms (the mobilization of resources), the operative code (goal implementation), and the integrative mechanisms (the compatibility of the institutional pat-

[16] Talcott Parsons, *Structure and Process in Modern Societies*, p. 17.

terns under which the organization operates with those of other organizations and social units).[17]

The problem with this model is that it tends to be static and does not allow the researcher to deal with the organization on a time basis.

A second social system construct is to be found in the prime beneficiary model developed by Blau and Scott. On the basis of who can be determined to be the prime beneficiary of the services of a formal organization, they establish four analytic typologies: mutual benefit associations, in which the membership receives the primary benefits; business concerns, in which the owners are the prime beneficiaries; service organizations, in which the clientele group is the primary beneficiary, and commonweal organizations, in which the public at large is the prime beneficiary.[18] These typologies are difficult to apply to existing organizations because they do not allow one to account for the movement within an organization as it moves from one form of action to another. They provide neither any way to limit nor to define explicitly the clientele involved.

The third model, that offered by Sherif, focuses on the small group and, within this context, the importance of group norms and values as a factor in individual behavior and in the emergence of conflict. Sherif states:

A group is a social unit (1) which consists of a number of individuals who, at a given time, stand [in] more or less definite interdependent status or role relationships with one another, and (2) which explicitly or implicitly possesses a set of values or norms of its own regulating behavior of individual members, at least in matters of consequence to the group.[19]

This model directs attention to relations between small groups rather than relations within the group. It raises the problem of shifting individual attitudes within and outside the group. One application of this model and its stress on the importance of group norms is to be found in an article by Faris. He points out that the individualistic explanation of conflict on the basis of the frustration-aggression formula and according to the concept of displacement (i.e., the use of a scapegoat) is insufficient. There is need, he says, for examining interaction among groups and the conflict stemming from group definitions of reality as a corrective to the excessive emphasis on individual

---

[17] *Ibid.,* pp. 20, 44, 47, 57, 164.

[18] Peter M. Blau and W. Richard Scott, *Formal Organizations: A Comparative Approach.*

[19] Muzafer Sherif (ed.), *Intergroup Relations and Leadership: Approaches and Research in Industrial, Ethnic, Cultural, and Political Areas.*

action as determining group behavior. The group perception of reality and its influence on individual perceptions is a part of what Faris calls the "universality and normality of ethnocentrism." Hostility is not entirely a personality component; it originates, at least in part, within the context of a specific group or groups. The reduction of hostility is likewise a collective process in which group perceptions and norms are modified to understand more fully the total context giving rise to the conflict.[20]

The fourth model centers around the concept of role analysis as a means of understanding the action of an individual in the group. In their study of Massachusetts school superintendents, Gross, Mason, and McEachern set up a closed-systems model in which they concentrated on role conflict and collision around a central position.[21] Four definitions are in order here: by "position," the authors mean the location of an actor or class of actors in a system of social relationships; by "role," they mean a set of expectations, or a set of evaluative standards applied to the incumbent of a particular position; by "role conflict," they mean a difference between the expectations of the incumbent of a focal position and those in counter positions; by "role collision," they mean to describe the situation which occurs when two persons, entertaining the expectations that each can do the same thing, act on it simultaneously. This model is intended to supply the researcher with a tool to get at the difference in individual perceptions of role expectations, the multitude of positions which exist in a given setting, and the possibility of conflict and discord stemming from role collision and role conflict. While it excludes the external environment, it offers a means of establishing a greater perception of individual behavior in institutional settings.

The foregoing discussion illustrates the variety and abundance of conceptual approaches prominent in administrative analysis in the United States. In Brazil, however, the alternatives open to the researcher, the student, and the reformer have been much more limited. Here organization theory has been confined essentially to three models: the Continental European legalistic model, the machine model of American public administration, and a sociological model developed from a synthesis of Weberian bureaucracy with the social setting of administration.

Throughout the major part of their history Brazilians have viewed

[20] Robert E. Faris, "Interaction Levels and Intergroup Relations," in Sherif (ed.), *Intergroup Relations and Leadership*.

[21] Neal Gross, Ward S. Mason, and Alexander W. McEachern, *Explorations in Role Analysis: Studies of the School Superintendency Role*.

the problems of administration within a legalistic framework that is founded upon a civil law tradition. According to Alípio Goulart and Alberto Guerreiro Ramos' categories of analysis—the juridical, the technical, and the sociological[22]—the juridical phase applies to virtually all writing on Brazilian administration prior to 1936, although it does not cease with this date. It is oriented almost entirely toward abstract legal problems and is closely related to the study of administrative law. The basic sources cited by Brazilian writers are primarily French and, secondarily, German, and the intellectual framework is similar to that developed in those countries for the study of administration. This is understandable considering that, besides the civil law tradition, cultural borrowings from France and the use of ideals based on French political and administrative institutions have preceded cultural borrowing from the United States and the use of North American political and administrative models.

For the purposes here, specific writers following a legalistic model are not nearly so important as the general framework for administrative analysis created by the civil law system in Brazil. This legal foundation is crucial to the development of administrative theory in that country and is closely related to the failure of American-style public personnel concepts to function in the Brazilian environment.

Brazil has received its civil law heritage from two major sources: Portugal and France. For this reason, it is of value to measure Brazilian experience along these lines, with a model taken from Continental Europe rather than from the Anglo-American world. Such a model is to be found in Herbert J. Spiro's writing.[23]

In comparing Roman law and common law systems, Spiro initially draws a distinction between lawfulness and legalism. While lawfulness "looks upon the legal system as one instrument among several for the attainment of the goal of constitutionalism," legalism ". . . looks upon the legal system, its consistency and its elaboration, as the goal itself. All other phases of the political process are considered mere means for reaching this goal. . . ."[24] While there are obvious differences in style between the major continental European countries, Spiro maintains that legalism is one of their basic characteristics. In discussing Roman law, he points to its exhaustive detail, its

---

22 This threefold division of organization theory in Brazil is based on the categories suggested by José Alípio Goulart and Alberto Guerreiro Ramos. Goulart, "Sociologia e Administração Pública no Brasil," *RSP*, XVI (March, 1954), pp. 38–41; Guerreiro Ramos, *Uma Introdução ao Histórico da Organização Racional do Trabalho* (Tese).

23 Spiro, *Government by Constitution: The Political Systems of Democracy*.

24 *Ibid.*, p. 187.

comprehensiveness, and its orderliness—all of which are expressed in the emphasis on codification. These characteristics, he says, result in a preference for anticipatory legislation prior to experimentation, a feeling that nothing should be undertaken without prior legislation or regulation.[25] This conception of the law leads to an emphasis on law as an ideal toward which one should aim, rather than as something to be applied to present circumstances with as much precision as possible. Another aspect is the machinery of justice, which is much more important on the Continent than in the English-speaking countries.[26] Spiro relates these contrasting approaches to the law to different notions of knowledge pervading the educational system and intellectual endeavors. On the Continent there is a preference for deductive thinking in which the individual starts from general "laws" contained in a given body of knowledge and proceeds to apply them to concrete events that fit. The thought process in the Anglo-American world tends to depart from a different basis; it is inductive and more dynamic in character. From the facts contained in a series of cases or case studies, one moves on to tentative conclusions.[27] Consequently, he maintains, in Continental Europe there is the feeling that

Just as all the law has been put together in a comprehensive, consistent, and closed fashion, so should all knowledge about other fields be ordered. Just as those who are learned in the law can dispense justice, so should those learned in the science of the state or of the economy or of society be able to dispense the fruits of their study. Just as progress was achieved by compiling the law in codes, so could progress be achieved by compiling knowledge in these other spheres into comprehensive, coherent, and closed systems. . . . [In contrast] in the English-speaking countries, lower expectations are placed on legal knowledge and political science. The law has never been systematized and, as a consequence, there is little encouragement for attempts to systematize the social sciences in general, or political science in particular. They, too, may more safely grow from precedent to precedent.[28]

Certainly, exceptions can be found to these statements when it comes to the matter of specifics; yet they are relevant here in that they help to explain the different environment in which administrative principles and practices, developed mainly in the United States, have been expected to function. Throughout Brazilian legal experience, a decided emphasis has been placed on the codification of the law. In fact, one of Getúlio Vargas' major claims to lasting fame lies not in creation of an authoritarian state and the ordering of Brazilian

[25] *Ibid.*, p. 219.   [26] *Ibid.*, pp. 220–221.
[27] *Ibid.*, pp. 223–224.   [28] *Ibid.*, pp. 224–225.

politics in the 1930's but in the fact that he was responsible for an almost complete reform and unification of Brazilian civil and criminal law during this era. In this respect, he followed what Spiro points to as an important aspect of the Roman law tradition: that of the great lawgivers who, in their codification of the law, have made a lasting contribution for the order and progress of their nations. Another fact which should be remembered throughout any analysis of Brazilian organization theory is the stress on the systematization of knowledge and the underlying belief that the science of administration could and should form a comprehensive, coherent, and closed system of knowledge. In this development of thought, based on deductive methods of analysis, Brazilian administrative writers have retained a close contact with civil law theory.

Thus, when extensive administrative reform, with a preference for technical solutions to the problems of administration, was first begun in the mid-thirties, the concern with abstract legal theory continued to exist. Writers pursuing legalistic models and those constructing technical models shared the same basic premises and goals. They both accepted the assumption that administration should be separated from politics. Likewise they both ascribed to the centuries-old idea in political theory that power ought to be divided among the executive, the legislature, and the judiciary to prevent its abuse by the State. But, because of the traditional predominance of the executive in Brazil and the continuation of a civil law system, the separation-of-powers principle was more akin to Continental European usage than to North American. This may be seen in the fact that administrative law in Brazil has always been concerned with the development of legal controls on administrative abuses.[29] Finally, both groups have also aspired to essentially the same goal: an efficient public service that would meet the needs of the State and which would provide status and security for the individual civil servant.[30]

The bulk of Brazilian administrative writing, however, has followed a technical model in which administrative reform has been perceived in terms of the development of specialized skills. The model is task-oriented; it substantially excludes human behavior from the study of administration; and it assumes away the importance of the human element by adopting the premise that human interests are passive in character.

[29] A recent example of this approach is Miguel Seabrá Fagundes, *O Contrôle dos Atos Administrativos pelo Poder Judiciário.*
[30] Themistocles Brandão Cavalcanti, "Direito Administrativo e a Ciência da Administração," *RSP*, I (March, 1940), pp. 73–74.

Because these writings are voluminous and the topic of organization theory too broad to be presented here in its totality, representative figures will be used to provide both a background and a broader framework for a more specific consideration of personnel theory in the next chapter. Three of the leading figures in traditional public administration who have followed the technical model—Benedicto Silva, Wagner Estelita Campos, and Beatriz Marqués de Souza Wahrlich— have been selected as illustrative. They express the most systematic thinking about these matters among writers belonging to their generation. An analysis of their ideas will be followed by a consideration of the ideas of two writers who have pursued a sociological model: Alberto Guerreiro Ramos and Nelson Mello e Souza, men whose writings are indicative of the intellectual ferment experienced in Brazilian public administration in recent years.

The first of these figures, Benedicto Silva, is the foremost representative of the school of scientific administration in Brazil. He is essentially a synthesist of the ideas of Frederick Taylor, Henri Fayol, Luther Gulick, and Lyndall Urwick. While the word "scientific" enters into much of his writing, the emphasis is on the development of a series of principles or norms which are scientific only in that they represent supposedly universal rules for public administration. This is characteristic not only of Silva's approach but also of this whole school of thought, both within and outside of Brazil. Accordingly, his first principle is the search for the "one best way" as developed by Taylor. From this follow the so-called principles of the division of labor, the hierarchy of authority, and the development of a chain of command and, also, the administrative theory of Fayol, with its distinction between administration and government and with the executive functions of command, coordination, and control. The fact that in his analysis Fayol is one of the guiding lights in the development of the field of public administration and that Gulick and Urwick represent little but the adoption and perfection of Fayol's basic concepts helps to underscore Silva's belief in the universal quality of these principles.[31]

The second personality, Estelita Campos, who was until recently the director-general of DASP, occupies a position in Brazilian public administration not unlike that of Chester I. Barnard in American public administration. In fact, his book *Executive Leadership: Its Techniques and Its Problems*,[32] recently published in a third and re-

---

[31] Benedicto Silva, *Uma Teoria Geral de Planejamento*, pp. 25–33, and *Taylor e Fayol*.

[32] Wagner Estelita Campos, *Chefia: Sua Técnica e Seus Problemas*.

vised edition, parallels to a considerable extent Barnard's *Functions of the Executive*. Both focus on the problems of executive management as crucial to the success of the organization; both are aware of conflict with the principles of traditional public administration and thus adopt a normative approach to these principles; both mark the transition to the human relations school in public administration, with its focus on the work group and the adaptation of the individual employee to his work situation; both are concerned with the maintenance of equilibrium in the organization.

Estelita Campos' sources, like Silva's, are primarily North American, with the exception of Fayol, and he seeks to reduce the art of executive leadership to a series of normative principles. One of the basic, if not the most important, values on which these principles rest is his belief in a moral reform, both of the individuals involved in administration and the environment in which they work, as a solution to the administrative problems facing Brazil. By "a moral reform" he means the removal of political patronage from the federal civil service and the employment of individuals who are honest, well-trained, and capable of fulfilling their administrative responsibilities without interference by political partisans. This value, which is present throughout so much of the writing on Brazilian administration, is not so much a part of the dominant Brazilian value system as it is one which has been transferred from the United States to the Brazilian scene. In terms of personnel administration, this leads Estelita Campos to assert that entrance into the civil service by any means other than merit is strictly immoral. The basic problem, he insists, is not so much the need for greater attention to the technical problems involved in administration as it is the necessity of a reeducation of the country's directing elite in order to establish the proper moral climate. Such a moral climate would be characterized by honesty, economy, efficiency, and the absence of external political intrusions.[33]

His conception of executive leadership is manipulatory. In this respect, it shows a close similarity with the theory of democratic leadership developed by Lewin in the experiments held at the University of Iowa in the 1930's. In one section, Estelita Campos enumerates the traits of autocratic and democratic leaders in parallel columns. The first and basic characteristic contrasting the two is that, while the autocratic leader sets the objectives of the group in terms of his own personal interests, the democratic leader always sets them in terms of the group's common interest. He emphasizes the importance of

[33] *Ibid.*, p. 138, and "Recuperação Moral na Administração Pública," *RSP*, LXIX (December, 1955), pp. 282–301.

maintaining group cooperation through persuasion instead of through compulsion,[34] but devotes little or no attention to the fact that this approach to democratic leadership does not necessarily allow for the expression of real grievances unless the leader is in sympathy with them.

Beatriz Marqués de Souza Wahrlich, the third writer in the Brazilian school of traditional public administration, is one of the few authors writing in Portuguese who is concerned with organization theory per se. While her work has been primarily in the field of personnel administration, *An Analysis of the Theories of Organization*[35] reflects both the framework for her approach to personnel administration and the general status of administrative theory in Brazil until the emergence of Guerreiro Ramos.

Wahrlich divides organization theory into four categories: that of the engineers, the "anatomists," the psychologists, and the sociologists. In the first phase she places the administrative engineers who look at administration from the bottom up and who are concerned with mechanical techniques. The leading exponents are Frederick Taylor and Henry Ford. In the second, the emphasis of administrative analysis is reversed and attention is focused at the top of the organization. Wahrlich claims it is "anatomical" because of a basic preoccupation with forms and structure. These writers are essentially rationalists, and Fayol, Gulick, Urwick, Mooney, and Schuyler Wallace are the best examples. In the third phase she groups administrative writers who are influenced by psychology and who "interest themselves in the study of the organization as a system of control based on the recognition of individual motivations."[36] The most important figure here is Mary Parker Follett. Wahrlich also cites Catheryn Seckler-Hudson, Roethlisberger, Leighton, Simon, and Redfield as other significant figures. In the fourth phase she includes those authors in public administration who are concerned with the individual and his social setting. The basis of this school is the Hawthorne experiments. Mayo, Whitehead, and Roethlisberger are its precursors; they are followed by Barnard, Simon, Smithburg, Thompson, Selznick, and Redfield. Wahrlich laments that some of these individuals, especially Simon, suffer from a prejudice against traditional organiza-

---

[34] Estelita Campos, *Chefia*, p. 112.

[35] *Uma Análise das Teorias de Organização* is based on the thesis completed by Wahrlich in 1954 in the Graduate School of Public Administration of New York University for a Master's degree in Public Administration.

[36] *Ibid.*, p. 45.

tion theory. She also criticizes their tendency to use esoteric expressions.[37]

Having examined North American organization theory according to these four categories, Wahrlich concludes that while these various phases represent different approaches to the study of organization, all are needed to formulate an adequate theoretical basis for administration.[38] She implies quite clearly that they are all reconcilable.

At the root of Wahrlich's perception of administrative theory is the search for norms and principles which are to guide human behavior in organization and which, in their emphasis on reforming organization and human actions, lack a real foundation in empirical analysis. It is this approach which explains to some degree her grouping of widely divergent writers into the last two categories and which overlooks the authors' movement away from and the dissatisfaction with traditional organization theory. Apparently, once the belief in the existence of a body of universal principles of a technical character is accepted as a basic premise, a certain circularity of thought ensues, from which it is difficult to free oneself. Yet this does not concern Wahrlich, for, like Silva and Estelita Campos, she is essentially a synthesist of knowledge in the administrative field.

The emergence of a sociological school, centering around the ideas of Max Weber and paralleling the type of bureaucratic analysis found in such North American writers as Peter M. Blau, Philip Selznick, Victor A. Thompson, and Robert Presthus, marks a breaking away from the technical model to pursue a sociological one. This school is concerned principally with the formation of a conceptual framework related to the understanding of Brazilian administrative reality. Although the ideas characteristic of this school of thought are to be found more in discussion with Brazilians engaged in the field of public administration than in writing at present, there are two men writing in this area who are representative of this approach to administration.

Alberto Guerreiro Ramos has done a great deal to make these new ideas known. For him, the administrative function is preeminently sociological and anthropological and only secondarily juridical and technical. That is, he says, because "it consists of initiating social change and administering it." He writes:

> When we elaborate laws, regulations, instructions for the provision of service and rules, we are bringing about changes in human relations and

[37] *Ibid.*, pp. 75–76.
[38] *Ibid.*, pp. 79–80.

institutions which need to be administered intelligibly on the basis of the teachings of sociology and anthropology.[39]

He maintains that it is not enough simply to import new techniques and ideas, for society consists of a series of interrelated parts and such new techniques and ideas must be adapted to the needs of a particular society. He cites, as an example of the use of new techniques and ideas without adequate attention to the social context, the Brazilian experience with a merit system transplanted from the United States. In this instance, the existing social system completely changed and distorted the concepts involved.[40]

In contrast to Wahrlich, Guerreiro Ramos is quite sensitive to the movement away from traditional administrative theory in the human relations school. For him, this school represents a new departure in North American organization theory and is unreconcilable with previous ways of thinking about administration; yet this approach is not without its limitations. He points out that in considering the enterprise to be a complete social universe, Dickson and Roethlisberger have failed to perceive "the umbilical ties that unite it with the surrounding socio-cultural environment."[41]

In a later essay, he has insisted that a sociohistorical view of administrative phenomena is much more necessary in underdeveloped countries than in the advanced ones. This is because, in the latter, the advance in administrative theory and techniques is concomitant with their sociohistorical development.[42] Such a lack of awareness of the importance of the social environment, he states, undercuts the administrative reforms begun in 1938 and the political reorganization occurring in the latter part of 1945.

Another approach to the social environment within which administration functions is to be found in a recent article by Nelson Mello e Souza.[43] Whereas in the area of public administration Guerreiro

[39] Alberto Guerreiro Ramos, "Fundamentos Sociológicos da Administração Pública," Part II, Jornal do Brasil (Rio de Janeiro) [hereafter cited as JB], November 11, 1956, sec. 2, p. 8.

[40] Ibid., p. 8.

[41] Guerreiro Ramos, Uma Introdução ao Histórico da Organização.

[42] Guerreiro Ramos, "Desenvolvimento Tecnológico e Administração a Luz de Modelos Heurísticos," p. 1 (chapter of the forthcoming book Administração e Estratégia do Desenvolvimento).

[43] Nelson Mello e Souza, with the collaboration of Breno Genari, "Public Administration and Economic Development," in Daland (ed.), Perspectives of Brazilian Public Administration, Vol. I, pp. 145–171 (first published in Portuguese in the following form: Mello e Souza and Breno Genari, "Técnicas de Organização, Científica em Setores Específicos para o Desenvolvimento da Administração Pública," IDORT, XXXI [November–December, 1962], pp. 10–19).

Ramos is more concerned with the general development of organization theory, Mello e Souza is more interested in applying this new orientation to an analysis of Brazilian experience with administrative reform. His article demonstrates an awareness of Brazilian problems lacking in the majority of administrative literature in Brazil, although his zeal for modern, economic, and efficient administration is not less than that of his precursors. He does not call into question the traditional values and goals of public administration; instead, he seeks to explain why the techniques and skills imported from abroad have not functioned in Brazil as expected.

Thus, he directs his attention to "the ecology of development." His general thesis is

... that the application of techniques of scientific management to public administration in underdeveloped countries is handicapped primarily by non-technical problems. . . , [for] the principal focus of resistance is socio-political and derives from the structural characteristics of underdeveloped societies.[44]

The techniques designed to reform Brazilian administration failed because they were unrelated to administrative necessities. According to his interpretation, the Brazilian administrative system is primarily a paternalistic one, dependent on the external political environment. But this system should not be considered "pathological." It becomes pathological only if judged by a scale of values taken from the developed world. The challenge lies not so much in the rejection of what he calls rationalized values as in the development of a sense of timing in the careful and gradual overcoming of the problems presented by the sociopolitical environment.[45]

Whereas the reforms begun originally in 1936 lacked any basis in the political and social reality of the country at that time, he claims that by the 1960's, through industrial development, such a basis existed. In the 1930's, the "reformist movement was led by a technical elite who thought they could resolve the problems of modernizing by transplanting theories and practices developed in other contexts, especially the United States." He says further:

Their motivation was not linked to the economic development of Brazil, but rather to the moralization of political behavior and the patterns of administration. In spite of good intentions, it neither resolved nor clarified the problems of administrative reorganization in Brazil.[46]

Today conditions have changed, he affirms, and an administrative

---

[44] *Ibid.,* pp. 138–149.   [45] *Ibid.,* p. 148.   [46] *Ibid.,* p. 162.

system which serves the needs of a paternalistic political system is unable to meet the demands placed on it by the pressures for economic development.

Both Guerreiro Ramos and Mello e Souza, in resorting to sociological analysis for the study of administration and in using a conceptual framework based on the work of Weber, reflect a trend that is basic to the development of the social sciences in Brazil. Sociology, joined with related aspects of anthropology, enjoys a preeminence in the social sciences shared only by economics, while political science has not yet developed as a strong, separate discipline. With the exception of Orlando M. Carvalho, political scientists have been tied either to a legalistic model of politics or to a social systems model that identifies them in the Brazilian setting with the subfield of political sociology. This has meant that the viewpoint that public administration is closely tied to the study of political science has been rejected. This is due, first, to the attempt by writers in traditional public administration to separate administration from politics; secondly, to the recent emphasis on sociology to explain the failures of the technical approach to the analysis of administrative problems; and, third, to the domination of the technical assistance program by a "trade-school" orientation toward the problems of public administration.

Although the sociological approach does represent a clear step forward, it has the weakness of failing often to account for the differences between administration in the field of government and administration in the private enterprise. This point of view is further reinforced, both within and outside Brazil, by those closely tied to the field of business administration, who see little difference between administration in public and private sectors. It is true that both operate in a particular social context, but a public agency or department functions in an environment preeminently political and is subject to a series of cross-cutting pressures and conflicting goals and objectives which are absent in the private enterprise. The social universe of the business firm is a much more limitable and definable one. Its goals are narrower and more explicit; boundaries are more sharply defined; and its population is more limited.

Nevertheless, it is, in a sense, only natural, now that there are signs of a shift away from the techniques of administration to interest in the administrative environment, that there should be a movement toward the development of a sociological school. Social and economic relationships have continued to undergo many changes during the last two decades. In contrast, the formal political system has been only slightly affected. Regardless of experimentation with modified parliamentarian institutions between September, 1961, and January, 1963, the political system, from late 1945 to the revolution of April, 1964, functioned essentially along the same lines. Subsequently, the gap between the style of politics in existence and the developmental needs of the country became increasingly greater. Although the analysis of this phenomenon, as it is related to public personnel policies and practices, is more appropriately the subject of later chapters, it is pertinent to organization theory because this particular situation can be used to explain in part the reason for emphasis on sociology to break the confines of traditional administration. Because political institutions are formalistic in character and the style of politics represents a carry-over from the period preceding the Estado Novo, it has seemed to many analysts that the social environment, as a consequence of changing economic relationships, has been the major determinant of political behavior, if not the sole one.

Basic changes which have taken place in American public administration in the last two decades have not been adequately transferred to Brazil in spite of heavy reliance on American writers in this field and the training of substantial numbers of Brazilians in American schools of administration. Much of this is due to the hold of traditional public administration on Brazilian intellectual thought and to the commitment to reforming Brazilian administration according to the standards set by the scientific management school. Another, and perhaps more basic, explanation is to be found in the contrast between deductive and inductive reasoning which was briefly drawn in terms of the civil law tradition. The whole educational and intellectual orientation of law and the social sciences in Brazil is quite different from that encountered in the United States, where the way of thinking tends to be inductive, to be pragmatic, and to show a preference for proceeding from one isolated case to the next. As such, North Americans often tend to view means as ends in themselves. This way of thinking also tends to reflect a quality of continuous debate joined with a willingness to compromise. The development of Taylorism and later the scientific management school is very much a part of this tradition; yet when transferred to the Brazilian milieu, it becomes something quite different. This alternation in the intellectual bases of this school of thought is most clearly reflected in Benedicto Silva's book *Taylor and Fayol*. Silva considers Taylor and Fayol to be the great masters of the science of administration. Supported by essays from other Brazilian figures in the field of public administration, he embarks on a path of textual exegesis. In this work, as well as in others, he strives to fuse the contributions of Frederick W. Taylor,

Henri Fayol, and their disciples into a comprehensive, coherent, and closed system of knowledge. The basic reasoning process manifested not only by Silva but by this entire school in Brazil is deductive. These men show a tendency to proceed from a set of first principles, and from them they develop a theory of how administration could and should be ordered. For this reason, they have been most receptive to the administrative theory of Fayol, the POSDCORB concept of Luther Gulick, the principles of traditional American administrative thought, and, more recently, the Weberian approach to bureaucracy.

By juxtaposing the status of organization theory in Brazil and the United States, it becomes clear that Brazilian public administration has been subjected essentially to a single analytic model, one which may be characterized as a machine model approach to administration. There is really only one exception to this statement: Guerreiro Ramos. He alone has been willing to leave behind the confines of traditional public administration to consider Brazilian bureaucracy as a social system. His model, which has been termed sociological, does not have any strict parallel with the models developed to analyze organizations in the United States, although he is quite familiar with recent developments in organizational analysis and has synthesized them. His is designed, after all, to form a construct which can be used to more completely analyze Brazilian public administration. In this respect, he has developed a bureaucratic model which, as a subsystem, is interrelated with the social environment.

In contrast, Mello e Souza, the other writer classified as following a sociological model, has not broken with the scientific management school. Instead, he has held its concepts to be valid for modern administrative systems and has moved in the direction of a bureaucratic model which will explain the failure to create a modern administrative system on the basis of a hostile environment. The model against which he measures Brazilian administrative experience is Weberian. His goal is the creation in Brazil of an administrative system which is economic, efficient, and rational and which will eventually fulfill the Weberian requirements for modern bureaucracy. In this regard, it should be remembered that Weber's bureaucratic construct is much closer to the machine model of human behavior than it is to other approaches to administrative analysis.[47] Given previous Brazilian experience in administrative theory and present trends, organization theory will likely continue along these lines. An attempt was made to introduce the human relations school. Another is now being made

[47] March and Simon, *Organizations*, pp. 36–37.

to introduce the case-study technique and the decision-making model into Brazilian administration, but it has not yet produced results.

Attention can now be turned to personnel theory, which, like traditional organization theory in Brazil, is closely related to developments in North American public administration. It furthermore complements the systematic, comprehensive body of knowledge which has been built up in the scientific management school.

CHAPTER IV

Personnel Theory

The developments in Brazilian personnel theory parallel, to a large extent, those of organization theory sketched broadly in the preceding chapter. Just as Brazilian leaders in the administrative field have approached organization theory through what is essentially a single model, so too have they subjected personnel theory to a single analytic framework. But, whereas some have begun to revise and adjust the machine model of traditional administrative theory to Weberian concepts and have attempted to explain its failure to function on the basis of a hostile social environment, personnel theory has remained static and formalistic.

Involved here is a further difficulty, related to the reliance of Brazilian writers on North American public administration source materials. Personnel theory in the United States has scarcely passed beyond the model provided by the human relations school. Yet even these ideas have failed to make an impact in Brazil upon traditional ways of thinking about the public personnel field. As in the case of organization theory, Brazilian writers interested in public personnel administration have not attempted to apply the inductive methodology inherent in the human relations approach to the analysis of related Brazilian phenomena. When they have drawn upon the findings of this school of thought, they have incorporated them into an intellectual framework which demonstrates a preference for principles and deductive reasoning in analyzing the administrative process.

This chapter is concerned with tabulating the results from a content analysis of 138 articles and books containing material relevant to personnel theory. Of this sample, fifty were classified according to a legalistic model, while eighty-seven were characterized as following a technical model. Although none was sociological in character, one article fell outside the confines of the two previous categories. Strictly speaking, it belongs to the human relations school.

Consideration of the legal framework within which personnel techniques and principles have functioned will precede a detailed examination of the assumptions, values, and goals found in Brazilian public personnel administration materials. This examination will encounter the same three basic developments that have occurred in traditional North American public administration: first, a concentration on the techniques of administration; second, the formulation of a series of administrative principles; and, third, a transition away from these principles toward an interest in the position of the executive as crucial to explaining the failure of these principles to produce the desired effects.

The fifty articles and books following a legalistic model for personnel administration are concerned primarily with such legislation as the statutes of the *funcionário público*[1] and with the interpretation of legal norms, either in regard to what the public employee should be doing and does not do or with reference to how better to protect the rights of individual civil servants against the State.

At the center of this concern for the legal status of the civil servant lies the concept of the *funcionário público*, the public functionary. It is a concept tied closely to Continental experience, particularly French, and quite remote from traditions in the American civil service. In Brazil, as in France, the term *funcionário* (Fr. *fonctionnaire*) is

... applicable only to those employees of the central government who (1) have received a commission from a public appointing authority and (2) belong to a cadre of *permanent* employees, all of which involves a fixed monthly salary and the right to a retirement pension.[2]

A separate terminology exists for other public employees. In Brazil, these are the *extranumerários* (supplementary personnel) and the *interinos* (temporary employees). In France the same distinction is made between personnel *ouvrier* and *temporaire*.

In Brazil the career civil servant has enjoyed in the past, and to a limited extent continues to enjoy, a legal status carrying with it certain rights and privileges. Among these are tenure, retirement, sick leave, vacation pay, and social welfare benefits. Until 1960 one of the major political battles in the area of public personnel policies was the constant attempt of *extranumerários* to obtain these rights and privi-

---

[1] The two statutes of this kind in Brazilian legislation (the *Estatuto dos Funcionários* [Decree-Law 1713] of 1939 and the *Estatutos dos Funcionários Públicos Civis da União* [Law 1711] of 1952) codify the rights, privileges, and obligations of civil servants with the status of a *funcionário público*.

[2] Walter R. Sharp, *The French Civil Service: Bureaucracy in Transition*, p. 15.

leges through special legislation. The *interino* has tried to achieve this status through another tactic—that of having his classification changed from interim employee to one with tenure. Hence, in principle the *funcionário público* has been a permanent government employee admitted to the career civil service on the basis of merit, as proven by examination; in practice, however, this has been a status position with a certain amount of security and a fixed income to which many persons outside the merit system have aspired. This concern with individual status in the civil service and the parallel with the organization of the French public service are important factors to remember when an American-oriented classification plan is superimposed on this foundation.

Another parallel with Continental experience in general and with French experience in particular is found in the desire of the civil servant to have his rights and privileges guaranteed by specific legislation and to have this legislation compiled into comprehensive legal codes. Thus, the French movement to obtain a *statut des fonctionnaires* was reproduced in Brazil. In both cases, the goal of an *estatuto* (Fr. *statut*) was related to the desire of the *funcionário* (Fr. *fonctionnaire*) to obtain a general code fixing rules for recruiting, promoting, paying, disciplining, and retiring state employees. There is, however, one basic difference. In France, this movement took some eighty years to achieve its goal and was largely the result of pressure created by the *fonctionnaires*. In Brazil, it was of much shorter duration and the first *estatuto* was largely the result of Vargas' initiative in the attempt to create an elite civil service.

As a consequence of this concern for the legal definition of the rights, privileges, and responsibilities of the civil servant, several books and articles deal with the statutes governing the *funcionário público* and with additional rights and privileges accrued through other legislation and executive regulations.[3] Until 1960, when the *extranumerário* category was abolished by law, this interest in legal status also gave rise to materials dealing with the *extranumerário*, which paralleled the material on the *funcionário*.[4] A third area of

---

[3] Examples of these are: Carlos Schmidt de Barros Júnior, "Direitos Adquiridos dos Funcionários Públicos," *Revista de Direito Administrativo*, LI (January–March, 1958), 19–28; Fernando Henrique Mendes de Almeida, "Os Deveres de Obediência e Sigilo do Funcionário Público," *Revista da Faculdade de Direito, Universidade de São Paulo*, LIV: 1 (1959), 131–148; José Augusto de Carvalho e Melo, "O Estado e Seus Servidores," *RSP*, I (March, 1949), 57–59; Armando Pereira, *Os Direitos e Vantagens dos Funcionários*; Eduardo Pinto Pessoa Sobrinho, *Manual dos Servidores do Estado*.

[4] For legalistic articles dealing with the *extranumerário*, see: Amílcar de Araújo Falção, "Extranumerário; Equiparação de Salários e Vencimentos; Princípios de

interest has been those court cases which have been significant in the protection of the individual civil servant against the State.[5]

To understand properly the juridical framework within which the Brazilian civil service has functioned, it is essential to place this concern with the defense of individual rights as opposed to the State in contrast with North American administrative practices where the right of the State in determining public employment is preeminent.

Astério Dardeau Vieira has drawn attention to the contrasting legal traditions of the United States and Brazil. Recognizing the legal systems of the two countries as a crucial variable in their approach to public personnel, he attempted to set down these contrasts in an article written in 1938.[6] In the matter of the rights and guarantees of the civil servant, he places Brazil and the United States at polar extremes. In Brazil the fact that the protection of individual rights is placed over and above his responsibilities as a public employee works against efficiency in the public service. In contrast, he points to the concept of a collective or public interest as the major element in determining the relations between the State and its servants in the United States. Within this wider framework, then, the rights and guarantees of public employment, rather than the prerogatives of the individual, are established.

To make this contrast clearer, the individual's attitude toward the requirement of competitive public examinations is compared. In the United States, once an individual has passed the required examination, the State retains the right to decide whom it will use for public employment. An eligibility list is prepared; when a vacancy appears, the Civil Service Commission selects three names on the basis of geo-

Isonomia [Parecer]," *Revista Forense,* CLXXIV (November–December, 1957), 98–102; Valmiro Rodrigues Vidal, *Extranumerários União-Estados-Autarquias: Direitos e Vantagens;* Paulo Poppe de Figueiredo, "Pessoal das Emprêsas Concessionárias do Serviço Público," *RSP,* I (March–April, 1948), 23–26; and Alonso Caldas Brandão (ed.), *Previdência Social (Legislação): Atualizada com as Alterações até 31-12-1957* (Rio de Janeiro: Serviço de Documentação do Ministério de Trabalho, Indústria e Comércio, 1958). The latter book contains all legislation and decrees applying to the social welfare institutes, but a substantial part involves personnel administration as well.

[5] Two books indicative of this concern with the status of the civil servant before the State are: Gilberto Spilborghs Costa, *Administração de Pessoal: Jurisprudência Administrativa,* and Francisco Oliveira e Silva (ed.), *O Funcionário e o Estado.* The first is a catalogue of *regulamentos* (regulations and rules) on personnel administration; the second contains a series of judicial decisions over cases brought into the courts by *funcionários públicos.*

[6] Vieira, "O Interêsse Público e o Interésse Privado na Administração de Pessoal: Estudo Comparativo dos Sistemas Brasileiro e Norte-Americano," *RSP,* II (April, 1938), 9–12.

graphical apportionment. Finally, the office concerned selects the candidate it wants from among the three submitted for the position. In Brazil such a system could not function. The legal system in public personnel matters is based on the negative concept of first protecting individual rights against the State as employer. Consequently innumerable cases have arisen in which individuals who have passed the public examination and have not been admitted to the civil service have gone to court to protect what are deemed to be their rights against arbitrary action by the State.[7]

In contrast to the protective character of the juridical materials on public personnel administration, the eighty-seven articles and books following a technical model are oriented toward the improvement of personnel administration through the institution of new skills and techniques intended to contribute to the goal of economy and efficiency in the administrative system. This technical material corresponds to the machine model approach of the scientific management school in both North American and Brazilian organization theory.

The machine model approach in the United States and Brazil has as its basic assumption the passivity of human interests; as its goal, maximum efficiency and economy; and as its basic value, the belief that there is a "one best way." In organization and personnel theory, the initial focus of this model is at the workshop level, and the technique advocated is the use of modern administrative tools and skills. In personnel administration, emphasis is placed on the importance of classifying civil service positions according to the duties and responsibilities of each job.[8] This stress on the mechanics of personnel administration is also seen in the techniques prescribed for recruitment, examination administration, and pre- and in-service training.

A common value expressed in traditional American and Brazilian literature on personnel administration is that the fundamental unit of analysis is the position, not the individual. Virtually all Brazilian

---

[7] *Ibid.*

[8] Brazilian examples of this orientation are found in: Adalmo de Araújo Andrade, *Diretrizes para Classificação de Cargos*; José de Nazaré Teixeira Dias, *Classificação de Cargos*; Kleber Nascimento, *Classificação de Cargos no Brasil*; Eduardo Pinto Pessoa Sobrinho, *Classificação de Cargos*, "Classificação de Cargos no Brasil," (*RSP*, III [September–October, 1948], 91–100), and *Curso de Classificação de Cargos (Cursos de Administração)*; Othon Sérvulo de Vasconcelos, *A Classificação de Cargos como Problema de Organização*; and Astério Dardeau Vieira, *Como Classificar os Cargos*.

This valuation of the classification of positions as the key to an efficient civil service is perhaps best expressed in the original classification proposal submitted by DASP (Brazil, Comissão do Plano de Classificação de Cargos, *A Classificação de Cargos e a Revisão dos Níveis de Vencimentos do Funcionalismo Civil da União*).

writers in the personnel field have accepted this value without question. From this basis they have proceeded to use the position as a basic unit in classification and to assert that it should serve as a building block for the whole administrative structure. It ought, however, to be stressed that this is a value which emerges from both the Weberian approach to rational bureaucracy and American standards and practices. The basic idea in position classification in the United States is that all those positions in an organization involving similar duties and responsibilities should be grouped for purposes of recruitment, compensation, and other personnel matters. The idea is "neutral" enough in itself, but it is based on the philosophy that the position is to be classified and not the person currently holding it. The notion that prestige and status stem from the public office occupied and are not inherent in the individual is one of the fundamental tenets of the "American creed."[9]

The emphasis placed on position as the basic unit in developing a classification plan is at variance with the entire evolution of the Brazilian civil service. There the individual traditionally has carried the status inherent in himself into the civil service and it, in turn, has reinforced his prestige as an individual. This development is not unlike the situation existing in the British civil service prior to the nineteenth-century reforms and that in the United States during the Federalist era. For this reason, while there is a shift in Brazilian personnel theory away from emphasis on protecting the status of the individual civil servant from abuses committed by the State, this earlier concern with the individual in the employment of the State continues and is found in all current legislation on the subject.

In the United States, the concept of position developed in connection with patterns of upward mobility during an historical period that has followed—not preceded or coincided with—the Jacksonian revolution. In Brazil, such an experience has been absent. The democratic revolution, in the terms described by Tocqueville, is only now being experienced in Brazil.

As T. Lynn Smith has pointed out, Brazil has traditionally had a highly stratified society, with a rigid system of social classes. In such a context, the middle class has emerged more as a product of downward social mobility rather than as a product of upward mobility, as in the case of the United States. One of the consequences of the extended family, the traditional upper-class kinship unit, has been the appearance of numerous offspring for whom it has been difficult to

---

[9] This "American creed" concept is based on Gunnar Myrdal, *An American Dilemma.*

provide sufficient source of income with which to maintain their upper-class origins.[10] Under such circumstances, many of these individuals have sought government positions as a way of defending the status they feel inherent in themselves. In essence, they still aspire to a series of values which are aristocratic in character and which reflect the dominant value system in Brazil. Certainly much of this is in the process of changing under the impact of urbanization, industrialization, and an extraordinary population growth. These traditional patterns, however, have had a great deal to do with the social character of much of the Brazilian civil service.

In the Brazilian civil service, as in other administrative systems, such as the French, the individual is more important than the position. The *funcionário público* is, above all, a middle-class individual concerned with maintaining his status. Joined to this is the fact that, as numerous individuals in recent decades have sought to move up on the social scale, employment in the public service has become one of the signs that they have escaped from their lower-class backgrounds. In the changing character of Brazilian society, the public service provides a focal point for comprehending the overlapping of older and more recent patterns of social mobility.

The fact that civil service reformers have sought to impose the concept of position as basic to the development of a rational public personnel system has merely increased the gap between policies and practices in the area of government employment. The solution for Brazilians trained in the techniques of personnel administration is not a more rigorous application of the position principle, but, rather, a greater understanding on their part of the dynamics of Brazilian society. If the techniques of classification in public service are to be made functional they must be adapted to a social system quite different from that of the United States. Even the value of a single classification plan for the federal civil service of a complex transitional society such as Brazil's is open to question.

The transition from the emphasis on techniques to a concern with the principles of scientific management, both in the United States and Brazil, is a slight, but important, one. The same basic assumptions, goals, and values remain; the major difference is that they take on a more sophisticated form. In addition, to the goal of economy and efficiency is added the subgoal of coordination. To achieve the objective of a rational, ordered administrative system in which the adminis-

10 T. Lynn Smith, *Brazil, People and Institutions.*

trator can get things done, these writers claim that there must be a coordination of the men and tools involved. Moreover, the basic value —that there is a "one best way"—is further developed to include the concept of the separation of facts and values, the division between administration and politics, and the necessity of generalist administrators. As a consequence of these modifications, attention is shifted from the workshop level to the top of the hierarchy, to the formulation of organizational charts, and to the manipulation of subordinate units. The coordination of administrative tools and skills is the technique advocated to achieve this. The search for universal principles of administration now becomes the belief that they have been discovered.

In the field of personnel administration, the emphasis on mechanics is continued and expanded by standardizing methods of examination and recruitment, position classification, and pre- and in-service training programs.

The fact that this approach is especially normative is nowhere better noted than in two articles by Benedicto Silva.[11] He is convinced that there is increasing evidence that personnel administration in many countries has been placed on a rational basis, or is moving in that direction. In contrast, disorder and arbitrariness—traditional characteristics of personnel administration—are being replaced, with greater or less success, by civil service laws, regulations, and scientific procedures. Specialists, he further asserts, are agreed that the principal objective of modern personnel administration is to foment increasing efficiency in government. Such efficiency is to be achieved by a rise in general efficiency, lower unitary costs, high employee morale, and better service to the public. In order to adopt modern techniques and methods in personnel administration it is necessary to create a civil service based on unqualified acceptance and rigorous observance of the merit system. But this introduction of a merit system depends ordinarily on the preestablishment of a central personnel organ responsible for the principal phases of personnel administration.[12]

On the basis of these values and norms, Silva reduces the characteristics of a career civil service to fifteen essential elements:

1. Merit as the ultimate standard for admission
2. A classification plan

---

[11] Silva, "A Moderna Administração de Pessoal," *RSP*, LXVII (May, 1955), 216–239, and "Missão e Problemas dos Serviços de Pessoal," Introduction to Tomás de Vilanova Monteiro Lopes, *Problemas de Pessoal da Emprêsa Moderna*.
[12] Silva, "A Moderna Administração," *RSP*, LXVII (May, 1955), 218–219.

3. Standardization of wages and privileges
4. Adequate remuneration
5. Recruitment only for initial positions and advancement through promotion or transfer
6. The linking together of recruitment and the educational system
7. Realism in the conceptualization of examinations
8. In-service training
9. A "true" system of vertical promotion
10. Evaluation of the individual's ability (in terms of promotion)
11. Automatic horizontal promotion
12. Tenure
13. Protection of employee interests
14. The certainty of retirement
15. Liberal and progressive conditions of work.[13]

From the normative emphasis of the scientific management school, Brazilian and North American personnel theory moves into a transitional phase, where attention is drawn increasingly to the importance of executive leadership and to the maintenance of equilibrium in the organization through executive manipulation. The emphasis on coordination is continued; however, stress falls more on the coordination of the human elements involved in the enterprise than on the techniques used. The role of the leader is to increase the participation of subordinates in the decision-making process and to obtain their compliance with the organization's demands through cooperative rather

[13] Silva, "Missão e Problemas," in Lopes, *Problemas de Pessoal,* pp. xiv–xix. Other examples of this approach are in the following: Urbano de Albuquerque, "Uma Política Segura na Administração de Pessoal," *RSP*, I (January, 1954), 75–77; Augusto de Bulhões, *Elementos para um Programa de Administração de Pessoal*; Ennor de Almeida Carneiro, "Avaliação de Cargos," *RSP*, III (August, 1954), 28–37, "O Plano de Remuneração: Fundamentos Teóricos e Técnica," *RSP*, LXVII (May, 1955), 240–262, "Salário e Relações Humanas no Trabalho," *RSP*, LXVI (January, 1955), 14–23, and "Política de Remuneração," *RSP*, LXVII (April, 1955), 41–47; Pedro Augusto Cysneiros, "Administração Pública e Administração de Pessoal," *RSP*, I (February, 1952), 139–145; José de Nazaré Teixeira Dias, *Administração de Pessoal: Algumas Sugestões para o Aperfeiçoamento do Serviço Civil*; Herson de Faria Dória, "A Seleção dos Servidores do Estado e a Diagnose das Contra-Indicações Profissionais," *RSP*, II (April, 1954), 29–33, and (June, 1954), 29–40; Paulo Poppe de Figueiredo, *Curso de Administração de Pessoal*; Lopes, *Problemas de Pessoal*, Maria da Conceição Miragaia Pitanga, "Administração de Pessoal e Planejamento," *RSP*, IV (December, 1946), 119–121; Arlindo Vieira de Almeida Ramos, "Base Científica da Administração do Pessoal," *RSP*, IV (December, 1951), 39–46; Luiz Guilherme Ramos Ribeiro, *Do Elemento Pessoal no Serviço Público.*

than through compulsive methods. In the personnel field, this orientation is expressed in the idea that there is a body of principles and norms to orient the administrator in his contact with employees.[14] There is an increasing awareness that the principles of scientific management as applied to personnel administration must be adapted to the specific set of circumstances encountered in each case. They are guidelines rather than directives.[15]

Precisely in this vein Eduardo Pinto Pessoa Sobrinho and José de Nazaré Teixeira Dias begin their book on personnel administration. They call attention to the fact that legislation regulating personnel administration—which began in Brazil with the Civil Service Law of 1936 and reflects the imitation of foreign models—has been excessively normative and abstract. They are also critical of the fact that debates over this or that piece of legislation have had little relation to the specific needs and problems of the individual administrator.

The human element in an administrative setting is the basic concern of their approach. The goal of efficiency is less an objective of personnel administration and more a consequence of certain other factors—the discovery and attraction of capable personnel, their training and perfection, and the maintenance of employee morale.[16] Moreover, they make a clear distinction between the individual and the position. They are critical of the traditional emphasis on the position as the fundamental unit of the organization to the exclusion of the human element. Their point of reference is Leonard D. White and

14 José de Nazaré Teixeira Dias, *Curso de Administração de Pessoal.*
15 Sixteen books and articles among the materials examined demonstrate these characteristics; one is listed in the preceding footnote. The others are: Adalmo de Araújo Andrade, *Introdução a Administração de Pessoal*; Brazil, Ministro Extraordinário para a Reforma Administrativa, "Normas para Preservação e Revigoramento do Sistema do Mérito"; Bulhões, *Curso da Administração de Pessoal*; Dias, "A Formação e o Aperfeiçoamento dos Quadros Administrativos de Chefia," *RSP*, LXVI (January, 1955), 11–13; Ary de Castro Fernandes, *Curso de Administração de Pessoal (Cursos de Administração)*; Byron Torres de Freitas, *Administração de Pessoal (Serviço Público, Indústria e Comércio)*; Anibal Maya, "Como Processar a Adaptação do Novo Servidor ao Ambiente do Trabalho," *RSP*, IV (December, 1943), 96–99; Raimundo Xavier de Menezes, *Elementos de Técnica de Avaliação de Cargos*; Hermínio de Miranda, "O Problema da Formação do Administrador," *O Observador Econômico e Financeiro*, CXL–CXLI (February–March, 1956), 57–59; Maria de Lourdes Lima Modiano, "Estímulo, Fator de Maior Eficiência no Serviço," *RSP*, III (August, 1949), 39–41; Antônio Fonseca Pimentel, *Alguns Aspectos do Treinamento*; Pessoa Sobrinho and Dias, *Princípios de Administração de Pessoal*; Wahrlich, *Administração de Pessoal: Princípios e Técnicas*, A *Importância de Formação de Pessoal*, "O Sistema do Mérito na Administração Federal Brasileira," *RSP*, XX (August, 1957), 237–254, and "O Ensino da Administração Pública e o Treinamento de Servidores Públicos no Brasil," *Revista Brasileira de Estudos Políticos*, XVIII (January, 1965), 57–80.
16 Pessoa Sobrinho and Dias, *Princípios de Administração de Pessoal*, p. 17.

his idea that the fundamental unit of the organization is the position *and* its occupant, the employee. Hence, position is defined as ". . . that body of functions and responsibilities which characterize a unit of the organization, attributed to an individual in virtue of the act of a competent authority."[17] They similarly modify the emphasis placed on the essentiality of a classification plan in scientific administration; it is simply a means to an end which is used in conjunction with numerous other techniques.

In the area of promotions, they advocate abandoning any rigorous adherence to mechanical procedure and replacing it with the idea that the method employed should be adapted to the particular needs of the organization. For example, the principle that promotions should be limited to those who have already served the organization needs to be modified when qualified personnel are lacking and when new blood is needed. If the principle conflicts with the needs of the moment, it should be abandoned.[18]

The same approach is applied to their examination of other principles and techniques advocated in scientific administration. The focal point is that employee interests must be brought into harmony with the fundamental interests of the organization through coordination, rather than compulsion, under the leadership of capable administrators. In this respect, they continue to advocate the necessity of a central personnel organ—one which will serve to coordinate the whole federal personnel system and which will establish harmony (or equilibrium) among the conflicting interests at play.[19]

A second example of this transition from the scientific management school is found in Raimundo Xavier de Menezes' book on the evaluation of positions as a basic element in the development of classification plans. At the outset he cautions against excessive certainty that positions can be evaluated according to sharp concepts and scientific precision: the method has its fallacies because in the final analysis it is subject to human judgment. Nevertheless, it is still the best method developed, and thus the administrator should be aware of the subjectivism inherent in it. Recognizing the limitations encountered, Menezes states that the evaluation of positions should be directed more toward the search for internal and external equilibrium in the organization than toward conformity with principles and methods not always valid in every context.[20]

[17] *Ibid.*, p. 56.
[18] *Ibid.*, pp. 185–186.
[19] *Ibid.*, pp. 191–192.
[20] Menezes, *Elementos de Técnica*, p. 104.

Several of the articles and books placed in this phase of personnel theory contain elements which, it would seem, would better warrant placing them in the human relations school. This is particularly true of the material just discussed. Although it is concerned with human relations as such, the focus on employee-employer relations is strictly from the viewpoint of the administrator—on how the human elements involved in the organization may be better utilized and how cooperation (in the sense of coordination) may be maximized. The one exception to this statement is an article published by José de Nazaré Teixeira Dias in 1942.[21] Instead of focusing on the executive or the administrator, Dias draws attention to the supervisor as the key man in the organization. However, the way in which he discusses the need for the training of supervisors is similar in outlook to the stress placed on the executive.

The distinctness of this transitional approach becomes clear only when contrasted with the work group and supervisor focus of the human relations school as developed in the United States. In the literature on Brazilian personnel administration, this change is further obscured by the fact that a number of writers in the transitional phase make reference to the Hawthorne experiments and draw on the writings of Mayo, Roethlisberger, and Dickson without altering basically the traditional framework of their analyses.

This use of materials from the human relations school within the framework of traditional public administration and personnel administration is nowhere better demonstrated than in the writings of Beatriz Wahrlich. Her most recent book is designed as a manual for the administrator at all levels.[22] It is essentially a representation of a traditional approach to personnel administration along technical, "how-to-do-it" lines, modified by ideas from writers in transition away from scientific administration (such as Barnard) and by concepts from the human relations school.

After four introductory chapters dealing with public personnel policies and practices in Brazil, Wahrlich moves into a discussion of the scientific techniques designed to contribute to the objective of a rationalized administrative system. Because of her wide experience in attempting to institute these practices in Brazilian administration, her constant reference to the successes and failures of these techniques in reality offers an insight lacking in most of the Brazilian literature on personnel administration. Throughout the book, underneath the specific techniques, is an interlacing of Weberian and American

---

[21] Dias, "A Formação de Supervisores," *RSP*, III (August, 1942), 27–29.
[22] Wahrlich, *Administração de Pessoal*.

values she seeks to apply to the reform of the Brazilian civil service. Wahrlich is very much aware of the conflict that has occurred in attempting to institute a functioning merit system. She points to the source of the problems, how they have been overcome or reduced, and the necessity of eradicating the sources of resistance. Despite an unfavorable set of circumstances, her belief in neutrality remains unshaken.

A further development in Wahrlich's ideas is found in a recent article,[23] originally presented as a paper at the 1963 Latin American Conference on Public Administration in Developing Countries held in Bogotá, Colombia. While the major portion of the article is devoted to the teaching of public administration in Brazil, the introduction and framework of analysis tie together major trends in Brazilian organization and personnel theory.

In this paper, the key role public administration has to play in the development process is stressed. This importance stems from the fact that State intervention and an increase in executive power characterize the present era. Never, says Wahrlich, has social well-being been so dependent on government. To meet this challenge, it is essential that public administration become efficient. In the face of the conditions created by underdevelopment, the question of efficiency, she maintains, passes beyond the academic limitations imposed by administrative theory and becomes an imperative.[24]

The pursuit of administrative efficiency involves two aspects, the organizational and the human. These are related to Wahrlich's orientation toward organization theory discussed in the preceding chapter. Here the four approaches she singled out—those of the engineers, the "anatomists," the psychologists, and the sociologists—have been reduced to two groups. The first applies to those who analyze the civil service from an anatomical and physiological standpoint and who try to detect and to pick out structural and functional deficiencies in administration. This approach, she states, is based on Taylorism and is characteristic of public administration during the first forty years of this century. The second involves trends that have been revolutionizing administrative theory and practice for the last twenty years. The psychologists and sociologists who make up this group conceive of administration essentially as an association of persons in which the pursuit of determined objectives depends, above all, on group inter-

---

[23] Wahrlich, "O Ensino da Administração Pública," *Revista Brasileira de Estudos Políticos*, XVIII (January, 1965), 57–80.
[24] *Ibid.*, pp. 58–59.

action. Crucial to this orientation is its concern with the variables which condition the equilibrium of human relations.[25]

Wahrlich points to the fact that the attempt to increase efficiency in Brazilian administration has come about almost entirely through an emphasis on the organizational aspects of public administration. Very little has been done in terms of considering the human elements, and this, according to her interpretation, has been the basic cause of the general failure to change Brazilian administration and to achieve efficiency. Given this set of circumstances, a major effort must be directed toward the teaching of public administration and, more specifically, toward the training of civil servants at all levels. These constitute basic measures in the struggle against underdevelopment.[26] Such training, however, should be basically oriented toward personnel at the executive level. The key to success, it would seem, lies in placing a proper emphasis on leadership in an organizational context.

Training should be *global*, that is, it ought to embrace all categories of civil servants and it ought to project itself *from the top to the bottom*, reaching initially both executive and upper level advisory positions. The support of persons in these positions is essential to any program. Qualitative deficiencies in schedules containing personnel in executive positions have a decisive role in the failure of initiatives to improve the functioning of administration. The search for efficiency in Brazilian public administration has called for, from the beginning, the training of personnel "at the top" with the objective of making them believers in the advantages of scientific administration.[27]

In short, Wahrlich asserts, the preparation of personnel at higher levels ought to be the immediate objective and retain priority in training.[28]

Thus, it may be stated in the way of a conclusion that Brazilian personnel theory has not progressed much beyond the limits imposed by traditional public administration. Although there is a substantial literature in North American personnel administration which can be analyzed according to the human relations model, and attention is given to this material in the *Revista do Serviço Público,* there is really only one article among the Brazilian materials surveyed that can

[25] *Ibid.,* pp. 59–60.
[26] *Ibid.,* p. 60.
[27] *Ibid.,* p. 77.
[28] *Ibid.,* p. 79.

properly be included here.[29] The explanation for this phenomenon is to be found in two factors: the continuing belief that there are universal principles of scientific administration which must be imposed on Brazilian administration—if a modernized system is to be developed —and the fact that the group focus of the human relations school, while related to developments in American society, has little or no basis in the Brazilian environment. In the latter case, no universal principles as such are asserted, for the concepts advanced are founded on a solid empirical basis.

Nothing in Brazil, to my knowledge, parallels the Hawthorne experiments; nor is there any attempt to test out principles asserted on the basis of best judgment to see whether they really lead to the results claimed for them. In the transitional phase, there is some awareness of the conflict involved between the principles of scientific management and the broad range of Brazilian experience with civil service reform, but the ultimate validity of this approach is never once called into question. Instead, the search is continued for guidelines which will lead the administrator to his utopia where the goals of economy and efficiency are to be had through the creation of a merit system and a neutral and impartial civil service.

For the most part, organization and personnel theory in Brazil are oriented toward work in terms of nonhuman objects. When the human element is taken into account, it is from a machine model approach. Thus, on the basis of the preceding analysis of organization and personnel theory, it may be concluded that conceptually Brazilian public administration still operates within the framework of a closed system of thought. Only in the area of industrial relations has a true human relations school begun to emerge in Brazil.[30]

The emphasis in the public personnel field continues to be on the development of skills and techniques which will contribute to the goals of economy and efficiency in administration. The passivity of the human element in an organizational context is an unquestioned

---

[29] Arlindo Vieira de Almeida Ramos, "A Moderna Administração de Pessoal e os Conselhos de Pessoal," *RSP*, II (April, 1952), 41–55. Indicative of the attempt to introduce the ideas of the human relations school are: Morton Grodzins, "Administração Pública e Ciência das Relações Humanas" [translated from English], *RSP*, XV (February, 1952), 24–36, and A. Fonseca Pimentel, "O Homem na Organização do Trabalho," *JB* (November 18, 1950), sec. 2, p. 8.

[30] Evaristo de Morães Filho, *Relações Humanas na Indústria: Lições de Sociologia Industrial*, and Pierre G. Weil, "An Experience in Psychological Counseling and Training of Personnel in Brazil," *Training Directors Journal*, XVIII (February, 1964), 3–9. This observation is also based on an interview with Weil (February 24, 1964) at the Banco de Lavoura's training center in Belo Horizonte, Minas Gerais, and on a tour of the center and conversations with the staff.

assumption. Cooperation is also assumed to be something which will result if the right techniques are employed, if the correct controls over employees are initiated, if the proper sort of person is admitted into the civil service. The nature of conflict within the organization is little understood; no group-centered orientation comes to terms with the problems created by human relations within the area of public personnel administration; and no one has attempted to develop a systematic model which will approach the problem of personnel administration on the basis of open systems analysis.

CHAPTER V

Conflicting Perceptions of the Civil Service

Another way of approaching the third independent variable (the imposition of scientific management techniques without concern for existing administrative behavior) is to concentrate on the personalities concerned with changing the nature of the federal civil service and to consider conflicting perceptions of what the civil service and its public personnel system entail and what relation should or does exist with the external political system.

The following perceptions of the civil service should be considered in relation to the data presented in the previous chapters and as an introduction to the civil service's political setting. The interview material on which the content of this chapter is based is in itself insufficient to offer a complete image of the civil service, for it was collected with a different purpose in mind: to broaden the viewpoint previously presented and to pinpoint the perceptions which individuals selected on the basis of reputation, position, and a relevant interest in these matters had of the civil service within a broad social matrix.

Before proceeding further it should be made clear what the limitations of this interview material are and what it is intended to demonstrate. Attention was focused only on the federal civil service. While some time was spent examining the administrative reform movement in the state of Minas Gerais, this material is not included here, nor is any subsequent effort made to evaluate other attempts at reform in state administrative systems, as for example in the case of Bahia. No effort was made to obtain geographic distribution, nor to examine the impact of administration outside the major urban areas. With the exception of a short trip to Belo Horizonte, the interviews were confined to Rio de Janeiro. These deficiencies are to be weighed against three facts. First, although Brasília is formally the capital of the country, Rio, for all effective purposes, is the administrative center. Secondly, one institution, the Fundação Getúlio Vargas, is overrepresented because it, more than any other, has been intimately involved in administrative change at the national level for the last twenty years. Finally, it should not be assumed that because the interviews took place in Rio they therefore represent individuals only from that area of the country. Those interviewed came from a variety of regions and in many cases still retained a strong sense of regional identification.[1]

If the interview material is classified according to what a public personnel system entails and what is involved in administrative change, thirteen of the interviewees may be characterized as technical and structural in orientation; one as normative; five as focusing on the functions of the executive as crucial to changing the administrative process; and eight as sociological in character—in that they consider change in the administrative system as a consequence of the external social system. Seven of the interviews fall outside the boundary imposed by the status of organization and personnel theory in Brazil.[2] The civil service is conceived of as an integral part of the political system in these materials. As might be expected, the men interviewed in these instances looked at the civil service from positions outside the administrative system, although they too were involved in civil service reform.

The thirteen interviewees classified in the first category represented a variety of backgrounds. Two were officials in the Ministry of Finance at the middle management level (one of these has written extensively in the field of public personnel administration); one was located in DASP; one in Petrobrás; one in the US/AID program in public administration; and one in the Conselho Nacional de Economia. A judge, formerly both a DASP employee and a member of the presidential staff, and a general in the army who was also the director of a governmental agency were interviewed. Three interviewees were professors of public administration in Rio de Janeiro with interests in personnel administration (of these, one had moved into business administration, while the others had concentrated their efforts in the public personnel field, the one teaching in this field and pursuing a government career and the other serving on a positions-classification commission in the state of Guanabara). A professor of public administration in Belo Horizonte and an active participant in the administrative reform program in the state of Minas Gerais complete the list.

These individuals perceived the civil service and the problems of

---

[1] The interview material and techniques are further discussed in the Appendix, which includes a facsimile of the interview guide.

[2] Seven additional interviews were held, but the material collected was not relevant to the purposes here.

administration in terms of structures and techniques. In each case their attention was focused on how to obtain personnel who were well trained, competent, and free of political association. They operated essentially from the premise that administrative matters were best left to the technician and should remain free from political influence. At the same time, none of them denied that this premise had not operated properly during the past two decades; nevertheless, in their minds its validity was not affected by this situation. Economic and efficient administration, they felt, was contingent on the exclusion of political influences from the normal functioning of administrative organs. The major task ahead was the restructuring of the civil service to achieve modern public administration and the construction of new and more effective barriers against external political intrusions. At the same time, they believed that a modern civil service would better serve the desires and needs of those directing the political system.

The single interviewee whose approach could be classified as normative was a professor of public administration and an official in the Ministry of Finance; he had spent his entire career in government. His approach, similar to that of the technicians, varied in that by focusing his attention at the top of the administrative hierarchy he saw the need to reorganize not so much according to the incorporation of modern techniques as through the application of principles universal in character. Yet these principles, he said, would become viable only as further progress was made in democratic development. He was quite cognizant of the problems raised by the external political system, yet his belief in the validity of the merit system and principles of administration remained firm. At the same time, he felt that what had previously been stated as "scientific principles" were open to question. A modern and efficient civil service in Brazil would, in his opinion, become operational as the political and economic system matured. His viewpoint also varied in that he saw no way in which administration could be separated from politics, even from a theoretical point of view. This was probably due to the focus of his attention at the policy-making level of administration. The administrative problems facing Brazil today, he said, were the equivalent of social engineering. Even though a transition in Brazilian administration was under way, there was still no audience, no clientele, to whom writers expressing new ideas or approaches could direct themselves.

The third set of interview materials focused on the civil service from the standpoint of those with executive functions and adopted the approach that the crucial area in administrative change centers around the recruitment, training, and proper use of those located in the higher civil service. If the right sort of direction and guidance could be assured in the civil service, these men felt that previous diffi- culties in creating a "modern" administrative system could largely be overcome. This orientation was expressed in interviews held with a ranking DASP official, an American professor participating in the US/AID program in public administration, a professor of political science in Rio de Janeiro who has long been active in the field of public administration, a ranking official in the Fundação Getúlio Vargas who has participated in every previous administration reform pro- gram, and an employee of the Ministry of Planning participating in the formation of a new administrative reform plan for the Castelo Branco government. The specific way in which this preference for focusing attention on executive functions was expressed varied—from those who saw the major failing in the civil service as the lack of leadership skills and the absence of an executive training program to those who asserted that a greater effort must be made to establish an administrative class which could properly direct, control, and coor- dinate the administrative process and function as the guarantor for administrative reform.

Those individuals who have adopted a sociological approach to the analysis of administrative phenomena determined the fourth group- ing of the interview materials. This group was composed of three pro- fessors of public administration in Rio de Janeiro, one of whom has previously been active in politics; two professors of sociology; one professor of history and sociology who has had thirty years' experience at the executive level in one of the social security institutes; and a di- rector of one of the government's *autarquias*. These men viewed the character of the Brazilian civil service as a consequence of the social environment within which it functions. According to these interpre- tations, the concept of a merit system and the use of administrative techniques borrowed from more advanced countries was dysfunction- al in the Brazilian milieu because of the absence of a social system which was supportive. To institute any meaningful change in the civil service—or in the political parties, for that matter—these people maintained that a basic change in the country's social structure must first come about. For them, the predominant characteristic of Bra- zilian society was its patrimonialism (i.e., its traditional nature). This was an element which they felt could be traced throughout the polit- ical and administrative systems. These men contrasted the character- istics of a patrimonial administration with those of modern adminis- tration. Within the Brazilian context this was related to a struggle between an old system based on a clientele type of politics and the pressures for economy and efficiency in administration. The patronage system as a traditional means for entry into the public service was likewise contrasted with the creation of a merit system in which selection is made on the basis of the most competent. In one instance, this led an interviewee to assert the necessity of an administrative class, one which, with the full awareness of the social environment, would play a crucial role in development and in consolidating the power of a political regime committed to modernization. In such a case politics and administration would be joined, instead of separated, and a dynamic movement led by a modern elite and challenging the traditional order would be created.

In contrast to the preceding perceptions of the civil service, one final group saw the civil service as functioning in a highly political environment. For these individuals, it was impossible to consider the civil service without being aware of the fact that it was a major element in the functioning of Brazilian politics. Two of these men were federal deputies who had been in Congress for the past two decades and had exercised an important role in the passage of legislation relevant to the federal civil service; one was a lawyer and professor who had held positions previously in DASP, the Ministry of Labor, and in the presidential cabinet; one was an ex-administrative official currently employed in private business and still active in the public personnel field; two were professors of political science; and one was an American official with an interest in labor and civil servant organizations. While their individual views of the civil service varied, they all held in common an interest in it as an integral part of the political process. For them, the character of the civil service was related to the problems of executive-legislative relations, the structure and organization of the political parties, the way in which interest groups acted in the Brazilian context, and the nature of syndicalist organizations.

As might be expected, the individuals constituting these various groupings perceived the major problems facing the civil service and public personnel administration in quite different terms. Certain common problems, however, were singled out by each group. All groups pointed to the persistence of patronage pressures in spite of numerous devices designed to establish a civil service based on merit. The individual terminology used and the explanations given varied considerably, but none denied that a mass of unskilled civil servants had gained entrance through various nonmerit channels and presented a serious barrier to any attempt to alter the character of the civil service. In addition, whether or not these groups, or the individuals comprising them, supported the premise that administration below the policy-making level should be separated from politics, they agreed that the political environment was at variance with the creation of a "modern" civil service. As one American official in public administration put it, the major problem in Brazilian administration, as in other underdeveloped areas, was how to eliminate nepotism and political opportunism, for without a merit-based civil service United States administrative technicians and Brazilian nationals trained in the United States could not be adequately utilized. In another instance, an interviewee stated the problem in these terms: In those cases in which individuals had received training in administration, whether in Brazil or in the United States or both, none of them was really prepared to deal with the highly politicized environment in which he had to function. Yet, he said, the structure of political power in the Brazilian system was such that pressure groups, in their effort to influence public policy, focused a major part of their attention on those departments and positions in the public service which they deemed crucial to their interests. Still other interviewees, in discussing the highly political character of the federal administration, emphasized the fact that in many cases interest groups preferred to by-pass the congress and the political parties (which were basically electoral organizations) so that they might focus their attention directly upon the administrative system—either to neutralize the enactment of decrees and legislation hostile to their interests or to bring about favorable action on their behalf.

Beyond this, there was little consensus on what constituted the major problems faced by the civil service. Those interviews classified in the first three groups viewed the problems within the framework of traditional public personnel administration. Theirs was essentially a closed systems approach. They stressed the obstacles presented by such problems as the inadequacy of current examination techniques; the difficulty of oganizing and carrying out in-service training programs; the failure to establish a rationalized salary scale in an inflationary economy; the incomplete character of the classification of positions plan and the delays in its application; the slow character of mobility within the civil service; and the excessive amount of paper work required for those going through the proper procedural channels. They also cited the insufficiency of governmental resources to provide adequate salaries for the number of civil servants employed, joined with the government's inability to reduce the number of employees where they were in excess and at the same time to keep better staffs in the offices where skilled personnel were needed. In one case, an administrative official, on the basis of his experience as a departmental director in one of the ministries, singled out as particularly vexing the difficulty of breaking the administrative routine and providing coordination among the ministers or within the same ministry. After a lifetime in administrative positions, he found that, in spite of efforts at introducing new techniques and methods, the bureaucratic process continued to function basically as it always had. For this reason he stated that the fundamental problem facing the civil service involved how to obtain and keep trained, competent personnel.

Those in the third category tended to focus the problems at the higher levels of the civil service to explain the difficulty of obtaining more qualified individuals. In one case, an interviewee explained that the major problem is not how to impose a viable merit system, but how to open up the development of leadership skills so that those without university training could be drawn upon and utilized. He stated that the belief in a merit system had been essentially learned in the United States and transferred to Brazil, where without a system of mass education it had become another means of locking in members of the elite and thus was utilized to maintain a closed administrative system. The type of examination required he viewed as a major bottleneck which further stimulated the desire of many to by-pass the legal requirements and to gain entry through more traditional means. Stopping the mass pressures for public employment was not the problem as he conceived it. Rather it was how to accept them as part of the push to open up jobs to the common man; how to focus attention on the means to best utilize these pressures; and how to advance people within the civil service on the basis of qualification, ability, and reward for new skills learned.

In every case, the interviewees explained the gap between formal public personnel policies and the functioning of the personnel system in practice as a consequence of the political environment within which the civil service has operated. Policies designed to restructure the civil service, to provide a more competent and highly skilled personnel, and to contribute to the objectives of economy and efficiency were most often viewed as incongruous with a political and social system that was basically patrimonial in character. The attempt to create a "modern" administrative system was contrasted with the traditional character of Brazilian society and politics. In several cases interviewees noted the fact that the techniques and concepts contained in the field of personnel administration, as imported from the United States, were most successful in modern industrial firms and, within the public sector, in the state of São Paulo, where an adequate social and economic basis made these concepts operational. Many of the interviewees explained this gap solely as a consequence of the unjustified intrusion of partisan politics into the administrative arena. They maintained that these imported policies offered the best way to achieve a "modern" civil service and that they could function properly only if effective barriers were constructed to keep out the politician and pressures for public employment. This viewpoint was not confined to any one particular group, but was to be found in different forms in all five. In many cases it was believed that these violations would disappear as the problems of economic development were overcome. In others, the emphasis was placed on the human factor: new administrative techniques were imported, but individual attitudes and orientations, both within and outside the administrative system, remained unchanged. Still others spoke of the fact that structural reforms and the introduction of new procedures and techniques really accomplished very little in the way of change. They were imposed formally, but individual offices and departments continued to function substantially along traditional lines. The formalistic character of the administrative system, the lengthy paper work and the delays involved, and the need to get certain things accomplished encouraged the development of informal lines of communication where matters could be expedited in much less time and much more efficiently.

Politically the gap between policies and practices was explained by the existence of clientele politics. The whole structure of Brazilian politics was viewed as one in which the major focus was on building a large number of political supporters who then required rewards and jobs. Under such conditions, a merit-based civil service, neutral and impartial in character, was deemed to be a fiction. This was particularly true, said one source, since the attempt at administrative reform was itself a kind of politics.

In six cases, attention was centered on the DASP experience. It was singled out as an example of what can happen when ideas and institutions are transferred from one country to another without regard for the environment within which they function. What occurred was simply the erection of a new administrative structure through laws and decrees unaccompanied by an attempt to create an understanding of the value of the new system in political channels. One interviewee stressed the fact that DASP was systematically formed on the basis of American experience and that the ideas behind the whole administrative reform movement had come basically from the United States.

This view, expressed by one looking at administration from its wider political context, contrasts with the opinion of an interviewee included in the technical-structural category, in which the validity of these imported concepts and the techniques inherent in them were defended. This individual emphasized the point that the technical aspects of public personnel administration must be incorporated because they represented the only proven way that efficiency and economy could be achieved in administration. He went on to say that it was absolutely essential that models be imported from abroad. After all, from his viewpoint, a body of techniques of universal validity existed. The responsibility of the Brazilian, then, was to develop forms for utilizing them. In this case, he said, we were dealing with science, and in science we turn to advanced countries for their models. The merit system is one of these, and it is a model which is of use to us. In essence, the great ideas are the same in any place. The great error is the failure to adapt these models to the particular situation at hand. The one proven body of techniques is international and neutral, though in each instance they are subject to social, economic, and political limitations.

Two of the interviewees, in discussing the DASP experience, focused their attention on difficulties which had arisen within the civilian bureaucracy. One indicated that the reforms became formal because of the shortage of qualified, trained personnel to carry them out and because those committed to administrative reform were too few in comparison with the total size of the civil service. After 1945, this situation was further aggravated by the decline in real salaries and the attractiveness of higher paying jobs in private business. The second interviewee cited three factors as relevant to understanding the DASP experience. First, he stated that too much emphasis was placed originally on preparing personnel in DASP without devoting adequate attention to the preparation of personnel in the ministries who would carry out the reforms initiated under the auspices of DASP. At the ministerial level there was no administrative class trained in the new skills and capable of exercising the leadership needed to alter the character of the administrative system. Under these circumstances the publication of personnel directives by DASP was not enough, for these directives had to be carried out essentially by the same people. Hence, they were internally sabotaged. A second factor was the nature of DASP: its responsibilities were too extensive in relation to its ability to carry them out. During the dictatorship, the emphasis was on control rather than coordination; to this day the organization has functioned very poorly as a coordinative apparatus, although this was one of the major reasons for its creation. The third factor cited was the absence of public opinion defending the merit system, a concept imported from abroad and imposed from above.

A politician provided still another explanation of the formalistic character of the DASP structure and the violation of the norms it set in the public personnel field. He explained the gap between theory and reality as a consequence of the fact that the DASP structure was entirely unrelated to the needs and desires of the mass of civil servants. As one who had been active in the handling of numerous pieces of legislation benefiting the lower ranks of the civil service, he visualized the objectives and desires of those at the top of the administrative hierarchy and associated with the DASP principle as incompatible with the needs and aspirations of the mass of civil servants. This was, he felt, a result of DASP's lack of concern with the human aspect of administration. In too many cases its views on technical administration and on the achievement of economy and efficiency were imposed regardless of the social cost. Thus, the lower ranks of the civil service found a more logical recourse to action in the political realm, where, in association with urban labor groups, they could bring pressure to bear on the government in such matters as, for example, salary increases. The conflict with DASP arose when it ceased to be purely a personnel organ, began to try to control all aspects of administration, and demonstrated an unwillingness to compromise and to have its policies questioned. In explaining patronage pressures, the politician stressed not its aristocratic character but the opportunity it provided large numbers of people to escape their poverty-stricken surroundings by seeking public employment. Patronage was an institution with a humanitarian side in a social and economic system full of inequalities. This he contrasted with a government which sought neither to understand nor to deal with the social inequities that gave rise to these conditions, but rather sought to construct a higher and more effective wall to bar such influences from the federal civil service.

Another politician, discussing the contrast between the policies regulating appointments to the civil service and the practices used in making them, explained the phenomenon of *empreguismo*—the excessive seeking of employment in the public service—as the consequence of not one, but a variety of pressures. On the one hand, traditional pressures, involving kinship and friendship ties, were brought to bear on a person in public life. These pressures he related to the strong sense of family in Brazil and to the desire of the large family to see all its members protected and provided for. In addition, many individuals lost in the turmoil, change, and instability of contemporary Brazilian life turned to the public service as a safe haven where a steady, if modest, income was assured. Yet another cause of *empreguismo* was the growth of the population of the country: the number of jobs available was insufficient to grant employment to all in the expanding potential work force. Finally, this politician discussed the patronage pressures experienced by a party such as the Brazilian Labor Party (Partido Trabalhista Brasileiro—PTB) in contrast to those faced by the Social Democratic Party (Partido Social Democrático—PSD), a party consisting of traditional elements. Although not a member of the PTB himself, he saw the party as one which was based on the lower classes and immigrant labor groups, including a sizable number of active participants with Syrian-Lebanese background. Although not as large numerically in their country as the Irish in American politics at the turn of the last century, their interest in politics is comparable, and the politician referred to the description of politics in *The Last Hurrah* to describe this interest. He went on to say that while the PTB has always had a special interest in the Ministry of Labor and in the social security institutes, the positions of treasurer and assistant treasurer in the various departments and ministries were among the most popular for all types of patronage.

The ideal model that emerges from this interview material is that of a civil service which will function with the autonomy of the French system but with administrative skills and techniques borrowed from the United States. In the majority of the interviews conducted, a sense of frustration was noted. The general feeling was that the Brazilian civil service, in spite of all the attempts to reform its character, has continued to function substantially as it always had and has remained responsive to external political influences, despite the efforts to exclude them. After some thirty-five years of emphasizing the techniques of administration, whether focused at the operational level or at the policy-making level, the need for some other solution has become obvious but the question of which direction to take remains. The major problem in Brazilian administration is no longer the development of administrative know-how, for the country possesses a group of quite sophisticated people, trained in administration and the social sciences, who have an understanding of the prerequisites of modern public administration as it has developed in the West.

Most of the interviewees took refuge in the idea that the goal of "modern," economic, efficient administration will become realizable only in time, as the social and economic system matures. But they are equally aware that there is not the time to wait. Administrators in

Brazil have increasingly emphasized the necessity for more effective public administration if further progress is to be made in the area of economic development. In general, the problems created by patronage and political influence throughout the administrative system have been considered an evil which must be removed at all costs, an embarrassing situation which, although recognized, should be dispensed with as quickly as possible. Little attention has been devoted to understanding these pressures and analyzing their causes. The major need, it would seem, is for innovative behavior—for a willingness to break with foreign models and, the total context within which the institutions of other countries function, being understood, a willingness to look for Brazilian solutions to what are, in the final analysis, Brazilian problems. This is hardly an original observation, for something quite similar was expressed over a hundred years ago when the Viscount of Uruguay discussed the application to Brazil of English, American, and French administrative institutions.[3]

3 Visconde do Uruguay, *Ensaio sôbre o Direito Administrativo*, Ch. XXXI.

CHAPTER VI

A Model for the Study of the Political System

Among present-day materials on Brazilian politics, three viewpoints developed by Brazilian writers are helpful in understanding the environment in which administration has functioned. These are the concept of clientele politics, with its correlate, the Cartorial State; the idea that there are five types of political action which may be isolated from Brazilian political experience; and the notion that a strong conservative tradition has existed throughout Brazilian history. When pulled together into a model, these concepts provide insight into the political understructure of the civil service system.

The first of these concepts is in Hélio Jaguaribe's discussions of the development of a clientele style of politics from the combination of a plantation system with representative political institutions. He visualizes each clientele group as centering around pacts of mutual interest which are tied to a single man who is representative of the interests of a particular area. These pacts are articulated first by municipality, then by province, and finally converge at the national level. While this style of politics had its origin in the Empire, it did not reach its full development until the unitary state of the monarchy was abandoned and a federal republic established. According to Jaguaribe, the First Republic was essentially a political order dominated by a marginal middle class, in league with a rural bourgeoisie. Because of a semicolonial economy centered around the production of coffee, the middle class remained marginal and was incapable of instituting the radical changes in the country's socioeconomic structure necessary to make its role functional. Although these political relationships were functional for the needs of the First Republic, after 1930 they were responsible for a "social parasitism" which "strangles" relations among all classes and for a political system entirely out of keeping with socioeconomic conditions.[1]

The correlate of clientele politics is the Cartorial State, a regime in which favors (usually in the form of jobs or special privileges) are bartered for votes.

The essence of the Cartorial State is found in the fact that the State is, in the first place, the maintainer or guarantor of the status quo. [It] . . . is a product of clientele politics and, at the same time, the instrument that utilizes and perpetuates it. . . . [In this system] public employment is not in actuality directed toward the rendering of any public service, but only toward the more or less indirect subsidization of clienteles in exchange for electoral support. This function, separated from social reality, unrelated to the need for rendering effective public service, results in an infinite pyramid of positions where innocuous papers are circulated and where the only activity exercised is the feeding of itself through self-benefiting practices. . . . Its objective is not the rendering of public services, but [instead] the provision for a marginal middle class, which, since it has little to do, becomes the predominant force in public opinion —an illustrious force which votes and orients itself within the mechanism of an indirect subsidy. The dominant class indirectly subsidizes the leisure and the marginality of the middle class, giving it a place within the Cartorial State, and [the middle class] pays a tax which the [State] returns in the form of favors for the maintenance of clientele politics and a semicolonial and semifeudal structure.[2]

In contrast to Jaguaribe's isolation of a single predominant political style, Alberto Guerreiro Ramos abstracts from Brazilian history five ideal-types of politics. These are: (1) clan-style politics, characteristic of colonial Brazil and focusing around patriarchal families; (2) oligarchical-style politics, most appropriate for the period between 1822 and 1930 and centering on regional political bosses; (3) populist-style politics, best exemplified by the Brazilian Labor Party (PTB) and representing a larger concentration of political support than the first two political styles; (4) pressure-group politics, appearing only within more recent years and concentrated around specific economic interests, and (5) ideological politics, which reaches its maximum development during the Quadros and Goulart governments. These types, he postulates, tend to constitute successive moments in the evolution of Brazil. They do not, however, necessarily disappear with the emergence of a new phase; instead, they continue as historical residues.

[1] Hélio Jaguaribe, *Desenvolvimento Econômico e Desenvolvimento Político*, pp. 154, 170–173, and *Condições Institucionais do Desenvolvimento*, pp. 14–22.
[2] Jaguaribe, *Condições Institucionais*, pp. 22–23.

Thus, before March, 1964, all five types of politics could be observed interacting simultaneously, although they rarely existed in pure form. In the rural areas, clan- and oligarchical-style politics continued to predominate, while at the national level, ideological politics set the scene.[3]

The approaches of both Jaguaribe and Guerreiro Ramos provide insights into the political framework; they need to be modified, however, to be useful analytic tools for the 1945–1964 period.

Jaguaribe's concepts of clientele-style politics and the Cartorial State are valuable in that they get at a traditional pattern in Brazilian politics: the existence of a closed system in which the mass of the people are apathetic, political power is monopolized by a landowning and mercantile upper class, and public employment becomes the prerogative of a dependent middle class at the service of an oligarchy. These concepts also help draw attention to the gap between the political system brought into existence with the 1946 Constitution and the socioeconomic changes Brazil has been undergoing. Certainly at many levels and in different regions a clientele-style politics was able to function in these years, with the use of positions in the administrative system for purposes other than the provision of public services.

The problem with the Jaguaribe model is that it is too static and that it oversimplifies changes in the social, political, and economic structure both before and since 1930. For example, he speaks of the revolution of 1930 as the second seizure of power by the middle class, the first being the revolution of 1889. Because the ideological disorientation of the middle class was greater on this occasion than in 1889, he claims that it became more pragmatic, comprehending the necessity for power, not only to provide itself with jobs, but also to utilize the machinery of the State to perpetuate its control.[4] This analysis does not draw sufficient attention to the shift from the predominance of rural interests engaged in monocultural agriculture to the emergence of urban groups, of middle- and upper-class character, interested in developing the national market and in achieving independence from the excessive reliance of the country on external markets.

Jaguaribe's model of the Cartorial State is much more operational when it is joined with Guerreiro Ramos' differentiation of several distinct styles of politics. This concept of various political styles offers the advantage of escape from the traditional-modern dichotomy present in so much of contemporary political and social thinking. It also

---

[3] Alberto Guerreiro Ramos, *A Crise do Poder no Brasil: Problemas da Revolução Nacional Brasileira*, pp. 49–67.

[4] Jaguaribe, *Desenvolvimento Econômico e Desenvolvimento Político*, p. 173.

provides a link with Riggs's model of a prismatic society which is to be imposed between the extremes of a developmental continuum. Not only does Guerreiro Ramos establish a framework for the changing patterns of patronage across historic periods, but he also offers categories for the analysis of heterogeneous and overlapping political patterns in the course of Brazilian political development.

The concepts of Jaguaribe and Guerreiro Ramos, then, provide a foundation for postulating a set of political relationships, based on Brazilian materials, which can operate within the wider framework established in Chapter I by models taken from Diamant and Riggs. In terms of the four major political styles suggested by Diamant, Brazil has remained essentially a limited polyarchy, but the expanding basis of political participation between 1945 and 1964 and its effects on administration can be better comprehended by distinguishing various subordinate political styles, which represent different degrees of limited polyarchy.

To begin, where there are historic residues of clan-style politics in the more isolated rural areas, use of local public office by members of the extended family should be found. In the case of oligarchical-style politics, in which the focus is at the regional level and rural interests predominate, Jaguaribe's Cartorial State should come into existence, with implications at the national level when conservative parties, such as the Social Democratic Party (PSD), are in the ascendancy. In contrast, in populist-style politics, where personalism continues simultaneously with the development of wider electoral support, the use of civil service positions should change considerably.

Riggs's model of prismatic society provides a means of clarifying these political relationships. Earlier attention was drawn to his concept of formalism and to his emphasis on heterogeneity and overlapping patterns as peculiar characteristics of transitional societies. If these ideas are kept in mind, they explain why Jaguaribe's and Guerreiro Ramos's interpretations are complimentary rather than conflicting. Thus, it is postulated, between 1945 and 1964 patronage patterns in the federal civil service reflected heterogeneous and overlapping political and social pressures.

Viewed from one perspective (Jaguaribe's) public employment helps to provide status and security for a dependent middle class, protection against downward social mobility, and an important link in a system dominated by an "elect-elite."[5] From another point of view

5 According to Riggs's definition, the "elite" refers "to the power-holders in a society"; the "ruling class" "to those members of a society from whom the elite may be recruited"; and the "elect" to "those who hold high positions in terms of

(Guerreiro Ramos') a populist-type party, such as the PTB, would be inclined to use civil service appointments as a means of reward for the urban working groups and the lower ranges of the middle class which form the basis of its power.

In this overlapping of Cartorial and populist political styles, positions in the public sector constitute, according to this model, a focal point in the whole process of integration through which new groups are brought into the political process. This would also involve the initiation of a movement away from a closed, elitist system toward a mass-based one in which political parties find it necessary to maintain and provide for cadres of voters. Since there is already a premium on jobs of any sort in a developing economy, the lower ranks of the public service may be viewed as a major means of employment and as a way to improve status for individuals outside the ruling class. Under this set of circumstances, the basis of the Cartorial State should continue to exist in the terms set forth by Jaguaribe, i.e., favors are bartered for votes and the public service is used to subsidize its employees instead of to provide services to the public at large. The class basis of the Cartorial State changes, however. If the relationships just postulated are valid, then the Cartorial State should provide a means of access to the benefits of urban society for groups hitherto excluded from the political process. It is further postulated that a substantial part of the difficulty in analyzing the federal civil service is located in the overlapping of these two distinct uses of patronage—the one the protection of an educated, conservative middle class with upper class values and the other reward to a much larger group of individuals, mostly undereducated, who are painfully aware of the privileges denied them.

The foregoing, viewed in the context of a predominant Brazilian conservative tradition, may be contrasted with the notion of an American liberal tradition, as developed by Louis Hartz.[6] The concept of a conservative tradition unconsciously underlies much of the writing of Brazil, but it is clearly expressed in concrete terms for the first time by José Honório Rodrigues in his recent book, *Conciliação e Reforma no Brasil*.[7] In the first essay, Rodrigues develops the theme of

---

all socially prized values, not only power, but also wealth, learning, prestige, skill, and so on." In a fused model, then, "where functionally specific structures are lacking, the elite are also the 'elect'." (*Administration in Developing Countries*, pp. 125–126). According to this framework, Jaguaribe's middle class becomes a part of the ruling class.

[6] *The Liberal Tradition in America.*

[7] *Conciliação e Reforma no Brasil: Um Desafio Histórico-Político.*

alternating periods of reform and conciliation in Brazilian history which have always been given a conservative hue. If, in Hartz's terms, one can speak of the frustrated conservative in the American tradition, so in Brazil, in Rodrigues' terms, one may refer to the frustrated liberal or reformer. This wider sociohistoric context is related in turn to the broad problems of Brazilian development during the transition from a society corresponding to Riggs's fused model to a prismatic one. Essentially Rodrigues maintains that all efforts at reform in Brazil have been modified or altered by the predominance of a conservative, elitist tradition, which, through conciliation, has always met and overcome the threat of basic change in the system— whether social, political, or economic.

With Rodrigues taken as a departure point, today's crisis may be seen as the inability of many Brazilian political leaders to come to terms with the demands for fundamental change in their society because of their ties to this conservative tradition. To this may be contrasted the changing character of the United States elites and the development during the Jeffersonian and Jacksonian administrations of an egalitarian ideology which, although not applied to the higher civil service appointments, prepared the way for greater and more open participation in government by those with nonelite status.[8] Equally important, in the United States the changes in ideology and the preparation for a more open system of government preceded the era of industrialization and modernization. In Brazil, the pressure for such changes has coincided with a substantial alteration in the country's socioeconomic character, and this has immensely complicated the problem.

This desire for basic change may well be called the arrival of the "democratic revolution"—if Brazil is placed in the context of Tocqueville's writings, including the general conditions in Western Europe and the United States during the past century to which he referred, and if the constraints imposed by the more popular dichotomy of the West and the non-West are avoided. Social and economic change sufficient to modify the elitist orientation of Brazilian political life and to provide an adequate basis for the expression of egalitarian aspirations has taken place in Brazil only in the last thirty-five years. The very fact that change along these lines—in the movement from an elitist to a mass-based system of politics—has been continually subverted by the power-holders in this society has merely increased

[8] Sidney H. Aronson, *Status and Kinship in the Higher Civil Service: Standards of Selection in the Administrations of John Adams, Thomas Jefferson, and Andrew Jackson.*

the possibility ultimately of a violent solution to the problem raised by this trend.

When the problems of administrative reform are placed in this wider, more embracing political context, it should not be necessary to belabor the point that it is not enough to speak of the conflict between merit as a "good" and patronage as an "evil" throughout Brazilian history[9] and of the gradual emergence of a merit approach to government positions which achieved its apogee during the Estado Novo, only to be destroyed by the return to party politics in 1946.[10] Instead, attention must be focused on change in social, economic, and political sectors, on the evolution of an elitist civil service as opposed to the formation of an open civil service system responsive to the external political system, and on problems of integration in Brazilian society at large.

If Riggs's models of fused, prismatic, and diffracted societies are applied to Brazil, a good case may be made for using the decade of the 1930's as a dividing point in that country's political development. Until that time, Brazil was essentially a traditional society resembling the fused model. This means that, since "functionally specific structures" were lacking, the upper class may be viewed as monopolizing what Riggs singles out as three basic values found in all societies— power, wealth, and education. While these three values tend to "agglutinate" in all societies, the unity or fusion of these values is most complete in a traditional society such as that of pre-1930 Brazil. Under such circumstances, power includes all forms of influence.[11] To this must be added the importance of kinship ties and the concept of the extended family as the dominant institution in Brazilian society. The continued importance of the large family, with implications in the social and political realm, is one of the primary indications of the persistence and vitality of a traditional order.[12]

---

[9] See Murilo Braga, "Problemas de Seleção Pessoal," *RSP* (May, 1941), 103–106; Tomás de Vilanova Monteiro Lopes, "A Seleção de Pessoal para o Serviço Público Brasileiro," *RSP*, IV (October, 1952), 19–23; Geraldo Eulálio Nascimento e Silva, "As Qualidades Diplomáticas e as Condições de Ingresso na Carreira," *RSP* LXXIX (April, 1950), 20–43; Armando Pereira, *Os Direitos e Vantagens dos Funcionários,* pp. 25–26.

[10] See Beatriz Wahrlich, *Administração de Pessoal,* pp. 23 ff., and "O Sistema do Mérito," *RSP*, XX (August, 1957), 237–254; Brasil, Ministro Extraordinário para a Reforma Administrativa, "Normas para Preservação e Revigoramento do Sistema do Mérito.

[11] Fred W. Riggs, *Administration in Developing Countries: The Theory of Prismatic Society,* pp. 124–127.

[12] Both T. Lynn Smith and Emílio Willems consider the family to be the major institution in Brazilian society.

The upper class in traditional Brazil may be considered other than in the framework suggested by Riggs. In this instance, its role may be seen in a more positive light—as the chief agent in the process whereby the masses have undergone and are still undergoing acculturation to the Brazilian variant of Western culture. In this respect, the integrative process underway is much more than just a political phenomenon.

This leads into a consideration of values if the wider sociopolitical context within which Brazilian administration has functioned is to be understood. The dominant value system in Brazil is closely related to the continuation of a conservative tradition. These traditional values, Portuguese in origin, developed largely in the context of a New World plantation economy in a preindustrial era. They are contained in what Charles Wagley calls the Brazilian Great Tradition.[13] They are also related to what John Gillin singles out as the values of the contemporary middle segments in Latin America[14] and to what is often known as the "gentleman complex"—whether in Brazil, as in the case of Gilberto Freyre's writings about the sugar-cane cycle in the Northeast, or in the traditional American South, as in James Cash's *The Mind of the South*. The most useful list of social values, however, is Gillin's. While they are developed in the context of Latin American middle segments, they are of much wider applicability and supply a convenient checklist for the dominant value system in Brazil. They include personalism as a central concept, kinship and the strength of family ties, the importance of hierarchy and stratification (the master-servant relationship), "tangible materialism," the weight of transcendental values, the high worth of inner states and the emphasis on emotion as fulfillment of the self, fatalism, "decency" in mode of life, and disdain for manual labor.[15]

The persistence of a dominant aristocratic value system in Brazil has direct bearing on the political system and on the civil service. This value system may in turn be related to the distinction Riggs makes among myths, formulas, and codes as distinct levels of symbolization in society. He uses "myth" to refer to "the underlying norms, the basic values or goals, the ultimate purposes, by which any human society guides itself"; "formula" to define the "ground rules, whether ideological or utopian, whereby a society distinguishes the elect from the reject, allocates rights and duties, separates groups from one an-

[13] *An Introduction to Brazil*, pp. 5–10.
[14] "Some Signposts for Policy," in Richard N. Adams *et al.*, *Social Change in Latin America Today: Its Implications for United States Policy*, pp. 28–47.
[15] *Ibid.*

other, decides who shall make and defend its rules, what may be possessed and alienated, or what means are acceptable"; and "codes" to conceive of the "specific policies, programs, and decisions which result from political and administrative action, and the general format which shapes them."[16]

If these three levels of symbolization are applied to Brazil, the dominant myth or value system is found to be aristocratic and traditional, the political formulas egalitarian and democratic, and the administrative codes Weberian and highly rationalistic. To this characteristic must be added the notion of competing value systems within Brazilian society which vary because of community differences, regionalism, and a sharply defined system of social classes. The dominant aristocratic value system has been subjected to many new pressures as socioeconomic change has taken place in Brazil. Wagley hints at the stresses which traditional values have been undergoing in Brazil,[17] but much of Brazilian writing in anthropology and sociology seems to concern itself more with the continuation of patrimonialism (i.e., the syndrome of traditional society) and to place the conflict in terms of a traditional-modern dichotomy.[18]

Viewed from a still different standpoint, the conflict among value systems according to heterogeneous and overlapping patterns is but another expression of the arrival of the "democratic revolution" and of the emergence of a new series of values centering around the demand for equality of opportunity and social justice, which, as such, have great implications for the political system.

[16] Riggs, *Administration in Developing Countries*, pp. 175–176.

[17] Wagley, *An Introduction to Brazil*, pp. 7–8.

[18] For example, see Emílio Willems, "Burocracia e Patrimonialismo," *Administração Pública*, III (September, 1945), 3–8; "Problemas de uma Sociologia do Peneiramento," *Revista de Arquivo Municipal* (São Paulo), LXXV (April, 1941), 5–63; "Brazil," in Arnold M. Rose (ed.), *The Institutions of Advanced Societies*. This dichotomy is also carried over into some of the writing on Brazilian public administration. See Daland (ed.), *Perspectives of Brazilian Public Administration*: Siegel, "Administration, Values, and the Merit System," and Mello e Souza and Genari, "Public Administration and Economic Development."

CHAPTER VII

The Political Understructure
(1945-1964)

The administrative atmosphere between 1945 and 1964 was politically charged. For this reason it is impossible to view the administrative problems of the country without developing some awareness of the political environment and its interaction with the administrative system. The crucial element in this interaction was the political party. Before 1945 national party organization was largely unknown, although parties certainly did exist before this date. Related to the emerging importance of the political party after 1945 and influencing the administrative system were the rapid, but incomplete, expansion of the Brazilian electorate, the organization of eligible voters within the framework of a national party system, and the emergence of egalitarian aspirations that vastly stimulated an already active desire for political employment.

The political party system in post-1945 Brazil reflects the conditions characteristic of a transitional society. Just as there are elements in Brazilian society (discussed in preceding chapters) which bear a direct relation to the prismatic model developed by Riggs, so, too, the typology offered by Riggs may be used for the analysis of political parties and related to Brazilian experience.

Riggs postulates that in the prismatic model political parties must appear, at least in name, but they fail to accomplish what is expected of them in more advanced societies: the provision of a channel for political mobility and access to elite status for those interested in achieving political power. Under prismatic conditions the attainment of power continues to take place to a considerable extent outside the formal political party structure. The bureaucracy offers one of the major channels through which political power can be achieved. Rather than being entirely an administrative apparatus for the execution of policy decided on in the political system, it becomes a "primary vehicle for elite recruitment." But this channel is not open to all social strata. Thus, many of those who fail to gain access to the bureaucracy seek to achieve elite status through political parties.

Riggs considers the power struggle to be particularly acute in a prismatic society because a relatively small number of positions are available in the power pryamid. In such a context "a bureaucratic elite cannot be expected to surrender power without a struggle to aspirants brought forward by the "parties." . . . Instead of serving as a channel to elite status, the "parties" become incubators of "counter-elites."[1] On this basis, he offers the proposition: "the narrower the communal basis of elite recruitment . . . the greater the potential 'mass' basis for the 'parties.' " He continues:

> The question then arises as to whether [the political leaders] will move toward greater diffraction by institutionalizing political parties as channels for continuing elite recruitment and control over the bureaucracy, or whether the situation will remain prismatic as a result of "blanketing" the followers of the victorious "party" leaders into the bureaucracy. When this happens, of course, the bureaucracy remains institutionally—though with a wholesale change of faces—the primary channel of social and political mobility. . . . The inability of "parties" to provide peaceful and legal channels of access to power for their leaders makes them combative, smarting to change the regime and to displace the elite strata as a whole.[2]

Within this framework Riggs develops a typology of political parties based on two variables: the type of organization and the length of time in existence.[3] Riggs's typology has been expanded here from three to nine possible combinations (see diagram below). If this diagram is applied to Brazilian parties, both past and present, another

Second Variable: Time Span[a]	First Variable: Type of Organization		
	Bureaucratic	Polyarchic[b]	Personal
Durable	*bureaucratic/durable*[c]	polyarchic/durable	personal/durable
Persistent	bureaucratic/persistent	*polyarchic/persistent*	personal/persistent
Fragile	bureaucratic/fragile	polyarchic/fragile	*personal/fragile*

  [a] "The life of a fragile party can be measured in years, of a persistent party in decades, and durable parties in generations, if not centuries" (Riggs, *Administration in Developing Countries*, p. 139).
  [b] Defined as "a form of collective personal leadership resting on consensus or voting procedures" (*ibid.*, p. 138).
  [c] The italicized syndromes are those developed by Riggs.

  [1] Fred W. Riggs, *Administration in Developing Countries: The Theory of Prismatic Society*, pp. 132–135, esp. 135.
  [2] *Ibid.*, pp. 136–137.
  [3] *Ibid.*, pp. 138–139.

link is obtained in the continued predominance of the conservative tradition discussed in the preceding chapter and in the way it has been mitigated by the emergence of mass-based politics.

By using these variables, the domination of conservative parties in the course of Brazilian political development can be demonstrated. Both the Conservative Party of the Empire and the Republican Party of the First Republic were personal and durable, while all the conservative-type parties since 1945—the Social Democratic Party (PSD), the National Democratic Union (União Democrática Nacional—UDN), the Republican Party (Partido Republicano—PR), and the Freedom Party (Partido Libertador—PL)—have been polyarchic and persistent.

In contrast, reformist parties have been relatively unsuccessful. The liberal-progressive type of parties during the Empire were personal and fragile, and hardly any parties of this sort can be discovered during the First Republic, except for the National Democratic Party (founded in 1927), which was both personal and fragile. The one major exception to this pattern is the PTB, which has been polyarchic and persistent. But its development was cut short by the military coup of March, 1964.

The conservative tradition dominating Brazilian political experience has provided that country with a national leadership which has been antireformist, elitist, and personalist.

Antireformist because, with the rarest of exceptions, it alone has proposed political reforms, especially electoral ones, and it alone has offered obstinate resistance to reforms in an archaic economic structure.

Elitist because it has kept the masses marginal [to the political process], whether through the exclusion of the illiterate, the urban worker, the inhabitant of the interior, the agricultural worker, or because until today the great national groups have not incorporated the civilian masses.

The personalism of its political action has always predominated. Rarely has it corrected this through emphasizing problems and not persons. Affective considerations have complicated the direction of public affairs and from this has stemmed nepotism . . . , other variations common to favoritism that are tied to personalism, and the boss-clientele relationship of the State—a relationship to which all politicians, from the most oligarchical to the most labor-oriented, have adhered.[4]

These three elements have been characteristic of the conservative parties in Brazil from the Empire to the present. During the nine-

---

[4] José Honório Rodrigues, *Conciliação e Reforma no Brasil, Um Desafio Histórico-Político*, pp. 114–115.

teenth century and down to 1930 these parties were to remain virtually unchallenged. While it has been more common to speak to the two-
party system of the Empire, within the framework of a factional, upper-class style of politics, it is more correct to refer to such groupings
of political forces within the context of a dominant one-party system
in which conservative agrarian interests predominated.[5] The term
"party," however, should be used with caution because parties were,
above all, alliances of provincial elites. Under the First Republic,
these patterns became clearer, for, although there was in name only
one party, it was a coalition of state parties in which the Republican
Party of Minas Gerais and the Republican Party of São Paulo were
the essential units. Small opposition parties, with little importance,
appeared and disappeared at the municipal level. The breakdown of
the political system in the late 1920's, the formation of the unsuccessful Liberal Alliance, and the Revolution of 1930 that brought Getúlio
Vargas to power reflected a further fragmentation of political groupings. It was impossible for even the semblance of a national party system to develop.

Following eight years of dictatorship, this pattern of political organization was resumed in the creation of the PSD. The party represented a regrouping of a substantial part of the regional elites that
had formed the basis of the state Republican parties. It was, in this
respect, the direct descendent of the Conservative and Republican
parties of earlier eras. Joined with this element were those associated
with the bureaucratic structure of the Estado Novo and without ties
to the labor movement.[6] The PSD thus reflected a reorganization of
conservative political forces in that its leadership consisted of a cross-
section of both privileged urban society and the landowning elite.[7]

In contrast, there was no such continuity between past and present
in the more liberal parties. Many of the difficulties of the PTB stem
from this legacy. Not only did it have to reconcile radical and liberal
progressive traditions,[8] but also it was faced with the problem of
building a national electoral coalition, based on state party organizations and a wide variety of group orientations, in the absence of any
cohesive forces left of center. A strong movement committed to so-

[5] Afonso Arinos de Melo Franco, *História e Teoria do Partido Político no Direito
Constitucional Brasileiro,* pp. 28–29, 33, 39, 44–46, 52, 55.

[6] For a discussion of the formation of the PSD, see Orlando M. Carvalho, "Os
Partidos Políticos em Minas Gerais," *Revista Brasileira de Estudos Políticos,* I (July
1957), 103–104.

[7] John J. Johnson, *Political Change in Latin America: The Emergence of the
Middle Sectors,* p. 171.

[8] Rodrigues, *Conciliação e Reforma no Brasil,* p. 238.

cial reform within the framework of representative political institutions and paralleling the rise of the democratic left or well-organized, reform-oriented Christian Democratic parties in other Latin American republics has never been experienced in Brazil. Various reformist groupings have appeared during the course of Brazilian political development, but they have been isolated and unsuccessful ventures for the most part.

Yet, regardless of its difficulties with party organization and with opportunism, demagoguery, and populism, the PTB did introduce a new element into Brazilian politics. As an urban-based party, appealing to laboring groups and the lower ranks of the middle class, it was tied to developments dating back to 1920, when the first significant urbanization and industrialization movements began to take place in Brazil. As it became more and more a national party, its support widened and it took in elements quite extraneous to its title as a labor party. While the dominant forces within the party placed it slightly left of center, as a national party it picked up support on a pragmatic basis all the way across the political spectrum.

The third major party to appear in the post-1945 period, the UDN, presents a special case, for at the outset it leaned in the direction of a frustrated liberalism, only to end up as a conservative organization. The UDN came into existence as a broadly based coalition of anti-Vargas forces. However, it soon lost this character as the left wing of the new party broke away and established the Brazilian Socialist Party. (Partido Socialista Brasileira—PSB). This development had the effect of pushing the UDN right of center. Although it has often been referred to as an urban-based party appealing to the middle and upper classes, it also had to depend for some of its support on the same elements attracted to the PSD in the rural areas of Minas Gerais and the Northeast. Otherwise, it would not have been able to retain its status as a national party. As a conservative party, it was distinguished by its strong commitment to political democracy and by its appeal to the urban middle classes.

The important point to remember in discussing these three major parties—the PSD, the PTB, and the UDN—is that the lines of division among them are often hazy. Being amalgamations of different groups, they varied considerably from one region to another. This condition was necessitated by the emphasis beginning in 1945 on the creation of national parties. As the largest party organizations, they were certain to reflect the heterogeneous character of Brazilian society. Since their primary reason for existence was the election of public officials and the development of sufficient party organization to be able to attract sizable numbers of voters, their orientation could hardly be any other than pragmatic.

The most significant regional cleavage cutting across these parties was that existing between the underdeveloped Northeast and the Southeast. In the Southeast the generalizations often repeated about these three parties were most valid. There the PSD tended to be the party of the traditional regional oligarchies, the UDN appealed more to the urban middle classes, and the PTB had mainly an urban working class basis.[9]

Joined to such regional differences was the division between pro- and anti-Vargas political alignments, despite the fact that Vargas committed suicide in 1954. Both the PSD and the PTB were Vargas creations, whereas the UDN was substantially an anti-Vargas coalition. This division was strengthened by the alliance Vargas developed between the PSD and the PTB in order to gain the presidency in the election of 1950. As a successful majority coalition which could insure control of congress and the presidency, it had every reason to continue to exist. Tremendously strained during the Goulart government, this alliance nevertheless survived until he was forcefully removed from office. And, despite the abolition of existing parties in October, 1965, by the military government of Castelo Branco, a substantial part of the alliance has reappeared in the form of a new congressional organization called the Brazilian Democratic Movement (Movimento Democrático Brasileiro—MDB).

Beyond these three major parties, which constituted the only truly national parties from 1945 to 1964, were a plethora of smaller parties. Of these, only two were broad in scope—the Progressive Socialist Party (Partido Social Progressista—PSP), which was the personalist party of the governor of São Paulo, Adhemar de Barros, and the Republican Party (PR), which consisted of a political organization in several states surviving from the First Republic. This group of smaller parties included a number of programmatic organizations, which, in addition to the PTB and the PSP, appealed to urban labor: the Brazilian Socialist Party (PSB), the National Labor Party (Partido Trabalhista Nacional—PTN), the National Social Labor Party (Partido Social Trabalhista Nacional—PST), and the Representative Labor Party (Partido Representação Trabalhista—PRT). Three other small programmatic parties should also be mentioned: the Christian Democratic Party (Partido Démocrata Cristão—PDC); the Party of Popu-

---

[9] Cláudio [sic] Ary Dillon Soares, "The Political Sociology of Uneven Development in Brazil," in Irving Louis Horowitz (ed.), *Revolution in Brazil: Politics and Society in a Developing Nation*, pp. 164–195.

lar Representation (Partido Representaçao Populista—PRP), the old Integralist Party of Plíneo Salgado; and the Freedom Party (PL), a party confined largely to Rio Grande do Sul and favoring parliamentary government. These parties were often only programmatic in the formal sense, were frequently subject to intense internal rivalries among personalities, and were fragile organizations. One final party, the Brazilian Communist Party (Partido Communista Brasileiro—PCB), ought to be mentioned, but it has been illegal since 1947 and has since split into two, if not more, factions—one Moscow-oriented, the other Peking-oriented.

In the period between 1945 and 1964, as Table 1 illustrates, the political party pattern was highly unstable. This was a consequence of two factors: first, the prevalence at the state level of purely pragmatic alliances and coalitions, which were continually being formed, disbanded, and reformulated; and, secondly, the splintering of the electorate as the smaller parties gained a larger share of representation at the state and national levels. During this period, the PSD generally declined in electoral support; the UDN substantially retained its representation at the national level, but lost support at the state level; and the PTB and the PSP increased in size. At the outset, the PSD and the UDN were clearly the major parties, but by 1955 the PTB also had joined them as a national party organization. For the most part, Northeastern politics were dominated by the conservative parties, among which the PSD and the UDN exercised a major role, and were subjected to a high percentage of party alliances and coalitions. Two qualifications, however, must be noted: this pattern was not entirely static and it did not apply to the larger cities where political radicalism was a major characteristic. In contrast, in the Southeast party lines tended to be more sharply defined and smaller parties appeared to be more prevalent.[10]

All this made for a highly incongruous mixture of political styles and parties, which gradually led to a decline of traditional political forces and the emergence of new groups committed to change.

Prior to the events of April 1964, perhaps the greatest advantage of the

---

[10] In addition to the information in Table 1, the bases for these generalizations are three detailed studies of the Brazilian party system, in which the substantial electoral data utilized provide a valid foundation for conclusions presented here: Orlando M. Carvalho, "Os Partidos Nacionais e as Eleições Parlamentares de 1958," *Revista Brasileira de Estudos Políticos*, [no volume no.] No. 8 (April, 1960), 9–19; Gláucio Ary Dillon Soares, "Alianças e Coligações Eleitorais: Notas para uma Teoria," *Ibid.*, XVII (July, 1964), pp. 95–124, and "The Political Sociology" in Horowitz (ed.), *Revolution in Brazil*.

Table 1.   Legislative Representation by Party (Number of Seats)[a]

Year	PSD	UDN	PTB	PSP	PR	PST	PL	PTN	PRT	PSB	PDC	PRP	No Party	Total Seats[b]
Federal Senate														
1947	36	14	2	—	—	—	—	—	—	—	—	—	—	52[c]
1950	28	11	5	2	1	1	—	—	—	1	—	—	4[d]	63[e]
	30	13	6	5	4	2	2	—	—	1	—	—	—	63
1954	22	13	16	4	4	—	2	1	—	1	—	—	—	63
1956	23	13	16	3	4	—	2	1	—	1	—	—	—	63
1958	22	17	18	1	1	—	3	—	—	—	—	—	1	63
1960[?]	21	19	17	1	—	—	3	1	—	—	—	—	1	63
Federal Chamber of Deputies														
1947	157	77	23	3	7	—	1	—	—	—	2	2	—	304[f]
1950	97	54	43	17	5	4	2	5	1	—	—	1	63[d]	304[g]
	112	81	51	24	11	9	5	5	1	1	2	2	—	304
1954	120	73	66	36	16	1	10	7	—	3	3	5	—	340
1955–1956	144	74	56	32	19	2	8	6	1	3	2	3	6	326
1958	115	70	66	25	17	2	3	7	2	10	6	3	—	326
1960[?]	115	70	66	25	17	2	3	7	2	10	6	3	—	326
State Assemblies (Deputies)														
1947	354	207	95	26	53	—	5	6	—	—	5	15	—	905[h]
1950	253	208	132	57	34	41	7	14	5	7	14	18	139	930[i]
	302	237	137	8	46	46	20	14	5	8	14	18	—	930[j]
1954	272	165	148	91	55	17	20	16	5	12	27	12	96[k]	936
1956[l]	—	—	—	—	—	—	—	—	—	—	—	—	—	—
1958	276	147	154	87	53	23	15	22	26	19	30	17	94	963
1960[?]	273	148	153	84	51	21	12	21	24	17	29	16	24[k]	943

[a] Based on Brazil, *Anuário Estatístico do Brasil*, Vol. X (1949), pp. 641, 638–639; Vol. XII (1951), pp. 563–564; Vol. XIII (1952), pp. 570–571; Vol. XVI (1955), pp. 615–617; Vol. XVII (1956), p. 471; Vol. XVIII (1957), pp. 536–537; Vol. XXI (1960), pp. 414–415; Vol. XXII (1961), pp. 456–457.

[b] All statistics were taken from *Anuário Estatístico*. In some cases a totaling of the figures for a particular year, including those in the notes, will not correspond with the total-seats figure given for that year.

[c] Distribution of other seats: UDN-PR, 2; PPS, 1; PCB, 1; UDN-PTB, 1; PPB, 1; PSD-UDN-PTB-PRP, 1; PSD-UDN, 1; PSD-UDN-PL-PDC, 1; PR-PTB-UDN, 1; PSD-PDC-PTB-PPB-PR-PTN, 1.

[d] Unspecified coalitions.

[e] Distribution of other seats: PSB-PTB, 2; UDN-PR, 2; PPS, 1; PSD-PSP, 1; PSD-PL, 1; PSD-UDN, 1; PSD-PTB, 1; PSD-PR, 1.

[f] Distribution of other seats: PCB, 14; PPS, 4; UDN-PR, 6; UDN-PTB, 2; PSD-PR, 3; PSP-UDN, 1; UDN-PR-PDC-PTN, 2.

h. Distribution of other seats: PCB, 1; ED, 6; PPB, 19; PRD, 1.

[g] Distribution of other seats: PSD-PDP, 4; PTB-PSP, 4; PSD-PSP, 4.

[h] Distribution of other seats: PCB, 1; ED, 6; PPB, 19; PRD, 1.

[i] Distribution of other seats: POT, 1.

[j] Distribution of other seats: POT, 1; PRB, 1.

[k] Coalitions and alliances.

[l] No state assembly elections held.

loose-knit, relatively undisciplined organizational structure of the political parties was that it permitted easy entry into the political process by newly articulate groups. . . . The "extremists" purged in 1964 were primarily the politicians who had become spokesmen for the lower classes; nationalism and basic reforms of the nation's social and economic structure had been their major appeals.[11]

The major threat posed to the conservative order, reorganized and broadened through new political institutions in 1946, came increasingly from the PTB, for its support stemmed from articulate urban labor groups and represented the first appearance of mass politics in Brazil. The resultant political style was populism—a phenomenon quite different from the previous styles of clan and oligarchical politics. Many commentators have preferred to interpret this urban phenomenon as a continuation of the personalist politics of traditionally oriented rural areas. Yet it was quite different in that it appealed to a relatively new social class, brought it into the political process, and did not organize itself around locality groups.

Populism does not appeal to consanguinity, to kinship ties in their various forms, to residential dependency, to [this type of] loyalty. It appeals to a vaguer form of social solidarity. The political boss, in this case, is a representative of interests and, once in power, his followers expect advantages to improve their social position, whether in the form of jobs or in assured favors or opportunities, obtained through the manipulation of the organs of the State. The tie that unites follower and boss is *personal confidence* and not *clan fidelity*.[12]

Although the Constitution of 1946 represented a return to federalism and democratic political institutions and provided for political participation and access to elected public positions on a scale previously unknown in Brazil, the country remained a limited polyarchy with developmental goals. The right to vote was still determined on the basis of literacy. This meant that a substantial part of the population was disenfranchised since the illiteracy rate for persons 15 years and older was 65.11 percent in 1900, 64.94 percent in 1920, 55.97 percent in 1940, and 50.49 percent in 1950.[13] Furthermore, these percentages

[11] Phyllis Peterson, "Brazil, Institutional Confusion," in Martin C. Needler (ed.), *Political Systems of Latin America*, pp. 463–509.

[12] Alberto Guerreiro Ramos, *A Crise do Poder no Brasil: Problemas da Revolução Nacional Brasileira*, p. 55.

[13] Brazil, Serviço Nacional de Recenseamento, *Brasil, Censo Demográfico: VI Recenseamento Geral do Brasil—1950*, Vol. I: Série Nacional, p. 1. The Brazilian constitution establishes eighteen as the voting age, but available statistical materials do not make it possible to state the illiteracy rate for those eighteen and over.

conceal the regional variations within Brazil. In the Northeast, according to one source, this average was probably nearer eighty percent in 1950.[14] It is difficult to substantiate this, however, since regional illiteracy rates are not contained in the census of 1940 and 1950. The only indication available is stated in terms of the illiteracy rate for those persons between the ages of five and fourteen years. In 1950, of a total school population (ages 5–14 years) of 3,377,048 in the Northeast, only 466,433 children could read and write.[15] For this population group, then, the illiteracy rate was eighty-six percent.

As a result of the modernization process, tensions in the social and political order increased. In a nation where regional integration had been imperfectly achieved, the contrast between traditional rural areas and modern urban ones was greater than ever because of the unequal spread of the benefits of urbanization and industrialization. This divergence between rural and urban areas, much more complex than a simple dichotomization, was reflected in the political parties. The mixture of political forces, paralleling a variety of economic and political development patterns, was made more visible by the nature of the political system: whereas the Estado Novo had maintained a closed system of government, the political structure of the Second Republic[16] provided for a relatively free play of political forces. This visibility was increased by the use of proportional representation and the subsequent emergence of a multiparty system. But in a transitional society with a low degree of consensus over procedural matters, this combination of proportional representation with a federalist system made it all the more difficult to integrate the mass of voters and divergent alignments, of both a regional and interest-group character, into effective national party organizations.

In spite of the literacy requirement, a great expansion of the electorate took place in these years, and it was the responsibility of the

---

Nor is it possible to give percentages based on the 1960 census because the complete results of that census have not yet been issued.

[14] Johnson, *Political Change in Latin America*, p. 117.

[15] *Brasil, Censo Demográfico . . . 1950*, p. 92. The Northeast includes the states of Maranhão Piauí, Ceará, Rio Grande do Norte, Paraíba, Pernambuco, Alagoas, and Fernando do Noronha (territory). This definition, used for census purposes, excludes two states usually included in the standard definition of the Northeast: Sergipe and Bahia.

[16] It is probably more accurate to call this the Fourth Republic, granted the nature of the Revolution of 1930 and the political reforms initiated under Vargas. However, because of the predominance of the executive, the rule by decree law, and the short duration of this period between the First Republic and the Estado Novo, I prefer to refer to it as a transitional phase between two very different eras, rather than to speak of the Second and Third Republics.

Table 2. Presidential Voting Totals[a]

Term of Office	Elected Candidate	Votes Received
1894–1898	Prudente José de Morais Barros	276,583
1898–1902	Manuel Ferraz de Campos Sales	420,286
1902–1906	Francisco de Paula Rodrigues Alves	592,039
1906–1910	Afonso Augusto Moreiro Pena	288,285
1910–1914	Hermes Rodrigues da Fonseca	403,867
1914–1918	Venceslau Brás Pereira Gomes	532,107
1918–1922	Francisco de Paula Rodrigues Alves	386,467
1919–1922	Epitácio da Silva Pessoa	286,373
1922–1926	Artur da Silva Bernardes	466,877
1926–1930	Washington Luís Pereira de Sousa	688,528
1930	Júlio Prestes de Albuquerque	1,091,709
1930–1945[b]	Getúlio Dorneles Vargas	———
1946–1951	Eurico Gaspar Dutra	3,251,507
1951–1956[c]	Getúlio Dorneles Vargas	3,849,040
1956–1961	Juscelino Kubitschek de Oliveira	3,077,411
1961–1966[c]	Jânio da Silva Quadros	5,636,623

[a] Brazil, *Anuário Estatístico*, Vol. XXIII (1962), p. 362.
[b] No elections were held during these years.
[c] These terms of office were not completed.

new parties to organize this electorate on a national basis. Whether they did so successfully is another matter. One way this growth may be examined is to look at the number of votes cast for the winning presidential candidate in elections held between 1893 and 1960 (see Table 2). Between the elections of 1893 and 1925 the total vote cast for the winning candidate scarcely doubled, but by the election of 1929 it had increased almost four times. Following the dictatorship, in the first free presidential election in fifteen years, the election of 1945, the vote cast for Dutra showed a nearly twelvefold increment. Fifteen years later, in the 1960 election, Jânio Quadros received a vote that had grown twenty times larger than the vote cast in the first election held under the Republic.

Another way of viewing the growth in the electorate is to consider the number of voters registered in the last two elections before the declaration of the Estado Novo and those registered since the end of 1945 (see Tables 3, 4, and 5). For the purposes here, it is sufficient to note that there were approximately 1.5 million registered voters in 1933; 2.7 million in 1934; 7.5 million in 1945; 11.5 million in 1950; 15.1 million in 1954; and 18.6 million in 1962.[17] Yet in 1950, the one

[17] These figures are to be compared with a total population of 9,930,478 in 1872; 14,333,915 in 1890; 17,438,434 in 1900; 30,635,605 in 1920; 41,236,315 in 1940 (*Brasil, Censo Demográfico . . . 1950*, p. 1 and Brazil, Serviço Nacional de Recenseamento, *Brasil, Sinopse Preliminar do Censo Demográfico: VII Recenseamento Geral do Brasil—1960*, p. 27).

Table 3.   Voter Registration, 1933–1934 and 1945[a]

States, Territories, and Federal District	Constituent National Assembly Election 5/3/33	Congressional Election 10/14/34	Presidential and Congressional Election 12/2/45	
	No.	No.	No.	% of Pop.
North				
Guaporé	—	—	2,902	12.13
Acre	1,968	5,130	6,895	7.63
Amazonas	4,389	9,884	31,948	6.67
Rio Branco	—	—	673	4.91
Pará	28,990	46,774	159,395	15.33
Amapá	—	—	3,365	14.07
Northeast				
Maranhão	12,432	45,658	109,101	7.90
Piauí	10,462	40,959	132,455	14.42
Ceará	30,478	75,509	369,550	15.82
Rio Grande do Norte	18,959	47,402	131,560	15.28
Paraíba	29,664	51,452	175,634	10.92
Pernambuco	69,318	122,849	321,736	10.75
Alagoas	23,742	34,730	82,068	7.71
Fernando de Noronha	—	—	140	11.77
East				
Sergipe	23,460	45,657	97,089	16.00
Bahia	91,118	185,483	440,621	10.06
Minas Gerais	311,374	530,654	1,231,251	16.29
Espírito Santo	29,731	51,994	122,281	14.50
Rio de Janeiro	69,522	158,574	383,100	18.50
Distrito Federal (Rio de Janeiro)	84,892	136,085	549,353	27.74
South				
São Paulo	299,074	534,487	1,688,598	20.98
Paraná	34,844	64,208	229,672	17.28
Iguaçu	—	—	16,733	15.42
Santa Catarina	36,187	88,839	248,086	19.57
Rio Grande do Sul	231,194	327,264	753,232	20.23
Center-West				
Ponta Porã	—	—	10,351	10.20
Mato Grosso	8,788	21,888	59,121	16.05
Goiás	16,114	33,691	103,079	11.13
BRAZIL	1,466,700	2,659,171	7,459,989	16.22

[a] Based on Brazil, *Anuário Estatístico*, Vol. VII (1946), p. 514.

year for which comparable census figures are available, the registered
electorate represented only forty-eight percent of the voting age
population.[18]

[18] In 1950, there were 25,002,999 persons 18 years of age and older (*Brasil, Censo Demográfico . . .1950*, p. 2).

Although the total size of the electorate had increased, malapportionment reduced its effects on congressional representation. Regionally, voter registration was distributed in such a way that, under federalism and bicameralism, traditional rural agrarian interests were able to dominate congress. This is an institutional factor often overlooked. A senate determined on the basis of three representatives from each state and from the Federal District, elected according to the majority principle, meant that agrarian-oriented, underdeveloped states were able to control that body. In the chamber of deputies proportional representation was manipulated in such a way that the same rural interests were the dominant elements. The representatives of each state were elected on the basis of its total population—a total at variance with the registered electorate. Because of the higher illiteracy rate among the Northeastern states, a voter in those areas cast a vote worth substantially more than that of the individual voter in the more highly urbanized, industrial states of the Center-South, where the literacy ratio was a great deal higher. This meant that the traditional oligarchical groups in the Northeast were able to achieve an importance far beyond their just share. Their control over the chamber was further insured by a constitutional provision limiting the representation of the more populous states: after a state reached twenty deputies on the basis of one deputy for each 150,000 inhabitants, each additional deputy was determined on the basis of 250,000 inhabitants. In addition, the exclusive right of congress to initiate changes in the Constitution was a final factor in this malapportionment by which the oligarchical groups insured their maintenance of a privileged position in the struggle to control political institutions and mass-based politics.

On the other hand, the direct election of the president of the Republic meant that he was not only more representative of the total electorate, but also much more subject to mass pressures.[19] In this case the areas which were highly urbanized and literate in comparison with the rest of the country were somewhat overrepresented in terms of the total population. An example of this situation is in the 1955 presidential election in which the state of São Paulo and the Federal District (now the state of Guanabara), representing about twenty percent of the total population, cast approximately thirty percent of the national vote. In this same election, the city of São Paulo, with some five per-

---

[19] The ideas contained here and in the preceding paragraph, although considerably expanded, come from Celso Furtado, "Obstáculos ao Desenvolvimento Econômico do Brasil," *Correio da Manhã* (Rio de Janeiro), February 24, 1965, p. 14, and February 25, 1965, p. 14.

Table 4. Voter Registration, 1950–1962*

States, Territories, and Federal District	Federal, State, and Municipal Election 10/3/50	Federal, State, and Municipal Election 10/3/54	Federal and State Election 10/3/55	Federal, State, and Municipal Election 10/3/58	Federal and State Election 10/3/60	Federal and State Election 10/7/62
North						
Rondônia[b]	5,181	11,283	6,995	8,126	8,339	12,759
Acre	12,284	18,421	17,284	14,941	14,941	19,544
Amazonas	75,367	121,565	119,771	88,712	91,929	137,317
Rio Branco	3,506	7,196	5,675	5,998	5,696	4,984
Pará	277,692	345,588	373,125	271,374	324,511	421,531
Amapá	6,737	9,982	9,229	7,718	7,875	10,649
Northeast						
Maranhão	262,295	403,586	426,046	278,094	384,327	497,436
Piauí	220,073	292,583	304,472	232,368	244,262	315,158
Ceará	683,465	683,465	509,085	656,716	668,703	853,282
Rio Grande do Norte	243,231	324,309	294,870	229,523	278,087	321,014
Paraíba	346,141	439,460	447,598	291,120	353,371	405,407
Pernambuco	452,545	837,377	873,070	614,537	676,179	851,398
Alagoas	146,182	195,016	189,977	134,959	154,621	192,223
East						
Sergipe	147,144	218,847	200,900	145,303	150,095	192,503
Bahia	867,292	1,090,000	1,093,808	920,249	943,317	1,206,453
Minas Gerais	1,936,691	2,366,606	2,458,361	2,036,003	2,151,283	2,565,505
Espírito Santo	180,607	261,969	249,194	233,053	235,056	307,009
Rio de Janeiro	631,872	911,081	842,988	790,546	827,338	1,115,176
Guanabara[c]	837,428	965,481	992,459	977,839	1,099,490	1,198,588

South					
São Paulo	2,041,840	2,757,309	2,784,717	2,855,751	3,412,611	3,822,235
Paraná	372,796	609,838	672,645	684,881	885,418	1,100,637
Iguaçu	—	—	—	—	—	—
Santa Catarina	367,695	474,379	493,928	524,109	581,358	641,582
Rio Grande do Sul	987,236	1,212,792	1,319,170	1,274,344	1,409,310	1,561,162
Center-West						
Ponta Porã	—	—	—	—	—	263,002
Mato Grosso	132,037	182,743	194,151	177,004	203,984	263,002
Goiás	217,812	363,728	363,728	326,976	407,667	510,135
Brasília (Federal District)	—	—	—	—	23,564	34,010
BRAZIL	11,455,149	15,104,604	15,243,246	13,780,244	15,543,332	18,560,699

a Brazil, *Anuário Estatístico*, Vol. XXIII (1962), p. 362.
b Rondônia is the equivalent of Guaporé in Table 3.
c Guanabara, the former Federal District, contains the city of Rio de Janeiro. The totals for the Territory of Fernando de Noronha, listed separately in Table 3 within the Northeast, are here included with Guanabara.

Table 5. Who Votes (1945–1963) [a]

Election	Population	Registered Voters	% of Pop. Registered	Actual Vote	% Turnout	% of Pop. Voting
1945 Presidential	46,215,000	7,459,849	16.1	6,200,005	83.1	13.4
1950 Presidential	51,976,000	11,455,149	22.0	8,254,989	72.1	15.9
1954 Legislative	57,098,000	15,104,604	26.5	9,890,475	65.5	17.3
1955 Presidential	58,456,000	15,243,246	26.1	9,097,014	59.7	15.6
1958 Legislative	62,725,000	13,780,244	22.0	12,720,897	92.3	20.3
1960 Presidential	70,967,000 [b]	15,543,332	21.9	12,586,354	81.0	17.7
1962 Legislative	75,271,000 [c]	18,528,847	24.6	14,747,221	79.6	19.6
1963 Plebiscite	77,521,000 [c]	18,565,277	23.9	12,286,173	66.2	15.8

a Brazil: *Election Factbook*, No. 2 (September, 1965), p. 19.
b Preliminary results of 1960 census.
c Estimates, *Anuário Estatístico*, 1962.

cent of the population, provided about eight percent of the national vote.[20]

Herein lies the key to the continued existence of the PSD-PTB coalition throughout the majority of this period. The PSD, as the most cohesive conservative party, was able to maintain the largest representation in congress because of the weight given to rural areas in this body—even though the increase of the urban vote and a decrease in PSD total representation over the two decades after 1945 could not be entirely mitigated. In contrast, the PTB was essentially an urban-based party whose support tended to rise over these two decades. The alliance of these two party organizations at the national level usually made it possible for them to elect the president and to capture a majority in the senate and chamber.

The era between 1945 and 1964 was above all one of patronage politics. In spite of the abuses introduced by political patronage and the negative effects it had upon public administration, the appearance of this phenomenon, in a form quite different from that existing prior to 1930, marked a step forward in the course of Brazilian political development—if the specific details involved are overlooked and not only the broad course of Brazilian political history but also the experience of other countries is considered. Such a statement may well represent an anathema to those committed to the goals of economy, efficiency, and rationality in administration or to those who would moralize the whole governmental process. Yet it shows that during these years Brazil reached a particularly crucial stage in the creation of a viable political system concomitant with the whole process of modernization. Once the pressures leading toward the formation of an egalitarian mass society begin to appear, as they have in Brazil since 1945, there seem to be but two ultimate courses open to a nation: the development of an open governmental system with representative institutions, institutionalizing the class struggle; or the development of a closed governmental system, imposing authoritarian controls over that society.

The major problem facing the political system in these years was how to effectively bring together heterogeneous political forces so that continued progress could be made toward the goals of an integrated nation-state and a modern economy. Within the framework of representative political institutions, the larger political parties played a crucial role. They were responsible for the aggregation of interests in such a way that the struggle for power could be institutionalized

[20] Johnson, *Political Change in Latin America*, p. 175.

and at least some decisions could be made on alternative lines for public policy, before immobilism set in. During the Vargas dictatorship the goals had been similar. To achieve a modern nation-state and a modern economy it was recognized that social changes were necessary in the structure of Brazilian society. What social changes were necessary, however, was a source of great disagreement after 1945. In general, during the Vargas dictatorship, emphasis was placed on controlled social change. The most potentially disruptive force was urban labor, but it was handled by Vargas in such a way that it presented no threat. After all, it formed one of the bases of his regime. With the return to an open political system, however, competing and disagreeing political forces entered into direct competition.

The political culture of Brazil was badly fragmented in the years following World War II. This fragmentation was a consequence not of Westernization impinging on "indigenous cultural heterogeneity,"[21] but, rather, of uneven developmental patterns and the continuation of political subcultures. These political subcultures, possessing common roots and sharing a common heritage, were of four major types: (1) the preindustrial, traditionally-oriented rural elites; (2) the older middle class components, which were the recipients of a frustrated political liberalism; (3) the industrial elements proper— the owners of industries, middle management, and urban labor; and (4) urban slum-dwellers who were for the most part marginal to the political process and alienated from the existing political order. Since political conflict came to involve the very survival of these subcultures and the basic form of the political system itself, politics became notably radical. This trend was increasingly visible after the end of the Kubitschek government. As the presidency passed from Quadros to Goulart, politics moved away from concern with specific bargainable differences toward the presentation or defense of "conflicting and mutually exclusive designs for the political culture and political system."[22] Participating in this process was a multitude of parties and also numerous fragile coalitions and alliances. In the meantime, as the center of political power moved from right to left, immobilism developed—the ultimate consequence of which was a "Caesaristic" breakthrough.[23]

[21] Gabriel A. Almond, "Interest Groups and the Political Process," in Roy C. Macridis and Bernard E. Brown (eds.), *Comparative Politics: Notes and Readings*, p. 131.

[22] Almond, "Comparative Political Systems," in Macridis and Brown (eds.), *Comparative Politics*, p. 452.

[23] The analysis used here is based not on Almond's model for the non-West, but on the model he has developed for Weimar Germany, France, and Italy.

Within this framework the focus of the political system was on elective office—whether the presidency of the Republic or a seat in the senate or the chamber of deputies. During the First Republic these positions were monopolized by the regional oligarchies, and appointive positions were filled on the basis of personal and kinship ties. By 1945, although the traditional regional oligarchies still exercised the upper hand in many areas and achieved an importance in the congress disproportionate to their numerical representation, the country had entered a transitional phase of development in which this old style of politics was no longer sufficient. The increasing size of the electorate and the effects of urbanization and industrialization led to the rise of a wide variety of groups with quite diverse interests. In the urban areas politics developed a mass basis. In contrast, apathy continued to characterize the people living in the countryside; when they did vote, it was usually in accord with the wishes of their *patrão*. Because of the transitional nature of the country, these patterns overlapped and interacted. Appointive positions in the public service were still filled according to personal or political criteria, but the way they were used, the numbers of individuals involved and their social class, varied considerably.

Where either a large or expanding electorate is involved, patronage politics has provided the interested individual politician of local or state party with jobs in the public service which can be used for reward to the party faithful. In the case of the United States during the latter part of the nineteenth century—a country with a two-party system existing over a lengthy time span—patronage supplied a means for coalescing state and local party organizations into national entities. Even then, patronage was a highly disruptive force, difficult to control, because it was primarily a local and regional phenomenon. In a loosely-knit multiparty system of recent origin, such as that in Brazil in this period, the dispersion of patronage among personalities and regional and interest alignments was even greater. Patronage politics was used to the greatest extent around the federal executive and those federal deputies and senators elected on the basis of urban support. In both cases mass politics was a dominating factor. This element, however, was absent to a considerable extent in the rural areas, where an oligarchical style of politics continued and patronage served more traditional purposes.

In a recent article Paulo Singer has described this system of political relationships between the elected official and the party follower especially well. While in this passage his comments are limited substantially to executive-legislative relations at the federal level prior to April, 1964, they are designed to apply to state and local levels as well.

The chief executive is elected with the support of certain political groups. Once he wins the election this support is repaid through positions with the government. Positions are distributed in proportion to the electoral force of each group, reflected in the number of congressional representatives that each group succeeds in electing to office. If the chief executive himself is the leader of a group, he will provide his group with the greatest share of positions, in such a way that it will make him stronger politically. Each position has a certain political weight, depending on the number of jobs that the person named to it can fill, on the size of the funds which can be manipulated by him, and on the degree of electoral yield obtained from public services provided through the position. For example, positions in the Ministry of Transportation and Public Works (the Ministério de Viação e Obras Públicas) and in its state offices are considered to have great political weight. This political weight is due to various factors. First, these positions permit the control of the railroads; they are considered to provide great electoral advantage because of the number of jobs available. Secondly, the construction of highways and public works . . . is controlled by these positions. This permits the persons occupying them to control sizable funds from which it is always possible to obtain considerable profit in collusion with contractors and suppliers.

Generally the chief executive attempts to increase his congressional support by attracting political groups that did not support him at the ballot box. By paying a corresponding price in positions, he can obtain this support without much difficulty. It is clear that the stock of positions and sinecures is limited. Some political groups will have to be excluded from the apportioning [of positions]. These will form his opposition. But for a professional politician, whatever his type, it is most distressing (and politically harmful) to stay too long in the opposition. Consequently, a third position has been invented which is neither among the "ins," nor in the opposition, but "independent" or in the "constructive opposition." This is a position which offers several advantages: its occupants are not subjected to the "wear and tear" of government, that is, they are not held responsible for the insufficiencies and shortcomings of those who are in the government and they are not able to fulfill even a minimum part of their preelection promises. At the same time they obtain numerous favors from the government, trading their votes each time the government does not have a sure majority for a particular project which interests it. It is necessary to note that even when the government's bloc is in the majority, it can never be sure that it can count on all its votes. This is because each deputy (councilman or senator) is faithful, above all, to the particular interests of the group he represents. If a certain measure de-

sired by the government hurts these interests, the congressional representative—even if he is a member of the government's bloc—will deny it
his vote.[24]

While patronage politics was the dominant characteristic of the
period between 1945 and 1964, it was most evident at the national
level in those cases in which the government was based on an alliance
between the PSD and the PTB. This alliance functioned in three
governments: the second government of Getúlio Vargas (1951 to
August, 1954); the government of Juscelino Kubitschek (1955–
1960); and the government of João Goulart (under a parliamentary
regime between September, 1961, and January, 1962, and a presidential one between January, 1962, and March, 1964). In the intervening periods the UDN was in the ascendancy. These were: (1)
the Dutra government (1946–1950), which was based on a conservative alliance among the UDN, the PSD, and the PR; (2) the Café
Filho government (August, 1954, to November, 1955), which was an
interim government completing all but three months of Vargas' term
of office after his suicide; (3) the government of Jânio Quadros (January to August, 1961), in which the UDN was considered to be the
party most closely allied with the government (although Quadros
tried to govern as a president above the parties), and the PTB was
the vice-president's party, and (4) the Castelo Branco government,
which was installed by the April, 1964, revolution and represented, at
least at the outset, a working relationship between the UDN and the
military, a pattern which also existed in the governments of Dutra
and Café Filho.

During these years of fluctuating governing coalitions, the most
stable arrangement was that established between the PSD and the
PTB under the influence of Vargas. The UDN was in the government
only for short periods of time. Its main orientation was a moralizing
one in which patronage politics were condemned as one of the great
evils to be removed. It was never in power long enough to begin to
blanket public positions with its own followers. This made it quite
feasible for the party to adopt a moralizing role and gave credibility
to the claim that it did not engage in patronage politics—at least in
terms of the open distribution of jobs in the public service. Yet, if
the action of the UDN at the state level is examined, its record was
not so perfect. The most obvious case at hand in recent years involves
criticism of the government of Carlos Lacerda in the state of Guana-

[24] Paulo Singer, "A Política das Classes Dominantes," in Octávio Ianni *et al.*,
Política e Revolução Social no Brasil, pp. 81–82.

bara (the former Federal District encompassing the city of Rio de Janeiro) for filling the state administration with large numbers of the party faithful during 1964.

The constant accusations against these practices and the expression of dismay at the disorder introduced into the administrative system have caused the functional side of the patronage system to be over-looked. In a highly dispersed political system based on party govern-ment, the distribution of jobs and favors provided an integrating func-tion for a wide variety of groups and interests in a country where the availability of jobs was limited, where public funds were scarce, and where the economy was undergoing the severe stresses and strains brought about by the attempt to industrialize as rapidly as possible. The heterogeneous and overlapping patterns and styles of politics prevalent throughout the country were made even more disparate under a highly unstable multiparty system joined to a federalist sys-tem of government. Under such a set of circumstances, ideology could hardly provide a unifying factor for a party and at the same time guarantee it sufficient electoral support to elect its candidates. Neither could effective alternatives in public policy be offered as a sole means for aggregating interests. The one available unifying factor able to bring these diverse interests and groups together was the use of public office to provide jobs and favors as rewards to those assisting in amassing the necessary votes and resources required for election. After election the same technique was necessary to pass legislation. It was a highly pragmatic system and it functioned most effectively during the government of Juscelino Kubitschek, for even more than Vargas he understood how and why the system functioned and in most cases was able to obtain a majority in the congress to pass the bills he favored. A product of the existing party system, he was a political leader who understood the bargaining aspect of politics in a sense that neither Quadros nor Goulart seemed to grasp.

As already mentioned, the one party which benefited the most from patronage politics was the PTB. Prior to the disintegration of the Goulart government and the coup of March 31 and April 1, 1964, it was farthest on the road toward creating a mass-based party. To maintain even the semblance of unity and to provide rewards for its followers' expenditures of time, energy, and funds, it depended above all on the maintenance of patronage in the Ministry of Labor and especially in the social security institutes under the jurisdiction of that ministry. These institutes were essential administrative units which the party desired to control also because of the fact that the social security programs above all benefited the urban worker, the major group to which the party appealed. At the same time, while patronage politics was crucial to maintaining what party unity there was, in the urban centers of the central and southern parts of Brazil some elements in the party had begun to move away from excessive dependency on personalities. These elements were interested in the formation of an ideological program in accord with the PTB's character as an emerging working-class party with a humanitarian concern for the conditions and problems facing the industrial worker. The social reforms it proposed presented the greatest threat to the continuation of an elitist-oriented social and political order.

CHAPTER VIII

The Civil Service and Political Patronage

Patronage patterns in the Brazilian civil service are closely related to the chief executive and the political party structure. As one president followed another and as the relationships among the parties altered between 1945 and 1964, so, too, the uses of the patronage power changed in character. During these years, despite the merit standards in Brazilian law, political patronage functioned as the predominant criterion in the selection of federal employees.

The bureaucratic system developed by Vargas, with its technical elite at the national level, corresponds to Riggs's model of prismatic bureaucracy. It was, if not the primary vehicle for elite recruitment during the Estado Novo, a major source of entry into the administrative system for those from among the "ruling classes" who had had the "proper" education. After the collapse of the Estado Novo, a struggle ensued between the bureaucratic elite, as represented especially by DASP officials, and the conservative parties supporting, first, Linhares' provisional government and, then, the Dutra government.

As acting president and as the representative of a new coalition of forces, Linhares proceeded to neutralize DASP. He published his decrees directly, without submitting them to DASP for review; he independently raised the pay scales of clerical employees in the Ministry of Education; he issued a decree placing regional police administrators in the Federal District within the classified civil service; and he supposedly distributed numerous jobs in the public service among friends and relatives.[1] According to Siegel, Linhares' "political" intrusion into the civil service was intolerable to Moacyr Ribeiro Briggs, the new president of DASP, who had been appointed by Linhares to fill the vacancy left by the resignation of Luis Simões Lopes. Consequently, after a little more than a month in office, Briggs resigned, and a

[1] Gilbert Siegel, "The Vicissitudes of Governmental Reform in Brazil: A Study of the DASP," pp. 148–149.

mass resignation of all division heads and chiefs of services in the
DASP followed. Linhares did not choose to act on the resignations and
simply suspended the management of DASP. In accounting for these
resignations, Siegel explained them as a consequence of both Linhares'
violation of the merit principles, contained in the Code of the Public
Functionaries and other civil service regulations, and the lack of
preparation on the part of most DASP officials for dealing with a
political system in which professional politicians were able to operate
freely.[2]

These events were joined by a decree-law, issued by Linhares,
which substantially altered DASP control over public administration,
although it left intact DASP's responsibility for setting norms and
standards. It declared that all executive and auditing powers over
public personnel were to be the exclusive competence of the ministerial staffs and stated that DASP's authority in personnel matters was
to be limited to the maintenance of the manning tables, position controls, and other central records. The Division of Personnel Studies and
Orientation and Audits of Personnel became simply the Personnel
Division.[3]

Within the year, under the Dutra administration, another assault
was made on DASP as an instrument of the Estado Novo. This time
it was in the form of a bill introduced in the chamber of deputies
which would have eliminated DASP by transferring its budgetary
and other functions to the Ministry of Finance. Although the bill had
the support of the UDN-PSD coalition, the basis of the Dutra government, it failed to pass. Its significance, however, does not lie in its
failure to pass, but, rather, in the fact that it was prepared by the
Minister of Finance.[4] As such, it is indicative of the attempt of the
Finance Ministry to recover its traditional position of power and prestige in the administrative system. During the Estado Novo its status
was considerably reduced. Nevertheless, even though the Ministry of
Finance failed to achieve its objective by a frontal attack on the DASP
structure, it was quite successful in regaining its original position of
influence because of DASP's loss of its control powers. DASP's budgetary functions, which in theory paralleled those of the United States
Bureau of the Budget, remained purely formal in character. This proposed legislation also points to the transferral to the political arena of

[2] *Ibid.*, pp. 150–151.
[3] *Ibid.*, pp. 154–155.
[4] *Ibid.*, p. 171, credits the Minister of Finance, Pedro Luiz Correia e Castro, with
preparation of the bill.

an issue which was, during the Estado Novo, defined purely in administrative terms.

Other than this measure, no major attempts were made directly to destroy the organization. Instead, DASP was simply by-passed whenever the chief executive desired to ignore it. Dutra was primarily concerned with reducing government expenditures and, supposedly as an economic measure, forbade DASP to conduct competitive examinations during his administration. While he is usually credited with making few, if any, extralegal appointments to the civil service,[5] when vacancies occurred and it was necessary to fill them, he did make use of the *interino* category. As already noted, these appointments did not require the use of merit criteria.

These alterations in the structure of DASP and the reduction of its power resulted in substantial destruction of the apparatus established to create and maintain an elitist career civil service. When Dutra took office as the first legally elected president under the new constitution, the way was thrown open for the resumption of political patronage. The main category through which the followers of the political parties supporting the new government were admitted into the public service was that of the *interino*. Even though DASP was still responsible for the administering of public examinations and the appointing of career civil servants, effective barriers to patronage pressures no longer existed. Without DASP's control mechanism and with the return to a more decentralized administrative system, the ministries exercised a considerable amount of autonomy, and regional political groups could establish influence over the federal government's field offices more easily. What happened essentially was that one elite structure replaced the other, while the federal bureaucracy remained a primary channel of social and political mobility. Thus, a clientele style of politics, similar to that existing prior to the dictatorship and based on the middle and upper classes, reasserted itself.

This arrangement, however, was of relatively short duration, for when Vargas returned to the presidency in 1951 his government was based on an alliance of the PSD and the PTB. Although DASP was nominally strengthened as a more complete and systematic classification plan was begun, *concursos* (civil service examinations) were reopened, and public personnel practices were again centralized, political patronage was not eschewed. In terms of the administrative system this meant that jobs were distributed not only according to

[5] *Ibid.*, pp. 168, 170, 172.

traditional patronage lines (that is, to those clientele groups in the upper and middle classes who had contributed electoral support and considered reward was due them), but also according to new ones. Because a substantial part of his support was dependent on the PTB and the maintenance of the loyalty of urban labor leaders, patronage was used in the Ministry of Labor and the social security institutes to benefit a new class which was both numerically larger and of a different caliber in terms of education and preparation that that which had previously been admitted to jobs in the public service. The combination of the working-class background of many of these individuals and the existence of an open political system meant that these newer patronage patterns were more visible than older ones. Hence, when the evils of patronage were pointed to in the press and by individuals interested in re-reforming the civil service, the focus was brought to bear most often on this particular area, while more traditional patterns of patronage were often overlooked or minimized.

Patronage benefiting urban labor and the lower ranks of the middle class operated within the framework of a political machine. This machine had its origins during the era of the Estado Novo in the labor bureaucracy created in the Ministry of Labor and in the social security institutes. There was, then, no really independent labor movement. Virtually all the laws aimed at the improvement of the working conditions of urban labor had come from governmental action. This meant that initiative had come from the top down, in an attempt to anticipate the demands of the worker. The most obvious part of this system was the syndical tax which was levied on all workers and employers and which was used to finance labor unions (*sindicatos*). With the organization of political parties in 1945, the PTB assumed a major function in maintaining and expanding this whole apparatus. In this context patronage played an important role and civil service appointments tended to fall in the *extranumerário* category, until this type of public employment was abolished in 1960.

The extent to which patronage prevailed in the civil service as the major criterion for admissions can be seen by examining figures compiled by Wahrlich on the number of civil service examinations administered and comparing them with the total number of positions legally subject to entrance on the basis of merit. Of a total of 695,499 candidates who signed up to take public examinations for entrance into the career civil service between 1937 and 1962, 285,852 persons actually presented themselves for examination. Of these, only 75,155 succeeded in passing. Within this group, 30,000 received their approval at a date no earlier than 1961. Unfortunately, the total number of appointments made from this list is not available. Nevertheless, even if all of those who had been approved for admission to the civil service had received appointments, they would hardly have contributed to the achievement of a career service. In the ministries alone, nearly 300,000 positions were involved.[6]

In the *autarquias* Wahrlich claims that more than 200,000 positions theoretically should have been filled on a merit basis. Yet, she points to the fact that only two maintained merit systems: the Instituto de Aposentadoriao e Pensões dos Industriários (IAPA—the social security institute for industrial employees) and the National Economic Development Bank (Banco Nacional de Desenvolvimento Econômico—BNDE). Until 1960 both were successful in establishing a tradition of admissions only through public examination. But these admissions amounted to a total of no more than fourteen thousand persons, and even here in 1960 and 1962 numerous admissions were made without public examination, especially in the case of IAPI. This small number of admissions on the basis of proven qualification, added to the approximately seventy-five thousand previously mentioned, amounts to a rough total of eighty-nine thousand persons approved through merit examinations in these years. This number is to be related, states Wahrlich, to a total of a half-million civil service positions. Thus, for these three years, if Wahrlich's figures are used, only approximately 17.8 percent of the civil servants gained admission through public examination.[7]

Another view of the civil service in terms of overall appointments is provided in a report prepared by DASP in July, 1961. According to the data it had collected, of a total of 300,000 federal civil servants, only 15 percent had been admitted through public examination. DASP attributed this divergence between legal norms and reality to the fact that by that time the mass of the federal civil servants consisted of those who had belonged to the old *extranumerário* category and to the fact that only a small part of these employees had taken the proper examinations required of them: the *prova de habilitação*. Also included in this large number not properly admitted were many employees who had entered under lump-sum appropriations (*verbas globais*).[8]

The post-1945 experience with patronage pressures confirmed the

[6] Beatriz Marqués de Souza Wahrlich, *A Importância da Formação de Pessoal*, p. 18.
[7] Wahrlich in Brazil, Ministro Extraordinário para a Reforma Administrativa, "Normas para Preservação e Revigoramento do Sistema do Mérito."
[8] *JB*, July 8, 1961, p. 5.

belief of those supporting DASP that efficiency, economy, and rationality in the civil service could only be achieved through the construction of effective barriers to keep out the mass of job seekers and to neutralize the politician's influence. Yet the objectives of preserving the civil service from political intrusions and insuring the selection of public personnel solely on the basis of merit became increasingly remote to the political environment. Nevertheless, the moral commitment of the civil service reformers remained and they zealously defended the concept of a merit system.

As a consequence of the struggle to defend the DASP system, a certain degree of intellectual rigidity set in. In this process the validity of the principles of administration that had been learned abroad, transferred to Brazil, and later reinforced by the United States' technical assistance program in public administration was never once called into question, for they had become a belief system. When the political structure of the country altered with the return to an open system of politics, those associated with DASP and committed to the goal of establishing a merit bureaucracy in Brazil attempted to create a public image of DASP as a democratic organization and to show that what it had set out to accomplish was really much more consonant with a democratic form of government. Emphasis was placed on DASP as a technical, administrative organ which was politically independent and neutral.

The fact that DASP was an instrument of the executive was both a source of strength and weakness. When Vargas was in office, whether as dictator or as a constitutionally elected president, the organization prospered. In the area of public personnel administration this meant that *concursos* were properly administered, appointments to the career civil service were made through legal channels, and the entire personnel process was centralized under the control of DASP. The other presidents, with perhaps the exception of Jânio Quadros, were not really committed to the goals of the organization, although they all, at least at the beginning of their presidential terms of office, gave lip service to administrative reform and to the role of DASP in this area. This was because it provided a convenient cover for executive action in the area of public personnel.

Consequently, the personnel politics of the organization changed in accord with the wishes of the executive, and these changes could be conveniently cloaked in terms of moral precepts. The point could always be made that DASP was neutral and impartial and above the realm of politics. At the same time, if the executive wished to by-pass the organization and meet patronage pressures directly, he had the power to do so. DASP's control over formal appointments also could be used to defend the executive's appointive power against legislative inroads.

Much of the hostility in the press and in congress stemmed from the use of DASP according to the desires of the executive. It was not uncommon to find the same individuals bitterly attacking specific policies of the organization because of their association with political moves by the president and at the same time defending its contribution in the area of setting norms and standards for the civil service. The problem was that the normative and the political had a way of getting mixed. From a functional viewpoint the organization contributed tremendously to increasing the problem of formalism in public personnel administration. The legal and theoretical dichotomization of administration and politics made it more difficult to face the fact that the two were in constant interaction in the Brazilian milieu.

Statistically it becomes very difficult to measure in precise terms the effects of patronage on the federal civil service. While data on the size of the civil service, the number of appointments made, and the various categories of civil servants are accessible, they are neither complete nor always comparable. Consequently, it is difficult to measure how much change the civil service has undergone in recent decades as a consequence of the changing structure of Brazilian politics.

When Brazilian sources concerned with public administration are examined, one of the topics commonly mentioned is the tremendous expansion of the federal administrative system and the excessive number of people who occupy civil service positions (see Table 6). In 1938, 131,628 employees were reported at the federal level; in 1960, the totals varied between 344,097 and 345,568 employees.

The difficulty in measuring the size of the civil service stems from the autonomous status of the numerous entities included in the *autarquia* category. Before 1938 the practice of creating independent or semi-independent agencies and institutes was of little consequence, for throughout the First Republic and down to the declaration of the dictatorship in 1938, the total size of the federal civil service varied little. For this reason the total given in Table 6 for the ministries and other federal organs subordinate to the executive in 1938 may be accepted as fairly accurate. After 1938, as administrative services expanded and the government took on new economic and welfare responsibilities, the creation of *autarquias* became common. By 1960 the growth of these institutions had become so chaotic that it was necessary to try to establish controls over them and to coordinate more ef-

Table 6. Size of the Federal Civil Service, 1938–1960[a]

	1938	1943	1953	1956	1958	An.[b]	1960 DASP[c]	JB[d]
Federal civil servants								
Administração direta[e]	131,628	145,991	180,410	217,135	232,632	231,504		224,000
Autarquias[f]						114,064	120,097	120,097
Both (entire civil service)			240,000[g]			345,568		344,097
Administração direta								
Vacant positions				72,829		42,141	21,411	
Occupied positions				217,135		231,504		
Total positions				289,964		273,645		
Autarquias								
Vacant positions						28,115	28,115	
Occupied positions						114,064	120,097	
Total positions						142,179	148,212	
Entire federal civil service								
Vacant positions						63,876		77,115
Occupied positions						318,914		344,097
Total positions						382,790		421,212

[a] Based on Mário Wagner Vieira da Cunha, *O Sistema Administrativo Brasileiro, 1930–1950*, pp. 129–130; Brazil, *Anuário Estatístico*, Vol. XV (1945), p. 463, and Vol. XXIII (1962), pp. 335–336; Brazil, Departamento Administrativo do Serviço Público, *Relatório das Atividades do DASP, 1960*, pp. 53, 56; Adalmo de Araújo Andrade, *Diretrizes para Classificação de Cargos; Jornal do Brasil* (Rio de Janeiro), January 25, 1961, p. 5.

[b] *Anuário Estatístico*, Vol. XXIII (1962).

[c] DASP, *Relatório das Atividades*.

[d] *Jornal do Brasil*. Figures are based on information released by DASP.

[e] Literally, "direct administration." The collection of ministries, agencies, and commissions directly responsible to the president of the Republic.

[f] A plethora of autonomous agencies, departments, and services; government corporations; and mixed enterprises.

[g] The 1954 *Anuário Estatístico* states that this figure is only approximate and is taken from the commission responsible for the classification plan, the Comissão do Plano de Classificação de Cargos. Questionnaires were sent to 180,000 civil servants, accounting, according to the Commission, for 72 percent of a total of about 240,000 civil servants (*Anuário Estatístico*, Vol. XVI [1955], p. 516).

fectively the whole federal administrative system. The major instruments making possible a broad, overall view of administration were a careful survey of the entire civil service as a new classification plan was prepared, the passing of a classification law in 1960, and the creation of a comprehensive law for the social security institutes that same year. For the years between 1938 and 1960, however, it is difficult to estimate the total size of the civil service because standard sources do not offer information on the total numerical *autarquia* employment. The one exception to this statement is 1953, for which the estimated figure of 240,000 for the whole federal civil service is available.

A second aspect of Table 6 which is relevant to understanding the context within which political patronage has functioned is the gap between the total number of civil servants listed and the total number of positions recorded. In 1956, 217,135 civil servants were reported in the category *administração direta*, while 289,964 positions were authorized by law. In 1960, according to figures supplied by the *Anuário Estatístico*, there were 231,504 civil servants and 293,645 available positions in the *administração direta* category and 114,064 civil servants and 142,179 available positions in the *autarquia*. This excess number of positions supplied the chief executive with sufficient freedom to make new interim appointments if he wished, thus by-passing the merit system requirement, and an argument against those who accused him of expanding the ranks of the civil service. It could always be pointed out that he had limited the expansion of the civil service and had kept the numbers hired below the maximum legal limits.

A further insight into the civil service is provided in Tables 7, 8, and 9, in which detailed figures are presented on the number of appointments made, vacancies occurring, and positions abolished during the government of Juscelino Kubitschek (unfortunately, such data are available only for his government). These figures give an indication of the way appointments were handled during his term. Where civil service positions created by law were involved, he cannot be accused of excessive patronage appointments, since all permanent appointments had to be made through the DASP apparatus and since the only area in which political patronage could legally be utilized was in the *interino* category. As far as the researcher has been able to ascertain, he did not violate this precept. Given his concern for legality, the major area open to him for political patronage was the *extranumerário* category; there no legal controls existed on the nature of the appointments made. An idea of the numbers of civil servants involved here is given in Table 10.

Table 7.   Positions Occupied, Vacant, and Abolished during the
Juscelino Kubitschek Government.[a]

	1956	1957	1958	1959	1960	Total 1956–1960
Administração Direta Appointments						
By commission (*em comissão*)	202	92	85	165	109	
For life (*vitalícias*)	—	—	—	132	—	
Permanent (*efetivos*)	906	1,368	2,497	2,852	5,007	
Interim (*interinos*)	673	59	686	1,047	1,883	
Interim substitutions (*substituições interinas*)	85	1,321	55	88	96	
Reinstatements (*reintegrações*)	3	9	9	7	8	
Readmissions (*readmissões*)	29	74	24	39	24	
Returns (*reversões*)	11	8	15	19	101	
Transfers (*aproveitamentos*)	22	3	23	5	11	
Admissions (*admissões*)	—	—	—	66	—	
TOTAL	1,931	2,934	3,394	4,420	7,239	19,918
Administração Direta Vacancies						
Retirements (*aposentações*)	2,575	2,881	3,350	3,718	2,249	
Dismissals (*demissões*)	27	48	219	203	133	
Resignations (*exonerações*)	769	460	749	2,478	512	
Releases (*dispensas*)	—	—	108	69	32	
Deaths (*mortes*)	85	147	92	188	319	
TOTAL	3,456	3,536	4,518	6,656	3,245	21,411
Positions Abolished						
Administração direta						33,000
Autarquias						
Cargos[b]						3,143
Funções[c]						2,890
TOTAL						39,033

[a] Based on Brazil, *Anuário Estatístico*, Vol. XXIII (1962); *Jornal do Brasil* (Rio de Janeiro), January 25, 1961, p. 5; and Brazil, DASP, *Relatório das Atividades, 1960*, pp. 53–55.
[b] Positions occupied by *funcionários*.
[c] Positions occupied by *extranumerários*.

While often accused of patronage abuses, Kubitschek cannot be held responsible for excessive appointments any more than Vargas can. In 1943, at the end of the Estado Novo, 91,827 *extranumerários* were listed, compared with 113,574 in 1958. In view of the intervening years and the changes in government, the increases in the numbers of federal civil servants in the *extranumerário* category are not proportionately greater than the increase for the civil service as a whole. What appears to have taken place is a gradual expansion in the size of the federal civil service from the time of the dictatorship through the end of the Kubitschek government. In these years each government made its contribution to the expansion of public employment— no one government is more responsible for political patronage than another.

How the Goulart government fits into this pattern cannot be determined numerically, since there is an absence of data on the size of the federal civil service after 1960. It is known, however, that by the time Goulart became president the *extranumerário* category, the one which provided easiest access to the civil service for political appointees, had

Table 8. Positions in the Ministries and Federal Commissions and Agencies Responsible to the Executive (1960): Number Occupied, Vacant, and Total Number.[a]

Entities	Total	Positions Occupied	Vacant
Ministries			
Aeronáutica	20,005	17,353	2,652
Agricultura	26,227	24,826	1,401
Educação e Cultura	18,411	15,691	2,720
Fazenda	26,034	19,868	6,166
Justiça e Negócios Interiores	14,561	13,249	1,312
Marinha	17,184	14,566	2,618
Relações Exteriores	915	785	130
Saúde	19,517	18,998	519
Trabalho, Indústria e Comércio	6,818	6,232	586
Viação e Obras Públicas	101,172	79,882	21,290
Guerra	19,564	17,492	2,072
Commissions and Agencies			
Comissão de Readaptação dos Incapazes das Fôrças Armadas	25	25	—
Comissão do Vale do São Francisco	989	835	154
Comissão Executiva de Armazens e Silos	9	9	—
Comissão Executiva do Plano do Carvão Nacional	18	18	—
Conselho Coordenador do Abastecimento	71	65	6
Conselho Nacional de Aguas e Energia Elétrica	54	43	11
Conselho Nacional do Desenvolvimento	20	20	—
Conselho Nacional de Economia	161	117	44
Conselho Nacional de Petróleo	332	207	125
Departamento Administrativo do Serviço Público	809	639	170
Escritório Técnico da Universidade do Brasil	114	114	—
Estado Maior das Fôrças Armadas	108	89	19
Secretaria da Presidência da República	29	20	9
Superintendência do Plano e Valorização Econômica da Amazônia	498	361	137
TOTAL	273,645	231,504	42,141

[a] Based on *Anuário Estatístico*, Vol. XXIII (1962), pp. 335–336.

Table 9. Federal *Autarquia* Positions Responsible to the Executive and to Ministries (1960) : Number Occupied, Vacant, Abolished, and Total Number.[a]

Autarquias	Positions (*Funções*)				Positions (*Cargos*)			
	No.[b]	Occupied	Vacant	Abolished	No.[b]	Occupied	Vacant	Abolished
Presidência da Republica								
Conselho Nacional de Pesquisas	—	—	—	—	122	85	37	—
Instituto do Açúcar e do Alcool	1,162	995	167	90	450	450	—	—
Instituto Brasileiro de Bibliografia e Documentação	—	—	—	36	66	36	30	—
Instituto Brasileiro de Geografia e Estatistica:								
Conselho Nacional de Estatistica	4,838	3,581	1,257	—	—	—	—	—
Conselho Nacional de Geografia	1,070	634	436	—	—	—	—	—
Instituto Nacional de Pesquisas da Amazonia	—	—	—	—	47	47	—	—
Ministério da Agricultura								
Banco Nacional de Crédito Cooperativo	346	274	72	—	64	52	12	—
Caixa do Crédito da Pesca	79	66	13	4	—	—	—	—
Instituto Nacional de Imigração e Colonização	746	625	121	30	128	122	6	—
Instituto Nacional do Mate	4	4	—	16	—	—	—	—
Serviço Social Rural	460	310	150	—	—	—	—	—
Ministério da Educação e Cultura								
Universidades:								
Da Bahia	2,432	1,454	978	10	—	—	—	—
De Minas Gerais	—	—	—	—	4,505	2,974	1,531	1,009
Do Brasil	—	—	—	—	742	731	11	106
Do Ceará	1,412	676	736	—	—	—	—	—
Do Pará	458	358	100	—	—	—	—	—
Do Paraná	2,830	1,332	1,498	—	—	—	—	—
Do Recife	2,453	1,887	566	30	—	—	—	—

[a] Based on Brazil, *Anuário Estatistico*, Vol. XXIII (1962), pp. 335–336.
[b] Excludes *cargos* and *funções* abolished.

Table 9—Continued

Autarquias	No.[b]	Positions (Funções) Occupied	Vacant	Abolished	No.[b]	Positions (Cargos) Occupied	Vacant	Abolished
Do Rio Grande do Sul	2,485	1,457	1,028	—	—	—	—	—
Rural de Pernambuco	509	332	177	8	—	—	—	—
Ministério da Fazenda								
Caixas Econômicas Federais:								
Amazonas	49	49	—	5	—	—	—	—
Pará	113	113	—	20	—	—	—	—
Maranhão	31	31	—	17	—	—	—	—
Piauí	28	28	—	—	—	—	—	—
Ceará	94	94	—	7	—	—	—	—
Rio Grande do Norte	24	24	—	1	—	—	—	—
Paraíba	79	79	—	8	—	—	—	—
Pernambuco	249	249	—	10	10	10	—	—
Alagoas	42	42	—	2	6	6	—	—
Sergipe	17	17	—	1	4	4	—	—
Bahia	266	266	—	84	—	—	—	—
Minas Gerais	858	858	—	39	—	—	—	—
Espírito Santo	82	82	—	7	—	3	—	—
Rio de Janeiro	464	464	—	68	—	—	—	—
Guanabara	3,073	3,073	—	547	—	—	—	—
São Paulo	2,802	2,802	—	—	—	—	—	—
Paraná	579	579	—	36	—	—	—	—
Santa Catarina	126	126	—	—	—	—	—	—
Rio Grande do Sul	656	656	—	203	—	—	—	—
Mato Grosso	43	43	—	9	3	—	—	—
Goiás	22	22	—	—	—	—	—	—
Brasília (Federal District)	552	258	294	—	—	—	—	—
Conselho Superior das Caixas Econômicas Federais	76	76	—	51	—	—	—	—
Instituto Brasileiro do Café (IBC)	4,313	4,010	303	—	—	—	—	—

Table 9—Continued

Autarquias	Positions (Funções)				Positions (Cargos)			
	No.b	Occupied	Vacant	Abolished	No.b	Occupied	Vacant	Abolished
Ministerio do Trabalho, Indústria e Comércio								
Conselho Federal e Regional de Contabilidade	34	29	5	—	—	—	—	—
Conselho Federal e Regional de Engenharia e Arquitetura (CERA)	85	79	6	46	10	10	—	30
Hospital Júlia Kubitschek	271	116	155	—	—	—	—	—
Instituto Brasileiro do Sal (IBS)	156	107	49	8	—	—	—	5
Instituto de Aposentadoria e Pensões:								
Dos Bancários (IAPB)	1,997	1,750	247	7	—	—	—	—
Dos Comerciários (IAPC)	6,639	6,005	634	788	4,410	4,410	—	—
Dos Empregados em Transportes e Cargas (IAPETC)	7,252	6,903	349	83	3,890	3,890	—	—
Dos Ferroviários e Empregados em Serviços Públicos (IAPFESP)	5,046	4,254	792	432	373	360	13	—
Dos Industriários (IAPI)	16,433	10,477	5,956	—	1,494	1,286	298	70
Dos Marítimos (IAPM)	2,304	1,932	372	71	516	433	83	—
Instituto de Previdência e Assistência dos Servidores do Estado (IPASE)	9,359	7,131	1,228	—	—	—	—	—
Instituto Nacional do Pinho	951	902	49	—	—	—	—	—
Serviço de Alimentação da Previdência Social (SAPS)	1,393	927	466	26	1,127	711	416	1,491
Ministério da Viação e Obras Públicas								
Administração do Pôrto do Rio de Janeiro	9,449	7,357	2,092	99	—	—	—	—
Comissão da Marinha Mercante	427	427	—	—	—	—	—	—
Departamento Nacional de Estradas de Rodagem	4,716	3,277	1,439	33	12,206	8,404	3,802	160
Lóide Brasileiro	7,711	7,711	—	211	—	—	—	—
Serviço de Navegação da:								
Amazônia e Pôrto do Pará (SNAPP)	—	—	—	—	2,111	2,032	79	7
Bacia do Prata (SNBP)	—	—	—	—	750	598	152	12
TOTAL	09,145	87,410	21,735	3,143	33,034	26,654	6,380	2,890

been abolished. Furthermore, controls on the social security institutes, another patronage area, had been established.

Yet, the newspaper accounts covering Goulart's period of office and discussions with knowledgeable citizens lend the inescapable impressions that this was a period in which political patronage reached new heights and the legal barriers constructed around the federal civil service were breached in unprecedented numbers. No doubt political patronage pressures reappeared after a brief lull in such activities while Quadros was in office, but the extent to which they occurred cannot be measured. Nor can it be determined whether the waves of new appointments were based upon rotation in office or whether the total number of civil servants was simply augmented once again. Similarly, it is difficult to state precisely what were the effects of the Quadros reforms on the federal civil service. The impression which emerges is of a breathing period between two governments in which manipulation of the patronage power was crucial to political survival, rather than of real civil service reform and reintroduction of the merit principle.

Table 10.   Civil Servants According to Major Categories (Prior to the Classification Law of 1960)[a]

	1943	1958
Funcionários:		
With permanent appointments (*efetivos*)		67,096
Other		51,963
Total	54,164	119,059
Extranumerários:		
Contratados	685	
Mensalistas	40,277	
Diaristas tabelados[b]	38,197	
Diaristas estimados[c]	6,762	
Tarefeiros	5,906	
Total	91,827	113,573
Total federal civil servants	145,991	232,632

[a] Vieira da Cunha, *O Sistema Administrativo*, pp. 129–130; Brazil, *Anuário Estatístico*, Vol. VI (1941–1945), p. 467.

[b] Jobs included in fixed pay schedule.

[c] Jobs not in fixed pay schedule. The figures are estimates only because of the difficulty of obtaining exact numbers for these employees. The total number of *diaristas* is 44,959.

CHAPTER IX

The Collapse of an Elite Civil Service

Between 1945 and 1964 the federal civil service changed from the guardian bureaucracy created by the Estado Novo into a patronage bureaucracy, providing systems supports for the Second Republic. The preceding chapter outlined the general patterns of patronage politics; here focus is on the pressures and strategies used during these years to undermine an elitist-oriented civil service.

Throughout the Estado Novo the DASP apparatus functioned as a mechanism for developing an elite corps of career civil servants and for closing off other civil servants from access to the rights and benefits of the privileged *funcionários públicos*. Yet, even then, one group within the *extranumerário* category, the *mensalistas*, was able to improve its status considerably. Through Decree-Law 1909 of December 26, 1939, the requirement of a competitive examination was extended to *extranumerário-mensalistas*. Next, under Decree-Law 5175 of January 7, 1943, the possibility of promotion to positions immediately above those currently held was made available to them.[1] A decision on the part of DASP to provide them with an improvement in salary according to the criteria used for the *funcionário* followed. This decision marked the beginning of a systematization of pay increases to the whole *extranumerário* category with the objective of rewarding these individuals in proportion to their competence.[2]

After 1945 controls on the *extranumerário* and on the *interino* were relaxed across the board. Article 23 of the Transitional Provisions of the 1946 Constitution provided for the granting of tenure to all *extranumerários* who had a minimum of five years' service. Em-

---

[1] A distinction in terminology, however, maintained the separation between the *funcionário* and the *extranumerário*: promotions for the *extranumerário-mensalista* were placed under the category of *acesso* (access); the term *promoção* (promotion) was reserved for the *funcionário*.

[2] Maria Joana de Almeida Fernandes, "Aspectos da Política de Extranumerários," *RSP*, II (May–June, 1947), 113–114.

ployees in jobs of a permanent character who had more than five years of service or who had passed a competitive public examination (*concurso*) or an examination demonstrating their ability to fulfill the responsibilities of a particular position (*prova de habilitação*) received benefits placing them on a level with the *funcionários*. These included tenure, retirement, vacations, leaves of absence, and accessibility to jobs at higher levels.

The extension of rights and privileges similar to those of the *funcionário* to other permanent civil servants raised the issue of whether they were granted to the individual public employee or whether they were assigned to certain positions. DASP's legal consultant argued that these provisions meant that those employees who afterwards accepted jobs of a temporary character lost any formerly acquired prerogatives. This attitude, expressed in several DASP reports, was based on the interpretation that these benefits were extended to individuals because of their occupancy of certain positions. In contrast, the viewpoint of those defending *extranumerário* interests was that these privileges were extended to the individual independently of a particular position. In general, those who favored the broadening of the rights and privileges of the *extranumerários* did so on the grounds that they were more numerous than the *funcionários*, that they were indispensable to the civil service, that in many cases they filled positions of importance equal to those of the *funcionários*, and that because they were no longer merely auxiliary personnel they deserved the same treatment as the *funcionários*.[3]

Whereas privileges were extended to a sizable number of *extranumerários* and limitations were imposed on entry into this aspect of the public service through the requirement of an examination establishing one's ability for the job at hand, the filling of vacancies in the career service by the appointment of interim employees (*interinos*) provided a side entrance into the *funcionário* category.[4] Temporary appointments, valid for only a year, had a way of becoming permanent, although legislation required that after that time the *interino* had to pass the *concurso*. Even more than the *extranumerário*, the *interino* appointment tended to undercut the attempt to create and maintain a technical administrative elite, for it offered those benefiting from personal and kinship ties a means of entrance into the career civil service without examination. This was possible because the ex-

---

[3] This argument, frequently presented to the legislator, is quite well summarized in José Medeiros, "Estabilidade de Extranumerário," *RSP*, III (July, 1950), 56–58.

[4] Oscar Vitorino Moreira, "O Interino em Cargo de Carreira em Face da Constituição," *RSP*, I (March, 1950), 14–16.

ecutive had the prerogative of making each public service appointment, appointments which were announced in the form of decrees in the *Diário Oficial.*

As already mentioned, the DASP apparatus, designed to assist the executive in making appointments on the basis of qualified personnel, offered the president considerable freedom for juggling positions according to his wishes. The Dutra government demonstrates this. In the name of economy, Dutra initially adopted measures to limit personnel expenditures by reducing the number of formal appointments to the career civil service. The formal selection process, carried out under DASP's auspices, was already a long and drawn out one. Often there was a considerable delay between the opening of registration for the examinations and the administering of them and between the announcement of successful candidates and their actual appointment to office. Related to this was the fact that the examinations were difficult and that they were often criticized for being too rigorous in relation to the positions and salaries offered. Of the total number of persons who signed up for the examination, only a small percentage passed. The limitations imposed by Dutra on the appointments made from these approved lists added a further frustrating factor for those attempting to obtain public employment through the proper legal procedures. In the meantime, however, Dutra made interim (*interino*) appointments to fill the vacancies available in the career civil service. This tactic was repeated often in subsequent administrations.

A further example of the delays and frustrations in the formal selection process is found in a petition presented to the President in 1948 through the president of the Association of Brazilian Civil Servants (Associação dos Servidores Civis do Brasil). This petition, prepared by some three hundred candidates approved in the last examination for administrative official (*oficial administrativo*) positions, protested the delays in their appointment to office. In a speech before the senate, Alfredo Nasser stated their case:

Registration for the examinations for administrative officials was opened simultaneously throughout the country in 1945 and was reopened . . . twice in 1946, but only during the last few months of 1947, three years afterwards, . . . were the examinations given. Of the 10,000 candidates who signed up initially, 7,000 gave up, and of the 3,000 who took the examination, only 620 succeeded in qualifying. Of these 620, according to a notice tied to responsible sources, only the first 50, on the basis of their classification, will be appointed. The rest may receive the appointments during the next two years, if present conditions in the country are modified. At the end of this period, those who have not been appointed will lose their standing, because the law prohibits the appointment of a candidate approved in an examination whose period of validity has ended.[5]

Joined with the frustration of the examination process and the use of interim appointments was a third factor: the destruction of the pay differential between *funcionários* (or *interinos* in *funcionário* positions) and *extranumerários*. This came about through the passage of Law 488, known as the *Tabelas Unicas*.[6] The crucial section of this law was contained in Article 2, which stated that pay for each position (whether *cargo*, *pôsto*, or *função*) and grade (*graduação*), except in the case of the president, the vice president, members of congress, and ministers of state, was to be according to the same basic pay scale. This law also established a single pay scale for personnel in the civil and military service. The elitist structure of the civil service was further modified in Article 13. There the four gradations to which *extranumerário* employees were submitted were abolished, and in other articles each of these four previous divisions was adjusted to the same general salary scale. With this general improvement in the status and financial condition of the *extranumerário* and without the DASP formal controls to contend with, new appointments were made to the public service under the heading of *funções* (jobs outside the *funcionário* category) during the final years of the Dutra government. This was done regardless of the government's original vocal concern with economy in salaries for public employees.

When Getúlio Vargas returned to the office of the executive as a constitutionally elected president in 1951, one of his first acts was to attempt to rebuild the structure of an elite career civil service on the basis of competence, not patronage, and to undo the alterations introduced by Linhares and Dutra. On February 20, he issued an executive ruling reenacting Decree-Law 5175 of January 7, 1943, and stating, in accord with Article 186 of the 1946 Constitution, that entrance into the civil service could be made only through examination. This ruling specifically prohibited the admission of *extranumerários* through a simple listing of names and revoked the *Tabelas Unicas* in the ministries and other organs directly subordinate to the presidency. The ruling also authorized DASP to act with urgency to revise the *Tabelas Unicas* in these agencies and to adjust also the pay schedules of all *autarquias*. This ruling further stipulated that all bodies affected

[5] *JB*, July 10, 1948, p. 1.

[6] Brazil, "Lei Número 488—De 15 de Novembro de 1948, Dispõe sôbre o Pagamento de Vencimentos, Renumeração ou Salário de Pessoal Civil e Militário da União," in República dos Estados Unidos do Brasil, *Coleção das Leis de 1948, Atos do Poder Legislativo (Outubro a Dezembro)*, VII, 55–77.

must provide DASP with the necessary data needed for the revision. New schedules were published, and the filling of all jobs by *extranumerários-mensalistas* was to be suspended, as were all other schedules and acts altering what was termed "the existing situation." Once DASP had completed its revision, it was to present to the Office of the Executive a report naming those areas in each schedule requiring the attention of the government.[7]

The ruling marked the initiation of an effort by the President to revive DASP and to once again centralize public personnel policies and practices under his control. DASP immediately went into action, studying the *Tabelas Unicas* and checking the validity of each appointment in question. Where violations were discovered, the individual was either removed from his position or ordered to prove his qualifications through a *prova de habilitação*.

By mid-April, 1951, however, criticism began to appear in the press and in congress against the solutions offered by DASP as it started to put into effect steps to end the *Tabelas Unicas* and against the delays involved while waiting for DASP to declare its view on particular cases. In the face of this criticism, DASP issued a news release stressing the purpose of the revision:

> The purpose of the government is not to harm or, even less, to provoke a wholesale dismissal of public employees because of a change of government. Instead, its purpose is to give prestige to the law, to impede arbitrary choice, and to dignify public employment. . . .
> This is the reason so much that, parallel to the corrective measures, the government is attempting to name to the existing vacancies candidates selected according to examination. It is promoting new written public examinations or examinations of ability [*provas de habilitação*] that will meet the needs of the public service. In other words, its purpose is to give new prestige to the merit system, moralizing and making more democratic entrance into public positions.[8]

Not everyone, however, accepted the justification offered by DASP. For example, Senator Hamilton Nogueira defended the *Tabelas Unicas* in a speech delivered in the senate in July. He pointed out that in the case of the *extranumerário* this law ended a most varied nomenclature by eliminating the distinctions among *mensalistas, diaristas, tarefeiros* and *contratados*. Furthermore, the *Tabelas Unicas* was an act passed by congress, authorizing the executive to carry it out. The executive, in turn, had consulted DASP and new pay schedules

---

[7] *JB*, February 20, 1951, p. 6.
[8] *JB*, April 17, 1951, p. 6.

were put into effect. When Vargas came to power, however, the law was annulled and DASP proceeded to undo its effects.

Drawing upon the fact that DASP was considered a technical organ above politics, Nogueira proceeded to call in question its policies as a purely administrative organ. DASP seemed instead a mere instrument at the service of the president, for under Dutra it had put the *Tabelas Unicas* into effect and now, under Vargas, in the name of moralizing the civil service and undoing the evils of patronage, it was destroying them. According to Nogueira's sources of information, these changes involved five thousand functionaries. In defending the cause of the *extranumerário*, he claimed that DASP had once again usurped the legislative capacity. The acts of President Dutra, when he made appointments under the *Tabelas Unicas*, were perfectly legal. Furthermore, the legality of this action was at least to some degree recognized by Vargas, for the day's *Diário Oficial* had just announced that Vargas, through a request from the Merchant Marine Commission, had made fifty appointments to vacancies under the commission's *Tabelas Unicas*.[9] These positions were *funções*, not *cargos*, which put them in the *extranumerário* category.

On July 25, Vargas issued an executive ruling, based on an explanatory report prepared by DASP, modifying his previous position. To avoid paralyzing some sectors of the public service and for reasons of "social equality," he announced that he was delaying the initiation of those decrees dealing with funds spent on public servants irregularly admitted until all the individuals affected had had the opportunity to pass *provas de habilitação* and thus gain a legal right to their positions.[10]

The next year Vargas once again moved forward in his effort to build a federal civil service selected on the basis of competence. On March 27, congress passed a law requiring examinations for the admission of new employees to the social security institutes and other autonomous governmental entities,[11] and on September 18, Vargas made it effective through the use of an executive decree. The next step in reorganizing the civil service was the passage of a new Statute for the Public Functionaries, on October 28.[12]

It is important to note, however, that Vargas' attempt to impose the requirement of public examinations (*concursos*, as distinguished from *provas de habilitação*) and to develop a corps of competent civil serv-

---

9 *JB*, July 20, 1951, p. 9.
10 *JB*, July 27, 1951, p. 9.
11 Law 1584.
12 Law 1711.

ants was restricted to those with the standing of *funcionários públicos*. At the same time that he was defending the merit principle, he was proceeding with patronage appointments in the *extranumerário* category. This was a practice he had followed during the Estado Novo. This time, however, he was acting in a political context characterized by a congress not always subservient to the wishes of the executive and by political parties in the throes of developing a mass basis.

This situation was reflected in a law passed by congress on July 24, 1954, under which all *extranumerários-mensalistas* with five or more years of service were put on a par with *funcionários efetivos*. The law contained a section prohibiting Vargas from appointing any new employees to this grade. When it came time to promulgate the law, Vargas used the item veto to remove this particular section. He justified his action on the grounds that it would frustrate the just aspirations of a sizable number of candidates already approved in examinations (*provas*). He also vetoed another article, requiring minimal examinations for *contratados* and *tarefeiros*; thus, these positions were left open to executive patronage. In this case, he stated that such a provision would alter the personnel selection process by upsetting the independence of autonomous government agencies and entities. Afterwards, however, he modified his position, for it was later stipulated that new *extranumerários* would be admitted only to temporary positions, that salary limitations would be imposed on *extranumerários* in the *contratado* and *tarefeiro* categories, and that new employees at these levels would be admitted only through an examination for aptitude or capacity administered by DASP.[13]

At the end of August Vargas committed suicide, and an interim government, led by Café Filho, followed. In the face of what were apparently almost overwhelming pressures for public employment, Café Filho issued an open letter to job seekers through his private secretary. In it he said that the government was unable to promise any jobs due to the excessive number of public employees already in service and to the Treasury's inability to assume financial responsibility for any new positions. As it was, the payment of existing salaries in many cases was being delayed because of lack of funds. He also made it quite clear that his government was committed to admissions on the basis of competitive examinations "without a regime of patronage and without political influence." He stated, "The Executive Office does not have, nor does it sponsor, candidates and it is firmly resolved to maintain this norm as an example. It is its intention not to channel

---

[13] *JB*, July 24, 1954, p. 6, and August 8, 1954, p. 5. The *diaristas* were not dealt with in this law because they had been advanced to the *mensalista* level in 1952.

requests to the ministries or any other administrative organs."[14] Eventually, however, Café Filho—as others before and after him—found it necessary to give way to patronage pressures.

An editorial published by the *Jornal do Brasil* at this time called attention to the fact that the Café Filho government was faced with this onslaught of job seekers after only twenty days of being in power. The situation it described was to be frequent in subsequent years. On the one hand, public finances were chaotic and it was essential that the new government limit expenses; on the other, political pressures for the distribution of jobs to friends, relatives, and political party associates were intense and were increasing. If the politician was to collaborate with the government, claimed the editorial, he had to be able to meet the demands of his electorate. In the case of the more powerful politician, the executive clearly could not afford to alienate his support. Yet, once patronage was allotted to these individuals, it became difficult to resist the pressures of the less important.[15] This dilemma seemed inescapable, maintained a second editorial, for each change of government brought with it a new army of reliable followers, replacing that of the preceding executive.[16]

Juscelino Kubitschek, the next president, was subjected to similar pressures on assuming office. Like his predecessors, he formally affirmed his belief in the merit system, took some legal action, and then proceeded to make appointments in those areas in which the heaviest pressures were brought to bear. Shortly after taking office, he gave lip service to DASP as an instrument of administrative reform, issued two circulars increasing ministerial and agency accountability to the executive, and authorized interim appointments according to political criteria. Wahrlich holds Kubitschek responsible for making an estimated seven thousand appointments during this period and ascribes a large part of them to the PTB as a payoff for support during the electoral campaign.[17] A similar figure was quoted when these appointments were debated in congress. Kubitschek did not try to deny them; he maintained only they were made within the limits of the law.[18]

Further patronage potentialities were provided several months later through a directive approved by him and applicable to all the *autarquias*.[19] Annulment of all appointments to nonclassified positions and

[14] *JB*, September 9, 1954, p. 6.
[15] *JB*, September 15, 1954, p. 5.
[16] *JB*, September 18, 1954, p. 5.
[17] Interview with Beatriz Wahrlich, cited by Gilbert Siegel, "The Vicissitudes of Governmental Reform in Brazil: A Study of the DASP," p. 256.
[18] *JB*, July 14, 1956, p. 5.
[19] *JB*, May 5, 1956, p. 5.

of all acts granting permanent status to *interinos* without examination, beginning May, 1952, conveniently cleared the way for many of Kubitschek's own appointments and could simultaneously be pointed to as an act rectifying previous violations of the civil service system. As if this were not enough, the director-general of DASP issued an official note defending the President's right to make *interino* appointments to the *autarquias*.[20]

Kubitschek continued to make *interino* and *extranumerário* appointments in practice, but in statements released to the press he claimed that he was really anti-*empreguista*—opposed to excessive appointments to the civil service. To back up his position he pointed to civil service vacancies that he had not filled and to the number of positions he had ordered abolished. Examples of how Kubitschek manipulated appointments to the civil service in order to maintain executive control over them and how he also retained an image of opposition to increasing the government's financial obligations to the civil service are demonstrated by events occurring in 1954, 1957, 1958, and 1959.

In July, 1957, Kubitschek, on the grounds of economy, vetoed a bill passed by congress granting a salary increase to civil servants. At the same time he made additional appointments to the public service in the *tesoureiro* and *ajudante de tesoureiro* categories. These appointments were to a number of positions which had been conveniently opened through retirements and which offered the executive complete freedom to appoint whomever he wished. This action reflected a pattern common in executive-legislative relations throughout the Kubitschek government. While he sought to defend his patronage powers and continued to make civil service appointments according to non-merit standards, congress, under pressure from civil servant groups and organizations, tried continually to provide salary increases to meet the demands of the lower ranks of the civil service, where the largest numbers were employed and where the effects of the continuous rise in the cost of living were heavily felt.

In May, 1954, Kubitschek adopted another tactic. He went on the radio to announce that he was issuing a decree suspending all appointments until congressional elections, scheduled for October 3, were complete. Adequate advance notice on exactly when the decree would be promulgated was given and, it seems, a wave of office seekers descended on the presidential palace before the Monday, May 19, deadline. News articles on the inside pages of the *Jornal do Brasil* the preceding Saturday and Sunday carried these headlines: "The Rush to

[20] *JB*, June 27, 1956, p. 6.

Catete[21]: They Want 20,000 Jobs before Monday," "400 Appointees Are Awaiting IAPI's New Schedule," and "In Less than 48 Hours more than 500 Appointments Have Been Made to IAPI."[22] Once elections were over, the government returned to previous appointments patterns, the majority of the jobs being distributed in the social security institutions.

By this time the accumulation over the years of political patronage in the social security institutes had led to a situation demanding immediate attention. Financial disorder in the retirement and welfare programs of the institutes was rampant and, although consideration had been given to their reform before Kubitschek assumed office, little had been accomplished in the way of reform. On becoming president, Kubitschek inherited a bill, previously introduced, which was intended to provide the social security institutes with a single comprehensive law and to prohibit new appointments without examination. While this bill continued in congress for the next year, Kubitschek proceeded to have drafted a new measure for which he could receive credit. On May 23, 1958, he issued a decree establishing a commission and giving it the responsibility of preparing a draft of a law reorganizing the institutes. Article 3 of the decree repeated the prohibition contained in the original measure: all new appointments, admissions, and adjustment of services to individuals under the form of installment payments or according to similar practices were made illegal. This provision differed, however, in that it applied only to the institute benefiting federal civil servants (the Social Welfare Institute for Public Servants [Instituto de Previdência y Assistência dos Servidores do Estado—IPASE]) and to three other minor welfare organizations; the institutes in which the major amount of job patronage occurred were not to be affected.[23]

In a new session of congress the following year, a majority in the chamber of deputies agreed to freeze the bill and to push for the passage of a substitute measure granting full retirement benefits to workers fifty-five years old or with thirty-five years' service (later changed to thirty years). This occurred at the time Kubitschek was preparing to ban new appointments to the social security institutes. He opposed the measure and ordered the government's bloc to remain absent from the chamber so that a quorum might not be present to vote. Nevertheless, the bill was passed a short time later, and Kubitschek, with-

---

21 "Catete" was the name of the presidential palace in Rio de Janeiro before the capital was moved to Brasília.
22 *JB*, May 17, 1958, p. 4, and May 18, 1958, sec. 2, p. 12.
23 *JB*, May 23, 1956, p. 6.

out offering further opposition, sanctioned it, vetoing only those sections prohibiting new appointments.

By November, after congressional elections had been held, Kubitschek had decided that, in the face of the UDN's advances in the election, it was time to impose limits on the PTB and to turn the institutes over to a team of administrative technicians. This attitude was revealed by him in a conversation with PSD leaders. By then he had become concerned with Goulart's political ambitions.[24] Thus began a push for legislation to reform the social security system.

Much debated and amended (184 amendments at one point) and finally considered as an emergency measure, a comprehensive law governing the social security system was at last passed and sanctioned without any vetoes by the President in August, 1960. Under the new law, the individual institutes retained administrative and financial autonomy; in the personnel field this meant the power to organize and to control their own employees. At the same time the whole system was to be better coordinated by two bodies: the National Council for Social Welfare (Conselho Superior de Previdência Social—CSPS) and the National Department for Social Welfare (Departamento Nacional de Previdência Social—DNPS). Their responsibilities were the overall supervision of the social security system and the establishment of similar conditions for all beneficiaries. Through the DNPS the institutes, while retaining substantial autonomy, were subordinated to the Ministry of Labor and through that department were to be given the same organization as the Ministry and were to be governed by the same norms.

Since the original measure had been introduced, more than ten years of congressional consideration had passed. The President's refrain from using his item-veto power to cancel a section limiting admissions only to those who had passed public examinations was a pleasant surprise to those interested in administrative reform and in seeing the institutes removed from the influence of patronage. They were, however, quite correct in feeling that if new patronage appointments were desired, a suitable means of entry could be found. Nevertheless, with presidential elections in the offing and with Quadros running strong, the focus of attention of the Kubitschek government was now on protecting its appointees in the institutes and in using the reform and the principle of neutrality to protect its interests from a change in government. The new law was designed to become effective in December. After that date, each institute was to be administered

---

[24] *JB*, November 11, 1954, p. 4.

by an administrative council with six members: two indicated by the government, two by those receiving benefits from the program, and two by the businesses contributing to the program.

With Quadros' victory in the October election, the Kubitschek government proceeded to make certain that its representatives would dominate the councils. Since the terms of the appointees would not expire until December, 1964, Quadros' influence on the institutes could be minimized.

This attention to the constitution of the new councils in the institutes was accompanied by one last flurry of appointments as Kubitschek made his "political testament" (*testamento político*). At one point the protest in the press against these appointments reached such a level that the minister of labor and the chief of the President's civilian staff held a joint interview to provide information on these matters. Allegedly, the number of appointments involved was over fifteen thousand. They proceeded, not to deny the appointments, but to show that they were much more limited than supposed. According to the minister of labor, the total number of functionaries appointed was 4,436, of which 2,779 were patronage appointments and 1,657 merit appointments (i.e., based on qualification through public examination). He went on to say that all these admissions were by order of the President, who had received great pressures from all sides at the end of his term of office. He made it clear, however, that the President was not responsible for the persons appointed; he had merely authorized the appointments.[25]

The success of the movement to reform the social security institutes and to remove them from partisan influence must, then, be considered within a particular political context. This is important to remember, for afterwards, once Quadros had resigned and Goulart was in office, there was a great cry against intrusions into an area supposedly removed from politics. This experience underscores once more the point that was made in considering the Estado Novo. When administrative reforms—or any reforms in government, for that matter—are made, attention must be given to those groups which stand to benefit from a change in the power structure and to those which will lose. Once again, the banner of merit system practices and administrative rationalization and moralization was raised to achieve what were essentially political goals.

One of the first acts of Jânio Quadros was to order an investigation of previous appointments made to the civil service and to begin a

[25] *JB*, December 20, 1960, p. 4.

program of administrative reform. On February 21 he issued a decree prohibiting further appointments—except for those filling *cargos em comissão* and using persons selected on the basis of examination—and ordered the dismissal of all functionaries admitted to the civil service after September 1, 1960. A provision, however, allowed twenty percent of those dismissed to retain their jobs if they could prove the necessity of their service. Included in this investigation was a reexamination of the schedules and tables of the *autarquias* so that "with due respect for the principles of economy and efficiency, they could be adjusted to the real needs of service."[26] On the 23rd, under the authorization of the President, DASP undertook a survey of all appointments, with the understanding that it was to prepare a list of those employees who were to be dismissed. Since the institutes presented a particular problem under the new law, a move was made to replace the government's representatives on the governing council.

On the 24th, a notice appeared in the *Jornal do Brasil* reporting dismissals within the institutes. According to this report, the institute which had been most affected by excessive appointments was the Social Security Institute for Railroad and Public Services Employees (Instituto de Aposentadoria e Pensões dos Ferroviários e Empregados em Serviços Públicos—IAPFESP). There numerous appointments had been made without publication in the *Diáro Oficial*, as required by law. The *Jornal* gave the following figures on the number of dismissals which were forthcoming: 1,800 in IAPFESP, 1,450 in the Social Security Institute for Transport Employees (Instituto de Aposentadoria e Pensões dos Empregados em Transportes—IAPTEC), 650 in IPASE, 200 in the Social Welfare Food Service (Serviço de Alimentação da Previdência Social—SAPS), and 95 in the Social Security Institute for Maritime Workers (Instituto de Aposentadoria e Pensões dos Marítimos—IAPM). In the case of IAPI and the Social Security Institute for Bank Employees (Instituto de Aposentadoria e Pensões dos Bancários—IAPB), it stated that no official numbers had been released, but that in each case between two hundred and three hundred employees would be affected. Besides the institutes, the Ministry of Transportation and Public Works had also been adversely affected by patronage. There the study was still going on, but to date in only two departments—the highway department (Estrada de Rodagem) and the department responsible for drought measures (Obras contra as Sêcas)—some five thousand employees would be affected. Similarly, in the Ministry of Health no final report was ready, but

26 *JB*, February 22, 1961, p. 1.

investigations had revealed that, in the department responsible for dealing with rural endemic diseases (the Departamento de Endemias Rurais), 8,500 new employees had been hired within the last few months. In the same period, supposedly more than two thousand new employees had been admitted to other departments.[27]

Following this announcement four sets of dismissals were reported in the *Jornal do Brasil*. On March 3, anticipating action by the President, the administrative council of IAPB (whose members had been in office only since January) decided to act on irregular appointments to the institute to avoid presidential intervention. Under the new law governing the social security system, which made all irregular admissions illegal after it went into effect on September 5, it annulled 269 appointments. Then, on the 25th, Quadros himself, through a decree, ordered 369 functionaries appointed by Kubitschek removed from IAPI. A third set of dismissals, involving 1,232 individuals, took place under the auspices of the president of IAPFESP. The last notice in the *Jornal do Brasil* regarding removals by Quadros in terms of concrete numbers referred to the removal of 1,291 functionaries in the Ministry of Transportation and Public Works from the State Secretariat for Transportation (Secretaria do Estado da Viação) and from the Mail and Telegraph Department (Departamento de Correios e Telégrafos).[28]

Before long, however, previous patronage patterns reasserted themselves, for Quadros, who remained in office only seven months, was followed by João Goulart. In terms of the size of the civil service, Quadros' total dismissals were negligible and marked but a brief interval in a political context where patronage was essential to the politician. Once Goulart was in the presidency, the distribution of civil service jobs according to political criteria reappeared.

There was one crucial difference, however, between the two presidents. Whereas Kubitschek had used the role of the president as the dispenser of patronage to build a fairly effective governmental machine and was able to use it to obtain the necessary majorities for crucial legislation he desired to see passed, Goulart was never able to use his vast patronage powers to advantage. Kubitschek certainly had his problems with the PTB and the distribution of patronage in the social security institutes, but he never lost control to the degree that Goulart did. Until January, 1963, Goulart's problems can be attributed in large part to the existence of a parliamentary regime, but this

27 *JB*, February 24, 1961.
28 *JB*, March 3, 1961, p. 5; March 25, 1961, p. 3; April 2, 1961, p. 4; and April 4, 1961, p. 5.

cannot account for the fact that members of congress, in particular those in Goulart's own party, gained the upper hand in the matter of patronage even more so after the country returned to a presidential regime.

The first indication of a new wave of appointments, reported by the *Jornal do Brasil*, appeared in November. The administrative director of IAPETC disclosed that the institute had 4,112 vacancies in the *função* category,[29] of which 2,056 were at the disposal of DASP. He was quoted as saying there was no reason why candidates for appointment through public examination should feel themselves harmed by the government's decision to grant tenure and full status to 1,021 *interinos*.[30] The next day a strong denial came from the administrative director of IAPETC, who said he knew of no government order involving the 1,021 *interinos* mentioned by the *Jornal do Brasil*, although he did confirm the existence of 4,112 vacancies. These, he stated, were reserved as required by law—half for promotions and half for new admissions through public examination.[31] The validity of the original report being assumed, the director's denial may be interpreted as necessary because, according to the classification legislation, such an action was legally invalid.

The *Jornal do Brasil* then called attention to violations in IAPI, Lóide Brasileiro (the government's cargo line), and IPASE. On the basis of appointments published in IAPI's internal bulletin, the *Jornal* was able to account for over three thousand irregular appointments of *interinos* to the permanent service within a three-day period.[32] Similarly, by examining the internal bulletins of Lóide Brasileiro, the paper encountered material substantiating over a thousand additional illegal appointments.[33] The number involved in IPASE, over two hun-

---

[29] In the 1960 classification plan (Law 3780), the distinction between *cargo* and *função* was maintained, although the distinction between *extranumerário* and *funcionário* disappeared. "*Cargo*" refers to those positions created by law which are to be filled by *funcionários* or *interinos*. "*Função*" applies to jobs held by persons outside the *funcionário* category.

[30] *JB*, November 10, 1961, p. 5.

[31] *JB*, November 11, 1961, p. 8.

[32] *JB*, June 16, 1962, p. 8; June 23, 1962, p. 8; June 26, 1962, p. 4. This information was based on IAPI's *Boletim do Serviço*, No. 104 (June 5), No. 105 (June 6), No. 106 (June 7), and No. 108 (June 11), all published with an earlier date to avoid violating a presidential decree prohibiting all appointments until December 31. These sources are also referred to in a report, protesting the appointments, prepared by employees of the Institute (*JB*, July 5, 1962, p. 5). Deputies Nei Maranhão and Ferreira Lima based their reference regarding these violations on *Boletim do Serviço*, Nos. 980106 [sic] (*JB*, July 4, 1962, p. 3).

[33] *JB*, June 20, 1962, p. 3. This information was based on Lóide's internal bulletins of June 4–8.

dred, was considerably less.[34] In this latter case, the *Jornal do Brasil* held three men primarily responsible for these appointments: Deputy Saldanha Coelho (PTB leader in the state assembly in Guanabara), Paiva Muniz (an ex-president of IPASE), and Dr. Raimundo de Brito (ex-director of the Hospital dos Servidores and UDN candidate for the assembly in Guanabara).

Protests against these appointments reached the point that Goulart found it necessary to issue an official statement, on August 21, 1962, through the chief of his civilian staff. It ordered a rigorous investigation of the institutes for violation of Decree 51504 (June 11, 1962), which had suspended all appointments until December 31 unless under presidential authorization. In this statement, Goulart disclaimed any responsibility for these appointments. The president of IAPI, in an interview with the *Jornal*, maintained that no appointments had been made since the decree, although one thousand had been made prior to its becoming effective, and these had been invalidated. Nevertheless, he claimed that his institute needed eight thousand new employees for the proper development of its social welfare services. Furthermore, he said Goulart could not be held responsible for appointments in this case because the institute was under the control of its council.[35]

In the coverage provided by the *Jornal*, no further instances of patronage were recorded until May, 1963, when a meeting between Goulart and the PTB representatives in the legislative assembly of São Paulo was covered. According to the report, Goulart agreed to name immediately seventy-three persons indicated by the state PTB to directive positions in the various organs of the federal government in the state of São Paulo. The appointments were broken down in the following fashion: eleven to the Ministry of Finance, eight to the Ministry of Agriculture, ten to the Ministry of Labor, ten to the Ministry of Transportation and Public Works, seven to the Ministry of Industry and Commerce, three to the Ministry of Education, two to the Ministry of Mines and Energy, two to the Ministry of Health, three to Petrobrás (the government's oil company), five to CES,[36] five to the São Paulo Steel Company (Companhia Siderúgica de São Paulo —COSIPA), one to the Superintendency of Agrarian Reform (Superintendência da Reforma Agraria—SUPRA), one to the National Educational Service for the Apprenticeship of Maritime Workers (Serviço Educacional Nacional de Aprendizagem dos Marítimos—SENAM),

---

[34] JB, June 26, 1962, p. 8.
[35] *JB*, August 23, 1962, p. 10.
[36] Identification of this organization could not be located.

one to Lóide Brasileiro in Santos (the seaport of São Paulo), one to *Costeira* (the government's passenger liner) in Santos, one to the Brazilian Institute of Geography and Statistics (Instituto Brasileiro de Geographia e Estatística—IBGE), and two to the Ministry of Justice. Furthermore, the leader of the group, Deputy Ivete Vargas, expressed their desire to have the minister of labor, Almino Alfonso, replaced. The principal reason cited was that he had made appointments in the state of São Paulo unfamiliar to the state PTB party.[37]

Several months later Goulart replaced the labor minister. Whether the appointment of a new minister (Amauri Silva) was related to the meeting cannot be ascertained, however.

Attention was next called to between fifteen hundred and seventeen hundred illegal appointments to the ranks of IAPFESP. These had occurred in the state of Guanabara, under the influence of PTB deputies in the state assembly. They were appointments made by individual deputies within the party, and no one wanted to accept responsibility for them.[38]

Then, on July 18, Goulart published in the *Diário Oficial* another decree for a second time prohibiting appointments for a year. The *Jornal do Brasil* interpreted this decree as another attempt by Goulart to gain personal control over all appointments. Given the surrounding circumstances, this was probably a correct interpretation. Appointments could be made in exceptional cases, but such appointments had to be authorized by the appropriate minister and by the president.[39]

The next day a new crisis over appointments arose with the publication of an official statement by IAPFESP, in answer to a formal request by two federal deputies, giving the reasons for its appointment of fifteen hundred functionaries prior to the new decree. IAPFESP offered five justifications for its actions: they were made according to strict necessities; they were authorized by the President, who had approved only forty percent of the original request; all persons involved had been approved by DASP in a public examination (although not necessarily the formal *concurso*); all were *interino* appointments; and all could be verified according to the standards set for the institutes.[40] This was followed by a denunciation, delivered by PTB deputy José Gomes Talarico, which accused the president of IAPFESP, General Aluísio Moura, of using the names of PTB state and federal

[37] *JB*, May 9, 1963, p. 3.

[38] *JB*, July 14, 1963, p. 12, and July 17, 1963, p. 4; Carlos Amaral, "As Controvertidas Nomeações de Interinos para a Previdência Social em 1963" (MS), p. 17.

[39] *JB*, July 18, 1963, p. 4; Amaral, "As Controvertidas Nomeações," p. 16.

[40] *JB*, July 19, 1963, p. 3.

deputies to make appointments to the institute. Moura countered with a statement to the effect that all his appointments had been made with presidential authorization and were entirely legal. Goulart in turn ordered the Minister of Labor to investigate the matter. The Minister then made a public announcement, saying that it was entirely unfair to attribute to the President any *empreguismo* (excessive appointments) because the admissions were made independently without any intervention on his part.[41] Ten days later the Minister issued an order which decreed federal intervention in IAPFESP under Article 133 of the comprehensive law governing the social security institutes and which named an *interventor*. The grounds for the intervention were that the council of that institute had named thousands of functionaries without presidential authorization.[42]

The federal *interventor* then prevented 1,271 new appointees from taking office. He reported that the majority of these appointments had been made by the institute's council without presidential authorization. The majority of these were in Guanabara, where 629 accountants, 300 doctors, and 40 treasurers were involved.[43] He gave assurance, however, that dismissals would occur only after proper investigation. In a televised interview on August 4, the Minister of Labor stressed the fact that this was not political intervention—it was purely an administrative matter.[44]

Because an excess of illegal appointments had taken place in virtually all the institutes, the Minister of Labor issued a memorandum which required all *interinos* admitted after June, 1962, to take a public examination within sixty days in order to gain admission to the permanent service.[45] Two weeks later, he signed a directive dismissing five thousand functionaries named to the institutes since January 1 and requiring the DNPS to submit a request to DASP asking for a report on the approved candidates who would have priority in placement in the institutes. The reason for the dismissals, he said, was financial.[46] The presidents of the institutes countered with the argument that the directive was illegal under the terms of the comprehensive law and therefore should not be complied with. That same day, after the meeting of the social security presidents, the chief of the Minister of Labor's cabinet called a meeting of all the presidents and officially handed over to them the Minister's directive. Joined with it

41 *JB*, July 20, 1963, p. 9.
42 *JB*, August 1, 1963, p. 10.
43 *JB*, August 2, 1963, p. 3.
44 *JB*, August 4, 1963, p. 3.
45 *JB*, August 21, 1963, p. 5.
46 *JB*, September 3, 1963, p. 4.

was a second directive dismissing all treasurers appointed since January. The presidents and the representatives of the councils claimed that it was illegal. A statement was prepared by those resisting the Minister's directives:

> The members of the councils consider the ministerial directive to be capable of creating a serious crisis in the social security system, because the *interinos* appointed since January are, in the majority, minor servants designated by parliamentarians, syndical leaders, and politicians who have been giving support to President João Goulart in his campaign for basic reforms.
>
> The president of IAPC, Jurandir Perachi, forms a part of the group who will not comply with the ministerial directive, on the basis of the thesis that it involves a profoundly inhuman and discriminatory aspect: It does not order the dismissal of those who benefit from *cargos isolados* [unclassified positions generally located in the upper levels of the Institute].[47]

This particular incident made quite clear the degree to which the PTB was divided internally over the matter of patronage. Goulart was unable to pull these conflicting elements together to provide sufficient support for his legislative programs. Eventually the presidents of the major institutes—IAPC, IAPETC, IAPM, and IAPFESP—sent official letters to the DNPS saying that they would comply with the two disputed directives. Following this, the director of the DNPS was able to make a statement to the *Jornal* which closed the incident: The councils, while considering the Minister's act illegal, would respect his decision in accord with the principle of the hierarchy of authority.

Thus, in the years between 1945 and 1964, a patronage bureaucracy responsive to the needs of the external political system came into being. Simultaneously, the administrative reforms enacted into law by Vargas during the 1930's not only remained in effect, but were supplemented by new legislation enacted during these years. The result of the interaction of these two orders—the one legal, the other functional—was an administrative system which became increasingly formalistic, one in which the divergence between prescriptive norms and human behavior steadily grew.

[47] *JB*, September 4, 1963, p. 8.

CHAPTER X

The Gap between Norms and Realities in Public Administration

With the course of administrative and political development in Brazil traced, attention can now be turned to the second independent variable in the central hypothesis: the use of norms governing administrative behavior which are exogenous to the sociopolitical system. Related to this variable are two propositions: first, the gap between the formal requirements of the merit system and the realities of public personnel practices is to be explained to a considerable extent by the irrelevance of these concepts to the functioning of the bureaucratic system; and, secondly, the imposition of these norms and principles upon traditional values has led to conflict within the administrative system as a whole. These propositions will be approached from three perspectives: (1) the values involved; (2) the nature of technical assistance in public administration; and (3) the character of Brazilian political and administrative institutions. In the last case the focus will be on comparative analysis.

Generally speaking, writers and commentators have dealt with problems of Brazilian federal civil service reform by contrasting the traditional and the modern, corruption and reform, morality and immorality, "patrimonialism" and rationalized administrative practices. This dichotomy of thought is reflected throughout organization and personnel theory which for the last thirty-five years has tried to impose an essentially Weberian value system. As pointed out in Chapters III and IV, the major part of Brazilian administrative thought has passed through a series of stages paralleling aspects of North American administrative theory without ever having considered the sociopolitical understructure of either country's administrative system. While technical concepts for improving administrative economy and efficiency have been transferred in their entirety and adapted somewhat to previous Brazilian traditions and outlook in administration, the whole debate over the proper relationship between administration and politics in a democratic regime—which emerged out of the civil service reform movement in the United States—has been overlooked.

Only relatively recently, since Brazilian administrative thought entered a sociological phase, has attention been devoted explicitly to the problem of values. In this case the values inherent in patrimonialism (that is, the traditional order) have been contrasted with those of Weberian bureaucracy. Such an approach was adopted by Emílio Willems in the field of sociology beginning in the 1940's. However, it is only now that Weber is in vogue in administrative circles that Willem's work on bureaucracy has been utilized.

Many analysts of the Brazilian scene have stressed the traditional role of the extended upper class in Brazilian politics and the continued existence in many rural areas of the local political boss, the *coronel*. The syndrome of patrimonialism as a basic characteristic of Brazilian society has been extended to urban movements, where the political leader who engages in a populist style of politics is seen as a modern-day inheritor of this tradition. This situation is contrasted with the need to rationalize the bureaucracy and to impose a Weberian value system.

Undoubtedly the family has been a major institution in Brazilian society, and this condition has considerably affected the nature of politics in that country. Nevertheless, developments since 1945 have reflected changes for the political and administrative systems which make it impossible to completely explain the problems of patronage in the civil service on this basis. It is not sufficient to consider the difficulties in reforming the civil service simply a consequence of patrimonialism and of the importance of personal and kinship ties stemming from the *parentela*, the twentieth century version of the extended family.[1]

There are indications that the extended family is more a prevailing norm than a social reality reflected throughout Brazilian society. Charles Wagley, for example, points out that the existence of the *parentela* has been substantiated really only among the provincial upper class in the Northeast, through community studies by anthropologists. He states that kinship ties are probably less extensive in recently settled frontier areas and among the lower classes in the larger

---

[1] Charles Wagley, "Luso-Brazilian Kinship Patterns: The Persistence of a Cultural Tradition," in Joseph Maier and Richard W. Weatherhead (eds.), *Politics and Change in Latin America*, p. 175.

cities. Yet, the ideal of the *parentela* continues to persist for all groups.[2] He accounts for this in the following manner:

> The persistence of the widely extended *parentela* in Brazil must be considered as the reflection of deep-seated Luso-Brazilian values. . . . The traditional emphasis upon the *família* and the *parentela* provides a model for human relations that is an aspiration for even those segments of the society that cannot live in this way. The predominance of kinship in ordering social life explains the relative absence in Brazil of such voluntary associations as parent-teacher groups, garden clubs, civic clubs, and the like. People give greater value to kinship relations than to relations based upon common interest or even occupation.[3]

Although community studies of large cities are lacking, Wagley suggests that large, elite kinship groups still dominate Brazilian economics and exercise an importance in politics. This view is confirmed in an article by Anthony Leeds in which he devoted attention to networks of personal relationships called *panelinhas*. He defines the *panelinha* as a "relatively closed, completely informal primary group, held together in common interest by personal ties and including a roster of all key socio-politico-economic positions." Leeds goes on to assert that "without knowing this informal organization, one cannot really understand how Brazil functions, economically or politically."[4]

This value placed on family and personal relationships is an important element in the dominant value system existing in Brazilian society and pervading the political and administrative systems. In Chapter VI the elements in this syndrome of values were spelled out as specifically as possible and linked to the persistence of a conservative tradition in the course of Brazilian political development. The continuation of the value placed on kinship and personal ties—originally in the context of the patriarchal family and today transformed into the *parentela*—alludes to the vitality of this tradition and its adaptation to the social, economic, and political changes which the country has been undergoing. It also suggests the degree to which politics has been dominated by a traditionally-oriented upper sector.

At the same time, the dominant value system has been subjected to pressures brought to bear by competing value systems that vary because of community differences, regionalism, and a sharply defined

---

[2] *Ibid.,* pp. 186–187.
[3] *Ibid.,* p. 188.
[4] Anthony Leeds, "Brazilian Careers and Social Structure: A Case History and Model," in Heath and Adams (eds.), *Contemporary Cultures and Societies of Latin America,* p. 387.

system of social classes. Prior to 1920 these value systems were relatively isolated from one another, and their congruency with the dominant value system was not questioned. During the 1920's and the early 1930's, under the impact of socioeconomic change, these interlocking and mutually exclusive relationships began to break down. With the inauguration of the dictatorship, however, potential conflict was limited and competing political groups were kept isolated from one another. But with the return to an open political system in 1945 and in the face of the movement toward national integration and pressures arising from urbanization and industrialization, diverse value systems, previously insulated from one another, were brought into close contact.

Potentially, the most explosive situation arose from the contact between traditional, upper-class political actors, with elitist and attainment-oriented desires,[5] and recently arrived, working-class or upward mobile political actors, with egalitarian and achievement-oriented aspirations. Certainly the aspirations of those belonging to the urban working class were often utilized for more immediate political gains by individuals outside the industrial labor force. But this should not obscure the existence of goals and values quite at variance with the existing political and social order and the presence of political actors committed to these goals and values. Furthermore, the emergence of a new value system stressing egalitarianism is a social as well as a political phenomenon. It is reflected in the post-World War II religious mass movements of Umbanda, Spiritualism, and Pentecostalism.[6]

This obviously oversimplifies a complex situation, but the purpose is to emphasize the importance of values as a variable for political and administrative analysis. The way in which any set of values is introduced into a nation's experience has a great deal to do with the degree of congruity between formal political and administrative institutions and human behavior.[7]

The fact that Brazil made the transition from colony to nationhood by maintaining on the throne a member of the House of Bragança as a symbol of political legitimacy and without altering substantially the traditionalist, aristocratic values inherited from Portugal had much

[5] Fred W. Riggs, *Administration in Developing Countries: The Theory of Prismatic Society*, pp. 126, 128–129.

[6] Emílio Willems, "Religious Mass Movements and Social Change in Brazil," in Eric N. Baklanoff (ed.), *New Perspectives of Brazil*, pp. 205–232.

[7] This importance of values in analyzing and comparing social systems has been stressed by Seymour Martin Lipset in *The First New Nation: The United States in Historical and Comparative Perspective*, pp. 4, 210.

to do with its ability to resist the internal conflicts and separationist movements that threatened to destroy the new nation. The political and administrative institutions of the Empire were thoroughly congruent with the dominant value system and with the objective of achieving societal integration among the nation's elite groups.

This same elitist orientation continued with the establishment of a federal republic, for the egalitarian potential inherent in the model adopted from the United States was in no way related to the needs of Brazilian society. Republican institutions simply provided a convenient framework within which each regional elite could operate fairly independently. It was only after 1945 that the values on which political democracy has been predicated were expanded to the social and economic realm and that a politically aware mass group—urban labor—appeared to exploit this potential.

In the meantime, a third set of values had been introduced in the administrative reform program adopted during the late 1930's. These values were essentially Weberian in origin, but because the emphasis was on technical efficiency and economy and on the premise that administration and politics could and should be separated, there was no particular problem in incorporating this system. With the return to an open political system in 1945, the conflict potential in these administrative techniques and principles first became apparent, for they were at variance not only with traditional elitist values, but with egalitarian ones as well.

Thus, the dominant value system, aristocratic and traditionalist in character, was challenged by the egalitarian aspirations of urban labor; the democratic possibilities inherent in the political "formulas" of republican government were first exploited; and the rationalistic basis of the nation's new administrative "code" was made more formalistic than ever.

Given this conflict among competing value systems, it may be said that the effect of technical assistance in Brazilian public administration has been to increase the problem of administrative formalism. Technical assistance programs sponsored by the United Nations and the United States have contributed to perfecting the techniques used in public administration, but they have not effected change in the nature of the administrative system nor have they made it more efficient, economical, and rational. Yet, these were the very objectives and goals the public administration programs hoped to help make operational and were the *raison d'être* for their creation and for the funds allocated for their undertakings. This situation is not unrelated to experience along such lines elsewhere in what is usually termed the "underdeveloped world," where technical assistance more often provides system supports than stimulates innovative behavior.

In evaluating experience with technical assistance in the public administration field, Edward Weidner has singled out three approaches to the administering of aid, which offer additional insight into the way the problems of Brazilian administration have been handled. Those administrators representing the first approach maintain that very little in the way of administrative know-how can be transferred between countries because of the tremendous divergence in conditions. A second approach has been that adopted by those who would reduce the very differences the first group points to. Their goal has been to export to underdeveloped countries as many modern administrative processes and practices as possible. Within this framework Weidner distinguishes three subgroups. One of these is committed to the initiation of administrative change through the use of the principles of administration. Another stresses techniques, while the third emphasizes the universal nature of the management process. Weidner includes within this latter subgroup the United Nations, the University of Pittsburgh, and the University of Southern California.[8] The third approach, he says,

... rejects both the do-nothingness of the first ... and the minimizing of cultural differences of the principalists, technicians, and universalists. ... It seeks a rich variety of institutions, practices, and values in the modern world and urges that a country work toward its own distinctive ends in its own distinctive ways. The purpose of technical assistance is not to transfer special theories, techniques, practices or processes, but to explore with host country personnel their own situations and problems and to develop their own distinctive solutions and courses of action. Visitor and host should examine together the history and situation of their countries to see if the experience of the more developed suggests lines of inquiry or directions for innovation in administration for the one that is less developed. In general, this school holds that points of stimulus are likely to involve approaches to learning rather than skills; motivations and attitudes rather than detailed content; ideas rather than gadgets.[9]

By and large, Brazilian experience in public administration has been confined to Weidner's second approach to technical assistance— with a heavy emphasis on the techniques and principles of administration. Virtually no attention has been given to in-depth analysis of

---

[8] Edward W. Weidner, *Technical Assistance in Public Administration Overseas: The Case for Development Administration*, pp. 221–223.

[9] *Ibid.*, p. 224.

the existing system. Rather, European, North American, and Brazilian participants in the various public administration programs have proceeded to devote a great deal of time and energy to the teaching or learning of administrative methods and to their application to administrative situations. Although they have made a considerable contribution to the perfection of the formal system, they have achieved very little real change in administrative practices.

This emphasis on technical public administration may be observed by briefly examining Brazilian experience with United States assistance. In the early 1950's the United Nations was also involved in a public administration program, but its aid was channeled entirely through the newly created Brazilian School of Public Administration. As such, it provided the service of experts in the field of public administration, fellowships for study abroad, and, to some extent, equipment.[10]

On December 19, 1950, the United States and Brazil signed their first bilateral agreement under the Point Four program. The section dealing with public administration provided that technical assistance was to be offered in personnel administration, budgetary and financial administration, and organization and methods. This aspect of the agreement became effective in May and July, 1952, when two public administration advisors arrived under the auspices of the Institute of Inter-American Affairs. This was followed by the organization of a Brazilian board of advisors on public administration, consisting of eleven prominent Brazilians interested in administrative improvement, who were not to be influenced by "political considerations." By November they developed a public administration program calling for the training of 646 Brazilian officials in 16 different fields of public administration over the next three years. Basic training was to take place in Brazil, officials being sent abroad only in those cases in which proper training facilities were not available in Brazil.[11] The three-year projected results of this program are contained in Table 11.

Eleven projects for administrative improvement were planned by the board, and by mid-1953, eight were underway. Six of the projects were defined as follows: (1) a survey of the federal personnel system in preparation for a new classification plan for the civil service; (2) a

10 Michael Loew, "The Brazilian School of Public Administration, 1951–1956" (report prepared for the United Nations [mimeographed]), pp. 10–12, and Edward J. Jones, Jr., "Brazilian School of Public Administration, Getúlio Vargas Foundation" (mimeographed report), p. 1.

11 "Technical Co-operation in Brazil," *Progress in Public Administration*, II (November, 1953), 2; João Guilherme de Aragão, *Resultados e Perspectivas do Ponto IV no Brasil*, p. 7.

Table 11.   Proposed Three-year Plan for Training Brazilians in
Technical Public Administration.[a]

Public Administration Activity	No. Trained		
	Brazil	Abroad	Total
Municipal Administration (General)	50	10	60
Financial Administration	50	20	70
Personnel Administration	90	15	105
Budget Administration	100	20	120
Organization and Methods	90	10	100
Public Relations	25	5	30
Supply Administration	20	10	30
Police Administration	—	15	15
Hospital Administration	—	9	9
Traffic Administration	—	6	6
Postal Service Administration	—	6	6
Governmental Accounting	20	10	30
Supervision	10	6	16
Indian Administration	—	3	3
Training Technicians	—	6	6
Public Administration (General)	25	15	40
TOTAL	480	166	646

[a] "Technical Co-operation in Brazil," *Progress in Public Administration*, II (November, 1953), 2–3.

survey of the public personnel system in the state of São Paulo; (3) a survey of the public personnel system in the city of São Paulo, with the objective of developing modern testing procedures and training programs for municipal employees; (4) a survey of governmental agencies operating in the Northeast to help provide a coordinated plan for dealing with the drought area; (5) the organization of a department of public administration at the University of Minas Gerais; and (6) a survey of the medical assistance service offered by the Institute of Retirement and Pensions for Commercial Employees (Instituto de Aposentadoria e Pensões dos Comerciários—IAPC) for the purpose of reorganization.[12]

In 1956 the United States signed a contract (PBAD Personnel-Project 512–72–016) with DASP for further improvement in administrative practices through the use of American technical specialists and through additional training of Brazilians in technical administration. Over a seven-year period beginning in June, 1956, and ending October, 1962, fifteen Americans were brought in for purposes of technical assistance in financial management, personnel administration, and organization and methods. Besides a chief and two deputy chiefs, this involved one program analyst, one specialist in budgeting, one in accounting, two personnel generalists, two in-service training experts,

[12] "Technical Co-operation," *Progress in Public Administration*, II (November, 1953), 3.

two technicians in position classification, and three in organization and methods.[13]

This program ran into difficulties from the beginning, perhaps mostly because it was based on DASP, which by that time no longer exercised the effective powers of an organ of general administration. Siegel, in referring to the difficulties of this contract in reorganization and methods, points out that the men assigned to DASP were rejected outright and were excluded from assisting directly in the ministries and other agencies of the federal government. Under the agreement, DASP was to direct and control these activities, but it lacked the real power to see that any changes were executed.[14]

Then, in May, 1959, the University of Southern California, participating in a six-year public and business administration contract negotiated between the United States and Brazilian governments,[15] undertook the training of public administration professors on the Los Angeles campus. They also set up missions at the Brazilian School of Public Administration in Rio de Janeiro (the main office), at the School of the Public Service (DASP), also in Rio, at the School of Administration of the University of Bahia, and at the Institute of Administration in the Faculty of Economic Sciences of the University of Rio Grande do Sul. In the 1960–1964 period, forty-five Brazilians were trained in public administration at the University of Southern California. No other universities in the United States were included in this program.[16]

Thus, in looking back over experience in the separate technical assistance programs since the early 1950's, a certain degree of continuity can be observed in joint U.S.-Brazilian attempts to improve public administration. These programs have made a valuable contribution in stimulating the further development of administrative techniques and practices paralleling those found in the United States and West-

---

[13] Harry Keen, "Fact Book" (a collection of materials on US/AID projects and contracts in public and business administration in Brazil), p. 14.

[14] Gilbert Siegel, "The Vicissitudes of Governmental Reform in Brazil: A Study of the DASP," p. 241.

[15] Michigan State University handled the contract in business administration. Besides the personnel portion of the contract discussed here, the multipurpose U.S.C. program also involved library development, curriculum development, translations, and publications.

[16] University of Southern California Contract ICAc–1138 in Keen, "Fact Book"; Edward J. Jones, Jr., "End-of-Tour Report" (mimeographed), p. 2; Escritório do Govêrno Brasileiro para a Coordenação do Programa de Assistência Técnica (Ponto IV), "Folheta-Relatório sôbre o Programa Unificado do Ensino de Administração Pública e de Emprêsas" (mimeographed draft of a report), pp. 16, 36–38. The number of participants trained in the United States was obtained from the US/AID offices in Rio de Janeiro.

ern Europe. Certainly a shortage of administrative specialists still existed in July, 1965, when the University of Southern California contract ended, but the situation was no longer as it was in 1936, when the need for a detailed classification plan was recognized but no trained personnel corps was available to prepare it. Yet, the problem for North Americans and Brazilians remained: in spite of the time, effort, and resources spent in the last two decades, the federal administrative system continued to function much as it always had.

The whole matter of values, examined briefly at the beginning of the chapter, enters into an explanation of this failure to achieve economy and efficiency in administration and to establish what was considered the necessary correlate—a neutral and impartial civil service, selected on the basis of merit. Also playing a part in the failure are the broader patterns of administrative and political development examined in earlier chapters. The technicians, the principalists, and the universalists in Brazilian administration have worked from a value basis essentially Weberian in character and functional only where the necessary economic, social, and political underpinnings that belong to modernized systems already exist.

Because Brazil has already entered the take-off stage of economic growth and because social relations have undergone and are undergoing alteration, it is important to turn to a comparative examination of political and administrative institutions in order to understand why it is the political understructure which has been the major obstacle to further development along economic and administrative lines and how this factor is interrelated with norms and values.

The predominately integrative function of Brazilian political and administrative institutions in the post-1945 era is one of the basic reasons American-style public personnel policies have remained formalistic and have failed to establish a neutral and impartial civil service conducive to the goals of economy, efficiency, and rationality in administration.[17] A second reason is that these institutions have had to simultaneously develop a welfare or distributive capacity. On the one hand, they have had to face pressures from urban labor for better working conditions and more effective social welfare programs. On the other, they have had to meet the demands of the business community for greater economy and efficiency in administrative proce-

[17] Bert F. Hoselitz, "Levels of Economic Performance and Bureaucratic Structures," in Joseph La Palombara (ed.), *Bureaucracy and Political Development*, pp. 170–171; pp. 202–203; and Riggs, *Administration in Developing Countries*, pp. 63–64.

dure and for stability in the political system at large. The problem has been that none of these demands has been met adequately for the whole society. Finally, because of the commitment to representative political institutions, the system has had to deal with an increase in political participation by the urban masses.[18]

This brings us back to the problems of administrative and political development. Bert Hoselitz has developed a model for the analysis of bureaucratic development which may be related to Diamant's view of political development, discussed earlier. To recapitulate, Diamant conceives of political development as a multinormative process in which the success or failure of a system depends on its ability to deal with a variety of demands and goals; as a continuing process it can move forward, stop, or be reversed.

Hoselitz takes Talcott Parsons' classification of socially relevant actions into four groups—the latency sector, the integrative sector, the goal-gratification sector, and the adaptive sector—and uses them to analyze bureaucracy as a social system. His treatment of the integrative and adaptive capacities of a bureaucratic system is most relevant here. In dealing with the integrative function, he points to the importance of the general norms prevailing in a society. He postulates that

. . . in societies with strongly held ascriptive norms in the distribution of occupational roles, i.e., in societies in which status considerations predominate in determining who gets what jobs, procedures of recruitment into the bureaucracy will also exhibit a strong admixture of ascription. . . . Hence, it should not surprise us if we find that such behavior as the appointment of relatives to official posts, succession to a bureaucratic office by a family member of the holder, and similar aspects of recruitment along ascriptive lines which are often encountered in societies at the threshold of political modernization are merely a transference of generally valid norms regulating social action designed to meet the integrative needs of the society as a whole to a peculiar institution in this society.[19]

Once a rationalized system of recruitment with an emphasis on achievement rather than ascriptive criteria is imposed on a bureaucratic system in such a society, double standards and conflict develop within the bureaucracy. In addition,

it creates conflict between the bureaucracy and other institutions, since

[18] Gabriel Almond, "Political Systems and Political Change," *American Behavioral Scientist*, VI (June, 1963), 7.

[19] Hoselitz, "Levels of Economic Performance," in La Palombara (ed.), *Bureaucracy and Political Development*, pp. 175–176.

there is a danger that alternative standards—i.e., integrative patterns—may be applied.

Finally, it creates conflict within the individuals who man the administrative apparatus, since the latent values governing action in the society as a whole may not apply to certain institutions in it, and antagonism may develop between the basic values of social life as a whole and those applying to a particular institution in the society. . . . These factors may lead to a fractionalization of the bureaucracy, i.e., the dual economy which is so often stipulated by some observers as necessary in modernizing countries may have its counterpart in a dual bureaucracy.[20]

Dual bureaucracy is also related to a modernizing country's adaptive capacity since a rationalized, achievement-oriented bureaucracy may well be developed in the capital and a few other large urban centers, while in the rest of the country officials conform to these principles externally and continue in fact to follow a set of traditional norms.[21]

Another way of viewing the difficulties involved in administrative development is to introduce the element of time. Hoselitz hypothesizes that a society passes through several phases in the process of modernization. In this process a society "is confronted as a major functional requisite [first] with problems of solidarity or integration, then with those of a systemic goal attainment, and finally with those of adaptation."[22] He further postulates that as a system becomes more concerned with the goal-gratification sector (out of which a greater degree of structural differentiation arises), it tends to destroy the primacy of the integrative subsystem.[23]

If this model is applied to Brazil and related to Diamant's concepts, the Brazilian civil service may be viewed as existing in a society in which integrative functions still predominate. Prior to 1930 civil service recruitment was carried out primarily according to ascriptive standards, congruent with the dominant value system. During the Estado Novo an effort was made to impose a rationalized system of recruitment, based on achievement criteria, in a society where the dominant values remained ascriptive. The consequence was a situation corresponding to Hoselitz's concept of dual bureaucracy, not only a duality between the major urban centers and the outlying areas, but also within the ministries and between the ministries and DASP. During those years the conflict inherent in this situation did not come

20 *Ibid.*, p. 176.
21 *Ibid.*, p. 183.
22 *Ibid.*, p. 188.
23 *Ibid.*, p. 198.

into the open, but once the dictatorship had ended and attention had shifted to the building of a representative political system, integrative patterns of recruitment reasserted themselves and the problems of dual bureaucracy became apparent.

One refinement, however, must be introduced. Formally during the Vargas dictatorship recruitment for the federal civil service was made on the basis of achievement criteria, but in practice selection was made on the basis of what Riggs calls "attainment." Achievement-oriented criteria introduced into a highly stratified society where the benefits of that society were substantially confined to the upper classes limited admission to the civil service to a minority of the country's population.

For Hoselitz's concept of integration to be useful in an analysis of Brazilian experience after 1945 it must be expanded to account for patronage along lines other than ascriptive criteria. In using the concept of integration, Hoselitz turns to the patterns of bureaucratic and political development in Continental Europe, especially France, and then suggests that the same developmental sequence is occurring in Asia and Africa. The problem in using the course of bureaucratic development in the major European countries for purposes of comparison lies in the fact that their experience in moving away from an integrative phase was confined to administrative change within the context of conservatively oriented political systems where political participation was limited. In France national integration and the creation of a centralized independent bureaucracy preceded the Revolution of 1789. In contrast, in Brazil the problems of political and administrative integration have continued on into an era in which mass-based politics have begun to develop.

To understand these interrelationships properly, it is necessary to consider the timing of the movement to change the recruitment patterns of the civil service from ascriptive to achievement-oriented criteria. It also makes a great deal of difference whether patronage meets integrative functions within an aristocratic or democratic framework —within the context of a conservative or liberal national tradition. The importance of these variables, patronage and the timing of changes in the recruitment pattern, can be demonstrated by briefly comparing the experience of three countries: England, the United States, and Brazil.

The term "patronage," however, requires some clarification before proceeding further. It is used in two contexts: the distribution of positions in the public service according to personal and kinship ties and distribution according to party service. In Portuguese the term usually employed is *pistolão*.[24] For example, when Wahrlich refers to patronage and the spoils system in American experience, she uses *"pistolão"* as the equivalent.[25] Another term sometimes used is *patronagem*, as in the case of patronage parties—*partidos de patronagem*.[26] In either case, however, the focus of the expression in Portuguese is on the individual who uses his prestige and influence on behalf of someone seeking a job, appointment, or promotion. It is usually interpreted as a part of the syndrome of "patrimonialism." Strictly speaking, the term is not the equivalent of the spoils system as generally understood in American politics. Furthermore, the association of patronage with political party organization and rotation in office has not existed in Brazilian experience until recently, and only then in conjunction with traditional patronage practices.

Paul Van Riper, in his history of the United States civil service, has introduced some clarification in the concept of patronage which is useful here.

Before the nineteenth century most civil servants were chosen upon what have been called, not always too appropriately, political grounds. That is, most public appointments were made on the basis of partisanship, influence, wealth, family, personal loyalty, blackmail, or charity, rather than intelligence or competence to do the work. This is the system of patronage as opposed to the merit system. It should not be inferred, however, that the latter, because of the implications of the word "merit," is necessarily more efficient than the former. . . . A patronage system, though it usually tends in that direction, is not necessarily a spoils system, a term reserved for the more personal and partisan varieties of patronage politics. Conversely, as evidenced in nineteenth century China, the merits recognized by a merit system may not be geared to the needs of the state.[27]

A further distinction is the use of patronage by the political machine in American politics. In this connection, James Wilson has added a definition which offers further refinement of the concept:

A "machine" is defined as that kind of political party which sustains its members through the distribution of material incentives (patronage) rather than nonmaterial incentives (appeals to principle, the fun of the

[24] *Pistolão* also has other meanings; for example, it is commonly used to refer to getting something "fixed," such as a document, a ticket, or a license.
[25] Beatriz Wahrlich, *Administração de Pessoal: Princípios e Técnicas*, pp. 17, 33.
[26] Emílio Willems, "Burocracia e Patrimonialismo," *Administração Pública*, III (September, 1945), 3–8.
[27] Paul P. Van Riper, *History of the United States Civil Service*, p. 8.

game, sociability, etc.). "Patronage" is customarily used to refer to all forms of material benefits which politicians may distribute to party workers and supporters. Here it will be used to refer (generally) to the fund out of which the patronage jobs and favors are provided and (specifically) to the jobs and favors themselves. "Patronage jobs" are all those posts distributed at the discretion of political leaders, the pay for which is greater than the value of the public service performed. This "unearned increment" permits the machine to require that the holder perform party services as well.[28]

Discussing the aristocratic character of patronage in Great Britain before the completion of civil service reforms between 1854 and 1879, J. D. Kingsley emphasizes its function as a part of the upper class monopoly on politics, stemming from the Settlement of 1688, until this monopoly was challenged by a rising commercial upper middle class. This patronage system served two functions: a charitable one, in that it provided jobs for indigent members of the aristocracy, and a political one, in that it provided a recognized means of securing and maintaining parliamentary seats. Initially, this first function was more significant, but as years passed, political organization became more important and patronage came to be used more according to political expediency than according to family fortunes and personal friendships.[29]

According to Finer, political patronage at this time was utilized for two purposes: (1) to get individual members of Parliament to support a particular measure brought forward by the administration and (2) to prepare the way for an electoral victory. This system provided a certain amount of stability, for there was no rotation in office. Until about 1804, Great Britain was governed by either one-party government, no-party government, or ministerial government. Alternation between parties developed only after 1832.[30] What made this system function was the fact that a small electorate was involved. At the close of the eighteenth century, observes Finer, the electorate was between 200,000 and 250,000. Thus ". . . throughout the century . . . the rare individuals who had a right to vote were given preference in appointment to the public service and as public officials they were expected to cast their vote as their administrative chiefs directed."[31]

[28] James Q. Wilson, "The Economy of Patronage," *Journal of Political Economy*, LXIX (August, 1961), 370.
[29] J. Donald Kingsley, *Representative Bureaucracy: An Interpretation of the British Civil Service*, pp. 33–35.
[30] S. E. Finer, "Patronage and the Public Service: Jeffersonian Bureaucracy and the British Tradition," *Public Administration*, XXX (Winter, 1952), 340, 356.
[31] *Ibid.*, p. 340.

In contrast, in the United States the patronage system developed to
meet democratic, not aristocratic, pressures. While stability, continuity, and relative efficiency were characteristic of the federal civil service in the period between 1789 and 1829, it was essentially an administration of gentlemen. There was, of course, a substantial difference
between the Federalists and the Jeffersonian Republicans, but both
were committed to the concept of a permanent public service removed
from the control of patronage. Yet at the state level trends developed
which were to be repeated at the national level with the election of
Jackson in 1828. As Carl R. Fish has indicated, the genesis of the
spoils system in the United States is to be found in the states between
1775 and 1828. By 1828 every state in the North and West was faced
with an established spoils system or with an element desirous of instituting it.[32] This element was absent in the South, where a government controlled by the upper classes, with both leaders and followers
but no party organization, still existed. This gradual extension of
party patronage went hand in hand with growing acceptance of
democratic doctrine after 1801, for one of the elements inherent in
this doctrine was the idea of rotation in office and fixed terms of
office.[33] "Rotation was imposed because it was demanded from below,
not merely because it was advocated from above."[34] What gradually
emerged was a new type of office seeker replacing the gentleman,
first in New York and Pennsylvania and then at the national level
with Jackson, who incorporated into the national administration men
from the West.[35] Both White and Fish emphasize the fact that the
emergence of patronage in American experience is simultaneous with
a rapid expansion of the ideas of democracy, with a growth of the
electorate, and with the development of mass-based party organizations founded on winning elections.

The most important influence on the administrative system during the
years from Jackson to Lincoln was the wide enfranchisement of adult
male citizens and their organization into a national party system, accompanied by a surge of democratic sentiment that fanned an already active
desire for office. . . . National party organization was hardly known before
the 1830's, although both Federalist and Republican parties existed and
strong party organizations became well established in some states, notably

---

[32] Carl Russell Fish, *The Civil Service and the Patronage*, pp. 79, 103.

[33] Leonard D. White, *The Jacksonians: A Study in Administrative History, 1829–
1861*, p. 397.

[34] *Ibid.*, p. 301.

[35] Fish, *The Civil Service and Patronage*, pp. 79, 103.

New York. The origin of the national party structure began with the end of the congressional caucus in 1824.[36]

When Great Britain's experience with patronage is juxtaposed with that of the United States, the mixed character of patronage in Brazil becomes clearer. In the period prior to 1930 the Brazilian pattern of patronage paralleled British experiences in broad terms. Both countries maintained what were essentially caste bureaucracies where administration and politics were closely connected and government was dominated by the upper classes. In light of this experience, Jaguaribe's concept of the Cartorial State contains aspects of both the general and the specific. It defines a situation peculiar to Brazilian experience which is at the same time made more meaningful by considering the experience of a country such as Great Britain.

In like manner, when the experience of the United States is considered, the limitations of this model in explaining patronage patterns in post-1945 Brazil become obvious. To date political and administrative studies of Brazil, especially those of its political parties, have missed the connection between patronage and the development of faltering, but nevertheless *national*, party organizations which have attempted to come to terms with the emergence of a mass electorate and to guide it in such a way that elections can be won. Similarly, egalitarian aspirations by large numbers of citizens have been voiced. This phenomenon also has certain parallels with American experience in the 1830's. It is different in that the transition was not gradual, with development of patronage patterns in the states which broke with previous party dependency on local notables. Clearly that was impossible under the Vargas dictatorship. Furthermore, the social classes expressing these desires were radically different. In America they were primarily an independent yeomanry, while in Brazil they consisted of politically conscious members of the urban working classes. But in both countries, mass-based national party organization began with the organization of machine politics and with the problem of properly controlling the state and local branches of the party to win elections. There is a similarity in the use of party patronage by political bosses in both countries.

In this connection the whole timing of the movement to reform the federal civil service and to impose values of economy and efficiency becomes crucial. Again this point can be best understood by comparing briefly the experience of Great Britain and of the United States with that of Brazil.

---

[36] *Ibid.*, p. 11.

In Great Britain the demands for civil service reform coincided with the rise to power of a commercially oriented upper middle class which demanded an economic and efficient civil service to better carry on its activities. Preceding these civil service reforms was a reform of the political system centering around the Reform Bill of 1832, an expansion of the electorate, and the institution of a competing two-party system beginning around 1804. Economically, Great Britain had already entered the take-off stage in development and by 1850 had reached technological maturity. The era of administrative reform followed these developments and extended from 1853 (with the reform of the Indian Civil Service) through 1854 (with the Northcote-Trevelyan report) to the Order in Council of June 4, 1870—an order which marked a turning point in the functioning of the civil service. From that time to the rise to power of the first Labor government in 1924, there existed a harmony of outlook between the permanent officials and the new governing class in which participants agreed on the value of a neutral civil service.[37]

In the United States the movement for civil service reform also began after significant political and economic alterations had taken place—during what White calls the Republican Era (1869–1901). Yet a functioning merit system really first achieved its success in the following thirty years, only to run into difficulties during the Depression and the organization of the New Deal programs. Then it moved forward again in the 1940's and 1950's. This development took place under an economy which entered the take-off stage between 1843 and 1860 and achieved maturity in 1900. In terms of politics, the expansion of the electorate, the growing acceptance of democratic doctrine, the formation of national party organizations, and the establishment of an open, representative federal bureaucracy all preceded the reform movement in administration. Furthermore, civil service reform was couched in terms of morality, not in terms of economy and efficiency, until relatively late. It was into a political structure where the problems of participation had already been substantially dealt with that first economic and then administrative development was channeled.

In contrast, in Brazil several patterns of developments have converged. The civil service was reformed according to the concepts of economy and efficiency during the Vargas dictatorship. This was the era when the preconditions for economic take-off were established (the take-off phase really did not begin until 1951, with the return

[37] Kingsley, *Representative Bureaucracy*, pp. 188, 278–280.

of Vargas to power). At the same time institutional instability remained endemic to the political system. There was the need to deal simultaneously with (1) a rapid expansion of the electorate, (2) the development of national party organizations (within the context of a new multiparty system following after eight years of a no-party system), (3) the rise of aggressive labor movement, and (4) the egalitarian potential of the representative political institutions adopted.

It is probable that, until the participation and distribution problems are resolved in Brazilian politics, institutional instability will remain a characteristic of the political system, with unavoidable effects on the nation's federal civil service. Whether those who now exercise a monopoly on political power opt for an open or closed system to solve this dilemma is another matter.

The political understructure of the country, then, is a fundamental factor in the success or failure of any movement to institutionalize rationalized recruitment methods for its civil service. The technicians, the principalists, and the universalists in American public administration have failed to draw attention to the fact that our administrative system rests on a particular political foundation, characterized by a competitive two-party system over a lengthy time span and an economic system that has expanded in opportunities for the educated.

This highly competitive two-party system, while resting upon certain values with respect to democracy in the United States, also, in turn, shapes democratic values. Unquestionably, the nature of that competition and the closeness of it to many states as well as in our national elections, coupled with the continuity of our parties and their progress and competition for people from the economy makes the demand for a merit system wholly rational and *functional* in our context.

In contrast, in traditional and/or transitional societies and nations, where real political competition is either nonexistent or sporadic at best, there is no political understructure for a merit system. Or, for that matter, for any other aspects of public administration as we know the administrative system in the United States. An administrative system, with its bureaucracy, becomes in the traditionals/transitional and/or traditional society a prime instrumentality for exercising dictatorial power and also for maintaining a party in power and heading off the possibility for political opposition parties developing.[38]

While exceptions to the above statement in its particulars may be found in the Brazilian case, it can be applied meaningfully to the broad lines of the analysis here. First of all, the inability of Brazil's political understructure to support a functioning merit system be-

[38] Personal letter from Professor Gladys M. Kammerer, September 22, 1964.

tween 1945 and 1964 should be obvious by now. During the Estado
Novo, in the absence of political competition, the bureaucracy functioned as a prime instrument for exercising dictatorial power and for
maintaining the Vargas government's political order for eight years.
The fact that it failed to head off the possibility of opposition parties
developing was simply a consequence of the deterioration of the Vargas government's political supports. Regardless of the desirability of
economy and efficiency in administration, the Vargas-initiated administrative reforms served the needs of a dictatorial state. With the
reemergence of the representative political institution in 1946, it is not
surprising that the administrative system should come under assault
from political groups outside that bureaucratic structure, particularly
when it attempted to retain its closed character by continuing to re-
strict entry to initial positions in the career civil service. Throughout
this period the goal of a closed, European-style civil service remained
constant among civil service reformers. In contrast, the fact that in
1966 the country was being governed by an authoritarian government, exalting the values of moral reform, economy, and efficiency
meant that the objective of a merit system and a civil service technical
elite had become functional once again.

Awareness of the political understructure is even more important
in the Brazilian context because of the nature of the model used. The
political institutions adopted in the Constitution of 1946 followed an
American model. This factor, joined with administrative reform begun around 1937 which was based on American administrative techniques, meant that some of the problems inherent in the American
system were transferred to Brazil. Granted that the two social orders
and their dominant value systems are quite different, there are
nevertheless some parallels with American experience which provide
additional insight into the problems of Brazilian administrative reform in the context of an open political system.

Paul Van Riper has contrasted the political understructure of the
American civil service with that of Great Britain and most Continental
European countries in these terms. Whereas in the latter case the civil
service developed under unitary, parliamentary governments, in the
United States it has developed from a constitutional system based on
federalism and the separation of powers. To this condition he adds the
fact that American political parties have not been integrated and centralized. Under its system state and local politicians not only have
possessed a substantial amount of independence, but also have tended
to try to control those parts of the federal government having a direct
influence on their own constituencies. The division of power between

the federal government and the states has worked against the formation of strong party organization and under such a set of circumstances patronage and spoils have traditionally been relied on more to maintain party unity than principles and policies.[39]

Van Riper argues that public personnel problems are central to the problems of power in the American system.

Under our Constitution, the value of the patronage to a Chief Executive who wished to obtain legislative approval of his political program can hardly be overestimated. We know that the Presidents, without exception, have deliberately used the patronage for political purposes. Actually, the executive authority to appoint and remove public officials is one of the few constitutional influences making for governmental decisions in terms of national rather than local interests. It could be argued, with considerable justification, that the value and use of patronage as a consolidating influence has up to now far outweighed the damage caused by the appointment of technically incompetent persons. Certainly, if our past is any indication, we may expect a continuation of our legislative-executive antagonisms, so often reflected in manipulations of the public service.

It is our constitutional situation which has hindered and probably will continue to impede the development of a full career service in governmental work.[40]

At the same time, the use of patronage in the United States political system must be considered over a long time span. When the development of parties and political institutions is considered on this basis, an obvious contrast between patronage patterns in the nineteenth and twentieth centuries appears.

To summarize this course of political development all too briefly, political patronage as an integrating factor within the development of party organizations based on an expanding electorate first began at the state level roughly in the two decades preceding the election of 1828. With Jackson's assumption of power in 1829, these practices passed on to the national level. The use of patronage as a politically integrating force continued to rise constantly until 1861 and then levelled off, not with Lincoln's first term of office, but with his second.

[39] Paul Van Riper, "The Constitution and the Patronage," *Personnel Administration*, XI (November, 1948), 1–2. The value of patronage as an integrating factor within the American governmental system and its political parties is also discussed by Harvey C. Mansfield, "Political Parties, Patronage, and the Federal Government Service," and Wallace S. Sayre, "Introduction: The Federal Government —a Possible Approach to the Topic," in The American Assembly, *The Federal Government Service: Its Character, Prestige, and Problems.*

[40] Van Riper, "The Constitution and the Patronage," *Personnel Administration*, XI (November, 1948), 5–6.

Then, from 1865 until about 1883, the political use of appointments in the federal civil service rose again before beginning to level off a second time.

By 1901 the concept of a merit system had taken hold—only to suffer a minor setback with Woodrow Wilson's first administration. This was followed by a rapid expansion of the merit system until it reached a high point under the Hoover administration, when it again received a setback with the Depression and the inauguration of the New Deal program. Once the social change initiated by the New Deal had achieved a firm foundation, it was possible to expand the coverage of the merit system to new heights, so that by the time there was another shift in political power—with Eisenhower's government—very few positions were left in the federal civil service which could be used for patronage purposes.

Thus, stability in the civil service seems to show a correlation with stability in our party system and expansion of our economic system. Furthermore, the greater percentage of jobs filled on a patronage basis during the nineteenth century and the gradual decline of patronage in the twentieth is related to the maturation of the American politico-economic system. The major problems facing our political and administrative institutions throughout the nineteenth century were integrative. Prior to the Civil War they were primarily regional in character. After the Civil War they were essentially ethnic, as the wave of immigration to the United States rose and changed drastically in character. By integrating newly arrived immigrants and their successive generations into the American political system, political machines and their dispensing of patronage served a real need in our major urban centers. In the same way, in impoverished rural areas with a relatively high illiteracy rate political patronage continued to supply jobs to the party faithful.

Even today, although political patronage has passed from the national scene, it continues to function in many areas of our country at the state, county, and local levels of government. The problem of patronage still exists at these levels because, as Eldersveld indicated in a recent study of political parties in the Detroit area, there remains the problem of how to deal with the "personal-reward motivated person at the grass roots" level.

. . . There was a clear-cut indication in both parties that the congressional district elite felt more people could be attracted to party work, and turnover in the precincts diminished, if party work was less altruistic and volunteer. The district chairmen were willing to admit that many people entered party work "to improve their own lot," socially or economically, and that it was difficult to satisfy these workers without more political largess to distribute.[41]

In this connection, one wonders what the effect of the civil rights revolution will be on both the political and administrative systems of our country as the anti-poverty program really gets rolling and by-passes the established structure of local government to create new jobs which bring in the poor. Our pressures for public employment through channels other than those provided by the merit system are by no means over.

Already sharp conflict over who gets appointed has emerged in many of our communities, both large and small, in connection with the Community Action Committees and their programs. The federal Economic Opportunities Act of 1964 has stipulated that the poor must be represented in these committees and programs through their neighborhood organizations. The Negroes, especially CORE and the NAACP, have capitalized on this. Adam Clayton Powell was at one time involved, and in the case of HAR-YOU, an organization created to help Harlem youth, he complicated matters because he wanted to name the people and run the program. Elsewhere, the NAACP wants to name the people and run the poverty program at the local level. Of course, they also demand the right to pick people for jobs under the program, as well as for committee positions. This is a new group that has been alienated and that is trying to enter the politico-socio-economic process; a program and jobs in it are regarded as no small part of their means to success.

None of the foregoing, however, should be construed to mean that Brazilian experience should or could parallel these developments exactly. What comparative analysis does show is that Brazilian polit-ical and administrative difficulties are neither entirely unique nor peculiarly characteristic of the non-Western world. The basic political and administrative problems facing Brazil are integrative in charac-ter, and it is within this context that participation and distribution capacities must be developed.

As has been demonstrated throughout the preceding chapters, Bra-zil has met its problems of administrative and political development within the context of a mixed system characterized by heterogeneous and overlapping patterns. The political culture of the country is in-creasingly drawing near to the model of a fragmented political cul-ture, along the lines developed by Almond for the analysis of the major Continental European systems. Institutionally, the political

[41] Samuel J. Eldersveld, *Political Parties: A Behavioral Analysis*, pp. 274–275.

system has followed an American model during the First and Second Republics. Administratively, the country has mixed the goal of a closed bureaucratic system along European lines with administrative techniques developed to meet American administrative needs as that system matured. Until October, 1965, its political parties approached the multiparty system as it developed in Weimar Germany, France, and Italy. Yet organizationally, prior to the coup of March, 1964, the role of the major parties had much in common with the integrative function of American parties throughout the nineteenth century. The dispersal of patronage along regional and interest group lines was not peculiar to Brazil. It was instead a consequence of the diffusion of power under federalism and of the creation of a system of checks and balances, limiting executive preeminence and requiring a bargaining style of politics. But even this analysis has shown an overlapping of aristocratic and democratic patterns which clearly goes beyond American experience. Finally, if Lipset's analysis is followed, the character of the dominant value system is closer, within the context of Anglo-American countries, to that of Canada and Great Britain than to that of the United States. The problems facing Brazilian government and administration have become even more complex because of the convergence of conflicting demands and pressures on the total system. Since March, 1964, the solution of these problems has merely been postponed.

CHAPTER XI

Politics and Administration

As a nation-state Brazil has followed an uneven course of political development. During the Empire, progress was made toward the goal of integrating a series of diverse Portuguese-speaking provinces into one nation where among the regional elites, at least, a sense of national consciousness had begun to emerge. During the Republic, this integrative process halted as a federalist system of government replaced a unitary state and the emphasis shifted to the regional capitals. Certainly this process was initiated before the declaration of the First Republic, but the nature of the political institutions imposed after 1889 heightened the forces favoring regional autonomy and worked against the effort to create a unified state. The absence of any external threat which might endanger the political union previously established left each state relatively free to pursue its own interests and to operate substantially as a self-contained unit.

The Revolution of 1930 and the emergence of Getúlio Vargas as the major political actor marked an incisive alteration of previous political patterns. After a short-lived effort to reform the political structure of the nation under republican institutions, Vargas abolished them and instituted a unitary state committed to the goals of nation-building and socioeconomic progress. This state, however, was autocratic in character. By 1945, faced with both external and internal changes beyond its control, it passed out of existence. Once again the country experimented with federalism, bicameralism, organized parties, and political democracy—with the qualification that only the literate could vote. The goals of the political system remained the same. The major difference was that a concerted effort was made to achieve them through the development of representative political institutions. Yet this experience with republican institutions, patterned after an American model, was quite different from the First Republic. Active political participation was no longer confined to a landowning and mercantile elite.

The socioeconomic changes of the 1920's and the 1930's engendered a new series of political forces. The basic change was the initiation of mass politics. While the rural laborer remained apathetic for the most part, the industrial worker developed a sense of political consciousness which, in turn, fundamentally altered the whole pattern of politics. Thus, the push toward industrialization and modernization coincided with the arrival of the democratic revolution, with its egalitarian aspirations. In spite of this, neither the traditional regional elites nor the technical modernizing elites seemed willing to accept as legitimate the demands of an expanded electorate and the institution of constraints on their prerogatives. During the Goulart government a notable radicalization of politics took place and the immobilist struggle among competing, irreconcilable political forces led eventually to the breakdown of the system.

Within this fluctuating pattern of political development, Brazil has experienced three different approaches to the organization of a national civil service: the caste bureaucracy of the First Republic, the guardian bureaucracy of the Estado Novo, and the patronage bureaucracy of the Second Republic.[1] The primary characteristic of the civil service prior to the Vargas-initiated reforms in the 1930's was its identification with the dominant social classes and the selection of civil servants on the basis of ascriptive criteria. The guardian bureaucracy of the Estado Novo, as personified in the DASP, was devoted to the common good as interpreted by a select number of individuals. Both were elitist systems, but they operated in totally different ways. The technical elite of the dictatorship was well trained, within the limits of the possibilities available during the 1930's. It was devoted to the principal of unity as essential to the creation of a coordinated, effective state. It was also committed to the goals of the Vargas government and to the programs designed to contribute to the realization of these goals. The technical elite took considerable pride "in being inflexible as well as benevolent in its relations with the public, and unimpressed by outside criticism."[2] Yet, before the institutions of a guardian bureaucracy could take root in the Brazilian environment and provide a parallel with the administrative systems of France and Germany, the political understructure changed once more. Under the impact of representative political institutions and the beginnings of mass

[1] These types of bureaucracy are based on concepts developed by Fritz Morstein-Marx in *The Administrative State: An Introduction to Bureaucracy*, pp. 55–71.

[2] *Ibid.*, p. 60. This quote is from a section which describes the character of the Prussian bureaucracy between 1640 and 1740; the comments are equally descriptive of the technical elite created by Vargas.

politics, the guardian bureaucracy gave way to a patronage bureaucracy. It was, however, a patronage bureaucracy combining both aristocratic and democratic practices. In the former case, it served the purpose of what remained of the traditional aristocratic social order. In the latter, it was closely related to the rise of competitive party politics, within the framework of representative governmental institutions, and to the attempt to use patronage as a means of political control.

Nevertheless, in spite of these changes, there was a substantial amount of continuity in Brazilian administration. This was particularly true in the more powerful ministries, which were able to remain relatively impervious to the external political environment. One such case was that of the Ministry of Finance. Since the days of the Empire, it has been a strong, relatively independent ministry, with its own personnel system, bureaucratization, and (although subject to patronage pressures) substantial insulation from political fluctuation.

Regardless of its importance as an integrative mechanism, the patronage bureaucracy of the Second Republic was not all-pervasive. What existed, as was the case in the United States during the Jacksonian era (1829–1861), was a dual public personnel system—"one sector partisan, rotating its personnel; the other, based in part on examinations and in part on custom, neutral and permanent."[3] Within the context of Brazilian experience, the first tended to dominate the personnel practices of the social security institutes, while the second appeared to be more prevalent in the Ministry of Finance. This distinction, however, should not be drawn too rigorously, because available material seems to suggest that the elements of a dual personnel system were found throughout all the ministries, the social security institutes, and many of the *autarquias*.[4] The ways in which these elements were combined contrasted considerably. In addition, the rotation of personnel received substantially less emphasis. Prevailing patterns seem to indicate that it was much easier to add new employees to the government payroll than to remove anyone.

The central hypothesis stated in Chapter I and the propositions constructed upon it can now be evaluated. Three independent vari-

[3] Leonard D. White, *The Jacksonians: A Study in Administrative History, 1829–1861*, p. 315.
[4] The research of John Rood and Frank Sherwood supports this notion of a dual personnel system. In studying various ministries and agencies, they found small clusters of public servants who, regardless of statutory position or formal authority and changes in government, took the responsibility for getting the work of government done ("The Workhorse Group in Brazilian Public Administration" in Robert Daland (ed.), *Perspectives of Brazilian Public Administration*, pp. 47–56).

ables were selected to see whether a possible relationship could be established between them and a dependent variable—the behavior of the Brazilian federal civil service system. To recapitulate, the independent variables were the political understructure of the civil service, the use of norms which conflict with the demands of the social and political systems, and the application of the techniques of scientific management without adequate attention to the functional requirements of the existing system and without sufficient consideration for the human elements. As this study has demonstrated, all three variables are related to the behavior of the civil service, but the first is by far the most important.

Examination of the political understructure has shown that the style of politics has been of crucial importance in Brazilian experience with administrative reform over a lengthy time span, a factor not sufficiently accounted for in the first set of propositions. Drawing on the work of Banks and Textor, the hypothesis stated that in instituting any program of administrative reform the presence of a strong central government insuring political stability is more important than the style of government, i.e., whether it was a dictatorship or a democracy. No evidence in this study supports the validity of this proposition. Instead, the evidence demonstrates the close relationship between political system style, on the one hand, and the degree of centralization in national government and the extent of political and social stability, on the other. Furthermore, it is more accurate to consider the degree to which an open or closed political system exists than it is to draw attention to the distinction between democracy and dictatorship.

The centralization or decentralization that has taken place at different points in the course of Brazilian political and administrative development is intimately related to the political system styles of the various periods. This should serve as a caveat both to those who assert that administrative development is best achieved through the mechanism of a centralized state and to those who claim that the solution is to be found through decentralization and the creation of "islands of development." The crucial variable is the sort of political system desired. Within that context, attention must be directed to the timing of the administrative reform movement. There are conditions under which reform through the mechanism of a centralized state is essential, just as there are circumstances conducive to substantial decentralization. In other words, at times the need for basic structural change in a society requires strong state action; at other times incremental change can be maximized.

What made it possible for Vargas to impose sweeping administrative reform during the 1930's was the monopoly he exercised on political power. Once this monopoly was broken and a political system style emerged which was based on a mass electorate, competitive party politics, and the division of power between the executive and congress, his administrative reforms assumed a purely formalistic character because they were unrelated to the attempt to develop a representative and competitive political system in which the administrative system would be responsive to its demands.

This point is important because, in the original conceptualization of this study, the distinction between representative government and the rise of competitive politics or a competitive political system was not clearly stated. Yet Brazilian experience has shown that this distinction is absolutely essential to understanding developments in the country's political system. What existed before 1930 was a decentralized political system which was representative, but not competitive, except for those individuals participating in politics who were either members of the upper class or of a small, conservatively oriented middle class. Between 1945 and 1964 a decentralized and highly competitive political system functioning within the framework of representative government emerged. As a consequence of this widening range of demands accompanying modernization, the possibility of creating an egalitarian mass society presented itself for the first time in Brazilian history. This development was cut short by the April Revolution, which, strictly speaking, was a coup d'état rather than a revolution. Since that time a representative form of government has been maintained, but the scope of competitive politics has been considerably reduced and subjected to stringent centralized controls.

The material does, however, support the validity of a subproposition: the success in instituting merit system practices under the first Vargas government is explained in part by the presence of a strong central government committed to the reform of the federal civil service. Yet this statement needs to be further refined by adding that the moratorium on competitive party politics made this possible. A qualification should also be amended to the second subproposition: "the post-1945 problems of both expanding and defending a rationalized public personnel system are explained in part by the excessive decentralization of authority (formal power) and control (informal power) and by the multiplicity of competitive groups in a society undergoing fundamental change, where there is a lack of consensus on the means for resolving conflict and on the basic goals of the state." It is the second part of this proposition that has had the greatest relevance in accounting for the difficulties encountered in making the formal personnel system functional between 1945 and 1964. The political understructure during these years was simply not supportive of a federal civil service governed by the values and the goals of economy, efficiency, and rationality. Consequently, the public personnel system imposed during the 1930's and strengthened by subsequent legislation became increasingly formalistic, a trend attributable to the authoritarian character of these controls and to the influence of the political party in opening up competition and their destruction of the autocratic origin of the reforms.

The second major proposition offered to explain the political understructure—"any program of basic reform in a traditional administrative system is certain to create opposition"—does not warrant separate consideration if the material in Chapters VII, VIII, and IX is taken into account. This statement, joined by a second ("the way this opposition is expressed depends on the interrelation between the degree of centralization within the bureaucracy and the style of politics"), only complements the preceding statements. Variations in these matters are determined by political system style.

The other relationships postulated in the second set of propositions proved to be valid in the form in which they were prepared. It was hypothesized that in a centralized system of administration opposition to reform is more difficult to express because of the existence of a more effective control system capable of overriding traditional patterns and values. It was also stated that this control is more "effective" because major policy decisions can be made only at the top of the hierarchical structure. This is precisely what occurred during the Estado Novo, for it was essentially an administrative state in which political decisions were made at the top of the hierarchical structure and the administrative control system created was used to see that they were carried out. The administrative reform program appeared to be a substantial success from the outside, yet, when materials from this period are examined, it becomes apparent that conflict and opposition to the reforms were present within the administrative system. The monolithic structure of the Estado Novo, however, obscured this situation. Conflict between traditional and modern administrative concepts and practices was simply internalized.

The Vargas-initiated administrative reforms were at best partially successful. Outside of the technical elite, the men called upon to serve the state were essentially the same as in the past. Their values and behavior remained much the same, in spite of the forcible introduction of new techniques and ways of doing things. Given the elite character of this society and the absence of any system of mass education from which new individuals might be drawn, it was impossible to dismiss the mass of older public functionaries and to replace them with others. Had the whole structure of the administrative system been effectively renovated and a new body of public functionaries substituted, the bureaucratic apparatus created by Vargas would not have collapsed so easily once competitive party politics were resumed. Once DASP was reorganized, its power curtailed, and its elite corps of civil servants disbanded, patronage politics resumed at a new and more intense level.

In spite of all this, the legal norms and principles governing public personnel practices remained operational—at least theoretically—and were reinforced by additional legislation. For this reason they have been termed formalistic; they did not correspond to the way in which personnel actually gained entrance into the public service, nor did they account for the pressures brought to bear by political parties during an integrative stage of development.

A further hypothesis stated that the reaction to administrative reform during the Vargas era was related to fear of the bureaucracy as a control instrument in a no-party, authoritarian system, a fear resulting from experience with such control. In addition, it was stated that an important motivation of the political parties emerging after 1945 was their desire to make the bureaucracy responsible to the external political system. The material in Chapters VII, VIII, and IX confirmed this conceptualization only in part. These statements are fairly descriptive of the immediate postdictatorship years, but they are not as applicable to the remainder of the period. By that time the feasibility of an elite civil service based on merit and determined through public examination had collapsed without much resistance. Once the control apparatus of DASP had been destroyed and a political system dependent on the extensive use of privilege had developed, this fear of the bureaucracy as a control system was no longer an important motivation. The struggle, rather, was one of seeing who could capture public office and gain control of patronage powers.

The size of the federal civil service, which was singled out as an intervening variable, was found to be an important factor in this study. Reforms or attempted changes in public personnel policies and practices have been complicated by the number of civil servants employed by the government. Any basic reform must come to terms with the whole administrative system, and that task is almost overwhelming. The size of the federal civil service during the 1930's presented no small obstacle in carrying out the original administrative reforms, and by 1964 the total civil service, in all probability, had doubled.

The third set of propositions, concerning the role of DASP as an agent of the executive, was also of considerable use in the analysis of the political understructure. The material in Chapters VII, VIII, and IX confirms the relationships hypothesized. An examination of the political system and the patterns of political patronage verifies the assertion that the close association of DASP and the whole administrative reform movement with the Vargas dictatorship was inimical to its goals and objectives after 1945. Chapters VIII and IX substantiate further the use of DASP according to executive wishes.

From the second independent variable—the use of norms governing administrative behavior which conflict with the demands of the social and political systems—two propositions were developed. First, it was postulated that the gap between the formal requirements of the merit system and the realities of current public personnel practices can be explained to a considerable extent by the irrelevance of these concepts to the functioning of the bureaucratic system. The second proposition stated that the imposition of these newer norms and principles upon traditional values has led to conflict within the administrative system as a whole. Of these two propositions, only the first was confirmed by this study (Chapters VIII, IX, and X). The patronage system that developed after 1945 made the formal personnel system inoperative. The values of economy, efficiency, and rationality could not function in an administrative system responsive to the integrative needs of the political and social systems. Furthermore, they conflicted with traditional values stressing personal and kinship values and with more recent ones emphasizing egalitarianism. However, nothing in this material can be used to prove the validity of the second proposition. The material collected suggests that this is so, but the only effective way of verifying this statement would be to take a representative sample of the civil service and collect new data through interviewing. The interview material in this study does not provide any valid basis for generalization along these lines; instead, it is of most use in providing closure with other materials collected within the general context of the independent variable.

The third independent variable—the application of the techniques of scientific management without adequate attention to the functional requirements of the existing system and without sufficient consideration for the human elements—was dealt with in considerable detail in Chapters III, IV, and V. On the basis of this material it may be concluded that in terms of the internal administrative system the basic deficiency of the scientific management school in Brazil has been its neglect of the prescriptive bases from which it has been operating and its failure to test empirically the principles it has asserted. But this is not a failing of Brazilian writers in public administration in particular. Rather, it is a consequence of the belief transferred from traditional American public administration that the hallowed principles it proclaimed were universal and scientific and that they represented the one best way of achieving economy and efficiency in administration. Nor can the premise that administration can and should be separated from politics be supported by empirical evidence in the Brazilian milieu. The unquestioning acceptance of this value has obscured the importance of the environment within which any administrative system functions. Yet an understanding of this environment is essential if the problems of administrative reform and change are to be faced realistically in Brazil. Brazilian administrators have instead preferred to concern themselves with the active role of public administration in the modernization process and have devoted little attention to the influence of the environment with which they are dealing on actual administrative processes—except to consider it a corrupting factor which must be excluded.

Scientific public administration in general, and in Brazil in particular, has not been able to adequately come to terms with the human element in administration and with the whole question of human values. It makes little difference whether people are trained in better and more effective techniques of administration if no attention is given to changing traditional values and to adapting them to the needs of modern society. The Vargas-initiated administrative reforms certainly implied a new set of values, but these values were simply imposed on the existing system through legislation and structural alterations. No attempt was made to come to terms with the conflict emerging between individual values and the new norms which had been forcibly applied to the administrative system. After 1945 it became apparent that the presence of these norms did not necessarily lead to any change in administrative behavior.

Training in the public personnel field must deal directly with the socialization of large numbers of students and in-service trainees so that they can become more aware of the new normative system which must be accepted if merit system practices are to become functional. Adequate handling of the problems created by the emergence of an egalitarian mass society requires no less than the abandonment of traditional aristocratic norms and the substitution of egalitarian ones of the sort spelled out by Tocqueville in the last century and by

Myrdal in the present one. After all, there is nothing inherent in this process, now underway in Brazil, which necessarily guarantees that it will assume either a democratic or a nondemocratic character.

Training must also prepare these individuals to face the fact that administration is not necessarily above the political arena but is very much a part of it. This is especially true when social upheavals are underway and new groups are seeking to gain entrance into the political process. Civil servants also must be trained to have an open mind for new ideas and concepts at variance with the accepted way of doing things in the more "advanced" countries and to be capable of innovative behavior of the sort that can meet the developmental pressures and needs peculiar to the Brazilian system.

In training programs an emphasis needs to be placed on preparing generalist administrators who can perform critical political roles. Until now emphasis has been placed on developing administrative techniques. In future training programs, a shift should be made from a technical approach to administration to one in which individuals have a general background and an awareness of the fact that they must be capable of dealing with conflict and politics. Although training programs are moving in the direction of preparing generalist administrators, little attention has been given to preparing these individuals to deal with political necessities. In addition, this present movement toward generalist administrators is based on a concept in traditional public administration which views administrators as a sort of democratic ruling class, Platonic in character and representative of an aristocracy of talent.[5]

At the same time that individuals with a general background are being trained for administrative careers, it is necessary, if the country is to move in the direction of providing an open system of government and developing political mechanisms for dealing with social change, that these same individuals be prevented from "impeding the development of countervailing centers of political power."[6] A return to a competitive style of party politics will require understanding of the pressures which made patronage so important between 1945 and 1964. Rather than attempt to exclude political influence entirely, mecha-

[5] This observation is based on one aspect of Dwight Waldo's critique of traditional American public administration (*The Administrative State: A Study of the Political Theory of American Public Administration*, pp. 89, 97).

[6] This statement is adapted from a proposition developed by Joseph La Palombara, "An Overview of Bureaucracy and Political Development," in La Palombara (ed.), *Bureaucracy and Political Development*, pp. 20–21. The same is true of the concept of "critical political roles" in the preceding paragraph.

nisms must be developed to meet the demands of those groups who have deemed it necessary to exercise an influence on the administrative system in order to assert and to protect their interests.

The examination of organization and personnel theory offered in Chapters III and IV, however, should not be interpreted to mean that Brazilian administration must pass through each of the phases developed in American administration. Instead, with an awareness of the various models that can be utilized for the analysis of organizations in the United States, emphasis should be placed on an empirical analysis of the Brazilian administrative setting and on the development of concepts descriptive of Brazilian administrative reality. The need in Brazil is one of coming to terms with the problem of instituting functional changes in the administrative system. The criticism of traditional public administration, which underlies much of the content of these two chapters, should not be interpreted as implying a total rejection of traditional concepts and techniques. Instead, this critique is but an attempt to bring additional factors into consideration. These concepts and techniques apparently have their greatest application in the modern industrial firm functioning in a capitalistic society, although, even here, their validity has been questioned at times.

Scientific administration in Brazil has made a substantial contribution in terms of the introduction of new ideas, skills, and techniques. But now that this foundation has been established, it is time to develop a greater understanding of the social context within which administration functions and of the fact that political interrelationships are of crucial importance. This amounts to an application of the dictum offered by Waldo in discussing the economy and efficiency movement in the United States. "The descriptive or objective notion of efficiency is valid and useful," he observed, "but only within a framework of consciously held values." To this he added the concept of an "hierarchy of purposes" and a "pyramid of values" as a means for developing a new philosophic basis for administration.[7]

A reexamination of the assumption that administration both can and ought to be separated from politics is fundamental. Far too often this assumption has functioned as a premise in the Brazilian setting, protecting bureaucratic interests and aiding in the erection of barriers to defend bureaucratic power from "political" encroachments. Notable in Brazilian public administration literature since 1945 are two sets of interrelated values: those of economy and efficiency and those of democracy. Those of democracy, however, have been weak

---

[7] Waldo, *The Administrative State*, pp. 203–205, esp. 203.

and by and large present only by implication. Yet the meaning and significance of democracy is a central problem to Brazilian political and administrative development. In contrast, those of economy and efficiency have been vigorously asserted so that, in combination with the premise separating politics and administration, they have been used to develop the goal of an administrative system independent of political controls. Between 1945 and 1964 the administrative system was made responsible, accountable, and responsive to the external political system through the use of patronage, but in theory this relationship has been categorically rejected as an evil.

The major bottleneck in Brazilian political and administrative development is not the lack of officials possessing the required knowledge and skills. It is, instead, the failure to create an accepted and legitimate set of controls stemming from groups active in the political process and the absence of a clear set of policies determining what the political goals of the nation are and how they will be achieved.[8] Throughout the discussion of the Brazilian political system, it has been stated that the two basic political goals have been nation-building and socioeconomic progress. Generally these two goals have been present in the country more by implication than by actual statement. What is lacking is a set of subgoals designed to relate these two elements to the political system and to determine how these objectives will be achieved.

It is probable that before a change can be effectively instituted in the civil service, assuming that the country will eventually return to an open political system, basic alterations must occur in the political institutions of the country. Because "there appears to be some incompatibility between rapid economic development, on the one hand, and democratic political development, on the other," it is of crucial importance that greater attention be paid to the whole problem of political development and that the political system desired become a "consciously sought goal."[9] Brazilian experience with an open political system between 1945 and 1964 demonstrates the impossibility of maintaining a separation between administration and politics in a society in which the predominant concern of the political system is still integrative. The objective of displacing the influence of the politician and at the same time retaining his support for a professional

---

[8] This observation is based on Fred W. Riggs, "Relearning an Old Lesson: The Political Context of Development Administration," *Public Administration Review*, XXV (March, 1965), 77.

[9] La Palombara, "An Overview," in La Palombara (ed.), *Bureaucracy and Political Development*, p. 27.

civil service involved goals that were incompatible. This was because political patronage was essential to the politicians' survival. In the effort to make an open, representative form of government operational and to develop a national political party system, based on a mass electorate, political patronage has played no small role.

The course of Brazilian political development has been hindered by a failure to develop two crucial mechanisms: a built-in structure capable of dealing with reform and a style of politics in which bargaining and compromise become possible. Both of these mechanisms are crucial to progress in political development. The political institutions emerging after 1945 represented a step forward in developing these capabilities—only to be frustrated by the lack of leadership and any really cohesive set of forces after the resignation of Quadros. For all the imperfections of the Kubitschek government, it still stands as the government which made the greatest progress in developing these mechanisms.

Given this close interaction between administration and politics in Brazil, it may be concluded that for Brazil the concepts and ideas developed in political science—in particular, those contained within comparative government and comparative administration—have a great deal to offer in comprehending the nature of the administrative system. In the Brazilian environment, neither the thesis that "public administration should be divorced from political science" nor the thesis that "we [should] proceed from a 'disciplinary' to a 'professional school' perspective or orientation"[10] is conducive to coming to terms with the administrative problems facing the country. If anything, past experience with administrative reform and with the difficulties presented by formalism in the public personnel field demonstrates that Brazilian public administration could profit considerably by a closer association with political science. This does not mean that there should not also be a reaching out into other academic disciplines for new concepts and data, but rather that the study of public administration in this particular case should join hands with the same quest that is now going on within political science as a whole. This observation could probably be extended to the rest of Latin America.

Finally, it should not be forgotten that historically and culturally Brazil is as much a part of Western civilization as the United States, Canada, and Australia. While our national experience, as well as that of Australia, has been governed by a liberal tradition, Brazilian experience has been tempered by a conservative tradition. Brazil's depar-

[10] Dwight Waldo, "The Administrative State Revisited," *Public Administration Review*, XXV (March, 1965), 28.

tures from its European heritage are no greater than those to be found in the previously mentioned countries. Much can be gained in understanding the Brazilian political order by starting from a European point of reference, particularly one oriented toward the Latin countries on the Continent.

APPENDIX

METHODOLOGY

Essentially two techniques have been used throughout this book: content analysis and interviewing.

Content analysis was employed, first of all, to collect material on organization and personnel theory in Brazilian public administration. The indicators utilized fall into three groups: (1) specific terms in Portuguese for explaining administrative phenomena (those terms which are distinct from American experience and those which parallel concepts prevalent in American public administration); (2) the value system inherent in traditional public administration, which has been transferred from the United States to Brazil, and subsequent developments in this school of thought; and (3) the way Brazilians interested in public administration handle the conflict between the techniques and principles of administration, on the one hand, and the ecology of Brazilian administration, on the other.

A specific set of indicators was used to check out the presence of Weberian values and the use of principles of public administration. The former includes rationality, impersonality, hierarchy of authority, formality, a rational set of rules, the importance of position, legitimacy, trained personnel, a career service, a monistic set of relationships, and the bureaucratization of society. The latter consists of span of control, the unity of command, the homogeneity of work, nonspecialist administrators, a dichotomy of staff and line, the development of a chain of command, the separation of administration from politics, the specialist as "on tap, but not on top," the division of labor, and the specialization of function.

Content analysis was used also to isolate issues and problems in public personnel administration raised in the press and in articles and books. Two broad categories were set up: the nature of the opposition to merit system practices in the federal civil service and the defense offered for the merit system. In the first instance this included: (1) the attack against DASP, particularly its personnel policies, as a consequence of its close association with the Estado Novo; (2) the justifications used for violation of merit system practices; and (3) the protection of *interino* and *extranumerário* interests and the defense of patronage practices. In the second case two subcategories were isolated: (1) the desire to reorganize the civilian bureaucracy along "modern" lines to achieve more efficient administration in keeping with the developmental needs of the country and (2) the appearance of some public support for merit system practices (the contrast between the absence of such support in 1946 and its beginning in recent years).

Because of the broad time period included, the absence of indexing, the necessity of obtaining reliable student assistants to aid in gathering the material, and the lack of funds to finance an extended stay in São Paulo or to remain in Brazil longer than nine months, newspaper research was restricted essentially to one source: the *Jornal do Brasil*. Such reliance on one basic news source is open to criticism from several standpoints, not the least of which is the reputation the Latin American press has for partial and conflicting reporting of news stories. In recognition of this limitation, the material drawn from the *Jornal do Brasil* was supplemented by spot checks of other news sources, examination of relevant books and articles, and interviewing of knowledgeable persons on matters pertaining to the civil service. In particular José Honório Rodrigues was most helpful in suggesting how news sources in Brazil might be utilized. Moreover, the *Correio da Manhã* was checked carefully for the years extending from 1945 through 1949.

The *Jornal do Brasil* was selected as a focal point for newspaper research because of the excellent reputation it has had in recent years for complete and reliable news coverage. One notable exception should be mentioned: within the state of Guanabara, the *Jornal* and the *Correio da Manhã* have provided very different and conflicting reporting on Governor Carlos Lacerda's handling of the *favelas* (the slum areas of the city). However, the years for which the *Jornal* was relied upon most heavily fall between 1954 and 1964. This was a period when, of the news sources available in Rio de Janeiro, it offered the most complete and systematic coverage of the interrelationships between the federal civil service and the political system. This was especially true of the patronage pressures prevalent during the governments of Juscelino Kubitschek, Jânio Quadros, and João Goulart.

Interviewing, the second major technique, was used to get at the problem presented by the conflicting perceptions of what a public personnel system entails, what sort of civil servants are desired, and what relation should or does exist with the external political system. Elementary role analysis was engaged in to understand the perceptions which individuals in positions of importance and with a relevant interest in these matters had of the federal civil service. Because of the size and complexity of the administrative system and because of the multiplicity of groups with an interest in some aspect of public administration, an attempt was made to capture an insight into these conflicting notions of what the federal civil service is.

However, it should be made clear that this information in no way represents a sample. The material contained in these interviews is complementary in character. Its value is that it supports and corroborates material obtained elsewhere. In the original research design much more attention was devoted to this aspect of the project than was carried out in practice. The problem was not access; instead, it was the vast amount of written material available, which it was decided had to be handled first, and the limitations of time and resources.

Out of a total of fifty interviews scheduled, forty-one were completed. The average interview lasted forty-five minutes, although some were as brief as half an hour, while others lasted nearly two hours. Of the forty-one interviews, three were not related directly to the federal civil service. One was restricted to the personnel system in the armed forces and in the military ministries; one to the administrative reform program in the state of Minas Gerais; and one to the in-service training program of the Banco de Lavoura de Minas Gerais. But these three interviews, as they developed, were not unrelated to the project under consideration.

The interview guide used was semistructured. A detailed questionnaire was prepared initially in English. It then was reduced to eight broad topics adjusted to the particular situation at hand. The interviewer considered this reduction necessary, first, to establish proper rapport and, second, to deal adequately with the variety of interviewees selected. For example, with DASP and Fundação Getúlio Vargas personnel much more technical language was used than with officials in public life. The majority of the interviewing was conducted in Portuguese and as complete notes as possible were taken during the course of each interview.

Because of the absence of previous work on the administrative system providing a view of its interaction with the political system, the absence of reliable basic data on the participants in the public service, and the size and complexity of the federal administrative system, much of the material contained in this book is more impressionistic than was intended. There is likewise a lack of statistics. The only area where hard data were located and collected was in the attempt to measure the growth of the federal civil service. Even there the figures reported are not complete and offer only a general indication of the size of the federal civil service and the breakdown of major groups of civil servants into broad categories.

Interview Guide

1. What have been the chief problems in the public personnel field?
2. How would you explain the gap between public personnel policies (as stated in theory and law) and the way the personnel system has functioned in practice? To be more specific, how do you explain the continued existence of patronage practices after some thirty years of attempting to develop a merit system? Have political developments since last April changed this? In what ways? Has Brazilian experience with patronage in the civil service been entirely negative and harmful to the needs of the administrative system? Should political party influence be excluded from the administrative system? What about the executive's appointive power —are controls to be imposed on it? Does *empreguismo* vary according to party?
3. What are the needs of the Brazilian civil service? What are the goals of Brazilian civil service reform? What policies and practices are designed to achieve these goals? Why have these policies and practices not achieved the ends for which they were designed? Where has the emphasis been placed on reform in the civil service? On techniques? On training? On human behavior? What is needed? Does administrative reform bear any relationship to political reform? If so, what? If none, why?
4. What has been the main source of ideas for the development of an efficient civil service? How effective has UN technical assistance in public administration been? US/AID? Is Brazilian experience unique—or can the experience of other countries be of assistance in public administration?
5. What is the role of the administrator in the higher civil service? What sort of relationship exists with the political system? What sort of relationship should exist? Is the concept of the public interest of use here? What is the public interest? What sort of civil servant is desirable? How does one go about recruiting him?

6. In studying the Brazilian civil service, are the civil servant organizations of any importance?
7. Which have been the most powerful ministries? Have *empreguista* pressures been exerted equally on all ministries or have they varied according to ministry?
8. What influence has the move to Brasília had on Brazilian administration? Which departments, agencies, and divisions have been involved? Does day-to-day administration continue to function in Rio de Janeiro for all practical purposes?
9. What is the future of DASP? Is there a need to revise the organization or should it be abandoned?

BIBLIOGRAPHY

Books

Adams, Richard N., *et al. Social Change in Latin America Today: Its Implications for United States Policy.* New York: Vintage Books, 1960. John P. Gillin, "Some Signposts for Policy."

Almeida, Fernando Henrique Mendes de (ed.). *Constituições do Brasil.* São Paulo: Edições Saraiva, 1961.

———. *Contribuição no Estudo da Função de Fato.* São Paulo: Saraiva, 1957.

Almond, Gabriel A., and James S. Coleman (eds.). *The Politics of Developing Areas.* Princeton, N.J.: Princeton University Press, 1960.

American Assembly, The. *The Federal Government Service: Its Character, Prestige, and Problems.* New York: Columbia University, 1954. Herbert Kaufman, "The Growth of the Federal Personnel System"; Harvey C. Mansfield, "Political Parties, Patronage, and the Federal Government Service"; Wallace S. Sayre, Introduction: "The Federal Government: A Possible Approach to the Topic."

Andrade, Adalmo de Araújo. *Diretrizes para Classificação de Cargos.* Belo Horizonte: Instituto de Ciências Econômicas, Políticas e Sociais de Minas Gerais, 1960.

———. *Introdução a Administração de Pessoal.* Belo Horizonte: Universidade de Minas Gerais, Faculdade de Ciências Econômicas (Estudos Econômicos, Políticos e Sociais), 1959.

Aragão, João Guilherme de. *Administração e Cultura.* Rio de Janeiro: Imprensa Nacional, 1951.

———. *A Justiça Administrativa no Brasil.* Rio de Janeiro: Escola Brasileira de Administração Pública, Fundação Getúlio Vargas, 1955.

———. *Resultados e Perspectivos do Ponto IV no Brasil.* Rio de Janeiro: Departamento Administrativo do Serviço Público, Serviço de Documentação, 1959.

Aronson, Sidney H. *Status and Kinship in the Higher Civil Service: Standards of Selection in the Administrations of John Adams, Thomas Jefferson, and Andrew Jackson.* Cambridge, Mass.: Harvard University Press, 1964.

Azevedo, Lahir Short. *Competência do Poder Executivo para Criar Funções Gratificadas.* Rio de Janeiro: Departamento Administrativo do Serviço Público, Serviço de Documentação, 1958.

Baklanoff, Eric N. (ed.). *New Perspectives of Brazil.* Nashville, Tenn.: Vanderbilt University Press, 1966. Emílio Willems, "Religious Mass Movements and Social Change in Brazil."

Baleeiro, Aliomar. *Uma Introdução a Ciência das Finanças.* 2 vols. Rio de Janeiro: Revista Forense, 1955.

Banks, Arthur S., and Robert B. Textor. *A Cross-Polity Survey.* Cambridge, Mass.: Massachusetts Institute of Technology Press, 1963.

Barnard, Chester I. *The Functions of the Executive.* Cambridge, Mass.: Harvard University Press, 1938.

Barros Júnior, Carlos Schmidt de. *Dos Direitos Adquiridos na Relação de Emprêgo Público.* São Paulo: Revista dos Tribunais, 1955.

Bastide, Roger. *Brasil, Terra de Contrastes.* São Paulo: Difusão Européia do Livro, 1959.

Bello, José Maria. *A History of Modern Brazil, 1889–1964.* Stanford, Calif.: Stanford University Press, 1966.

Bernstein, Leova (ed.). *Legislação de Pessoal Civil da União e Autarquias Federais, Reunida, Atualizada e Anotada.* 2 vols. Rio de Janeiro: José Konfino, 1955.

Blau, Peter M. *The Dynamics of Bureaucracy: A Study of Inter-personal Relations in Two Governmental Agencies.* Chicago, Ill.: University of Chicago Press, 1955.

——, and W. Richard Scott. *Formal Organizations: A Comparative Approach.* San Francisco, Calif.: Chandler Publishing Co., 1962.

Braga, Murilo. *Seleção de Pessoal: Seus Objetos e Seus Problemas (Conferência).* Rio de Janeiro: Imprensa Nacional, 1942.

Brandão, Alonso Caldas (ed.). *Previdência Social (Legislação): Atualizada com as Alterações até 31–12–1957.* Rio de Janeiro: Serviço de Documentação do Ministério de Trabalho, Indústria e Comércio, 1958.

——. *Repertório da Previdência Social: Notícia, Histórica, Legislação, Jurisprudência.* Rio de Janeiro: A. Coelho Branco Filho, 1953.

Brant, Celso. *Teoria Geral do Serviço Público.* Belo Horizonte: Edições Acácia, 1951.

Brazil: Election Factbook (No. 2, September, 1965). Washington, D.C.: Institute for the Comparative Study of Political Systems, 1965.

Bulhões, Augusto de. *Curso de Administração de Pessoal.* Rio de Janeiro: Departamento Administrativo do Serviço Público, Divisão de Aperfeiçoamento, 1944.

——. *Elementos para um Programa de Administração de Pessoal.* Rio de Janeiro: Imprensa Nacional, 1945.

Cantanhede, Cesar. *Curso de Organização do Trabalho.* São Paulo: Editôra Atlas, 1953.

Carneiro, Alaim de Almeida. *Estudos Brasileiros de Direito e Administração.* Rio de Janeiro: Departamento Administrativo do Serviço Público, Serviço de Documentação, 1957.

——, et al. *Curso de Legislação de Pessoal (Secção III).* Rio de Janeiro: Departamento Administrativo do Serviço Público, Divisão de Aperfeiçoamento, Cursos de Administração, 1943.

Carneiro, Ennor de Almeida. *Alguns Aspetos da Administração do Pessoal.* Rio de Janeiro: Departamento Administrativo do Serviço Público, Serviço de Documentação, 1955.

Cash, W. J. *The Mind of the South: Its Origin and Development in the Old South.* New York: A. A. Knopf, 1941.

Cavalcanti, Themistocles Brandão. *O Funcionário Público e o Seu Estatuto*. Rio de Janeiro: Livraria Editôra Freitas Bastos, 1940.

———. *O Funcionário Público e o Seu Regime Jurídico*. 2 vols. Rio de Janeiro: Editôra Borsoi, 1958.

Chambers, William Nisbet. *Political Parties in a New Nation: The American Experience, 1776–1809*. London & New York: Oxford University Press, 1963.

Costa, Gilberto Spilborghs. *Administração do Pessoal: Jurisprudência Administrativa*. Salvador da Bahia: Imprensa Oficial, 1947.

Cunha, Euclides da. *Rebellion in the Backlands (Os Sertões)*. Trans. Samuel Putnam. Chicago, Ill.: University of Chicago Press, 1957.

Dahl, Robert A. *Who Governs? Democracy and Power in an American City*. New Haven, Conn.: Yale University Press, 1963.

Daland, Robert T. (ed.). *Perspectives of Brazilian Public Administration*. Los Angeles: University of Southern California Bookstore, 1963. Vol. I: Nelson Mello e Souza (with the collaboration of Breno Genari), "Public Administration and Economic Development"; John Rood and Frank Sherwood, "The Workhorse Group in Brazilian Public Administration"; Gilbert B. Siegel, "Administration, Values and the Merit System in Brazil" and "The DASP: A Study in the Deterioration of an Organizational Power Base"; and Siegel and Henry Reining, Jr., "The DASP and the Parliamentary System."

Deutsch, Karl W. *The Nerves of Government: Models of Political Communication and Control*. New York: The Free Press of Glencoe, 1963.

Dias, José de Nazaré Teixeira. *Administração de Pessoal: Algumas Sugestões para o Aperfeiçoamento do Servico Civil*. Rio de Janeiro: Departamento Administrativo do Serviço Público, Serviço de Documentação, 1955.

———. *Classificação de Cargos*. Rio de Janeiro: Escola Brasileira de Administração Pública, Fundação Getúlio Vargas, 1955.

———. *Curso de Administração de Pessoal*. Rio de Janeiro: Departamento Administrativo do Serviço Público, Divisão de Aperfeiçoamento, 1944.

Dimock, Marshall E. *The Executive in Action*. New York: Harper & Bros., 1945.

Dines, Alberto, and Antônio Callado. *Os Idos de Março e a Queda em Abril*. Rio de Janeiro: José Alvaro, Editôra, 1964.

Eldersveld, Samuel J. *Political Parties: A Behavioral Analysis*. Chicago, Ill.: Rand McNally & Co., 1964.

Estelita Campos, Wagner. *Chefia: Sua Técnica e Seus Problemas*. Rio de Janeiro: Fundação Getúlio Vargas, 1964.

Etzioni, Amitai. *A Comparative Analysis of Complex Organizations*. New York: Free Press of Glencoe, 1961.

Faoro, Raymundo. *Os Donos do Poder: Formação do Patronato Politico Brasileiro*. Pôrto Alegre: Editôra o Globo, 1958.

Fernandes, Ary de Castro. *Curso de Administração de Pessoal (Cursos de Administração)*. Rio de Janeiro: Departamento Administrativo do Serviço Público, Divisão de Aperfeiçoamento, 1944.

Fettermann, Oswaldo. *O Sistema de Pessoal na Administração Brasileira*. Rio de Janeiro: Fundação Getúlio Vargas, 1952.

Figueiredo, Paulo Poppe de. *Curso de Administração de Pessoal*. Rio de

Janeiro: Departamento Administrativo do Serviço Público, Cursos de Administração, 1954.

――――. *Estatuto dos Funcionários Públicos Civis da União.* Part 1. Rio de Janeiro: Imprensa Nacional, 1953.

Fish, Carl Russell. *The Civil Service and the Patronage.* New York: Russell & Russell, 1963. (Rev. ed.; first published, 1904.)

Freitas, Byron Torres de. *Administração de Pessoal (Serviço Público, Indústria e Comércio).* Rio de Janeiro: Editôra Aurora, 1953.

Gaus, John M., Leonard D. White, and Marshall E. Dimock (eds.). *The Frontiers of Public Administration.* Chicago, Ill.: University of Chicago Press, 1936. Gaus, "A Theory of Organization in Public Administration."

Glaser, Comstock. *Administrative Procedure: A Practical Handbook for the Administrative Analyst.* Washington, D.C.: American Council on Foreign Affairs, 1941.

Golembiewski, Robert T. *Behavior and Organization: O & M and the Small Group.* Chicago, Ill.: Rand McNally & Co., 1962.

Gross, Neal, Ward S. Mason, and Alexander W. McEachern. *Explorations in Role Analysis: Studies of the School Superintendency Role.* New York: John Wiley & Sons, Inc., 1958.

Guerreiro Ramos, Alberto. *A Crise do Poder no Brasil: Problemas da Revolução Nacional Brasileira.* Rio de Janeiro: Zahar Editores, 1961.

――――. *Uma Introdução ao Histórico da Organização Racional do Trabalho* (Tese). Rio de Janeiro: Imprensa Nacional, 1950.

Gulick, Luther, and Lyndall Urwick. *Papers on the Science of Administration.* New York: Institute of Public Administration, 1937. Gulick, "Notes on the Theory of Organization."

Haire, Maison (ed.). *Modern Organization Theory: A Symposium.* New York: John Wiley & Sons, Inc., 1959. Chris Argyris, "Understanding Human Behavior in Organizations: One Viewpoint."

Hambloch, Ernest. *His Majesty, The President of Brazil: A Study of Constitutional Brazil.* New York: E. P. Dutton & Co., 1936.

Haring, Clarence Henry. *Empire in Brazil: A New World Experiment with Monarchy.* Cambridge, Mass.: Harvard University Press, 1958.

Hartz, Louis. *The Founding of New Societies: Studies in the History of the United States, Latin America, South Africa, Canada, and Australia.* Harcourt, Brace & World, Inc., 1964.

――――. *The Liberal Tradition in America.* New York: Harcourt, Brace & World, Inc., 1955.

Heady, Ferrel. *Public Administration: A Comparative Perspective.* Englewood Cliffs, N.J.: Prentice-Hall, 1966.

Heath, Dwight B., and Richard N. Adams (eds.). *Contemporary Cultures and Societies of Latin America.* New York: Random House, 1965. Adams, "Introduction [to Social Organization]"; Anthony Leeds, "Brazilian Careers and Social Structure: A Case History and Model."

Herrman, Lucila. *Alguns Aspetos do Problema do "Turnover": Estabilidade da Organização.* São Paulo: Instituto de Administração, 1954.

Horowitz, Irving Louis (ed.). *Revolution in Brazil: Politics and Society in a Developing Nation.* New York: E. P. Dutton & Co., 1964. Claúdio [*sic*] Ary Dillon Soares, "The Political Sociology of Uneven Development in Brazil."

Hower, Ralph H., and Charles D. Orth. *Managers and Scientists: Some Human Problems in Industrial Research Organizations*. Boston, Mass.: Division of Research, Graduate School of Business Administration, Harvard University, 1963.

Ianni, Octávio, *et al. Política e Revolução Social no Brasil*. Rio de Janeiro: Editôra Civilização Brasileira, 1965. Paulo Singer, "A Política das Classes Dominantes."

Jaguaribe, Hélio. *Condições Institucionais do Desenvolvimento*. Rio de Janeiro: Ministério de Educação e Cultura, Instituto Superior de Estudos Brasileiros, 1958.

————. *Desenvolvimento Econômico e Desenvolvimento Político*. Rio de Janeiro: Editôra Fundo de Cultura, 1962.

————. *O Nacionalismo na Atualidade Brasileira*. Rio de Janeiro: Ministério de Educação e Cultura, Instituto Superior de Estudos Brasileiros, 1958.

————. *O Problema do Desenvolvimento Econômico e a Burguesia Nacional*. São Paulo: Federação e Centro das Indústrias, 1956.

Johnson, John J. *Political Change in Latin America: The Emergence of the Middle Sectors*. Stanford, Calif.: Stanford University Press, 1958.

Jurema, Abelardo. *Sexta-Feira, 13: Os Últimos Dias do Govêrno João Goulart*. Rio de Janeiro: Edições O Cruzeiro, 1964.

Kingsley, J. Donald. *Representative Bureaucracy: An Interpretation of the British Civil Service*. Yellow Springs, Ohio: The Antioch Press, 1944.

Kluckhohn, Florence Rockwood, and Fred L. Strodtbeck. *Variations in Value Orientations*. Evanston, Ill.: Row, Peterson & Co., 1961.

Lambert, Jacques. *Os Dois Brasis*. Rio de Janeiro. Instituto Nacional de Estudos Pedagógicos, Ministerio de Educação e Cultura, 1959.

La Palombara, Joseph (ed.). *Bureaucracy and Political Development*. Princeton, N.J.: Princeton University Press, 1963. Merle Fainsod, "Bureaucracy and Modernization: The Russian and Soviet Case"; Bert F. Hoselitz, "Levels of Economic Performance and Bureaucratic Structures"; La Palombara, "An Overview of Bureaucracy and Political Development."

Leal, Víctor Nunes. *Coronelismo, Enxada e Voto: O Município e o Regime Representativo no Brasil*. Rio de Janeiro: Revista Forense, 1948.

Lipset, Seymour Martin. *Agrarian Socialism: The Cooperative Commonwealth Federal in Saskatchewan, A Study in Political Sociology*. Berkeley, Calif.: University of California Press, 1950.

————. *The First New Nation: The United States in Historical and Comparative Perspective*. New York: Basic Books, 1963.

Lobo, Eulália Maria Lahmeyer. *Processo Administrativo Ibero-Americano: Aspectos Sócio-Econômicos—Período Colonial*. Rio de Janeiro: Biblioteca de Exército, 1962.

Loewenstein, Karl. *Brazil under Vargas*. New York: Macmillan, 1942.

Lopes, Tomás de Vilanova Monteiro. *Problemas de Pessoal da Emprêsa Moderna*. Rio de Janeiro: Escola Brasileira de Administração Pública, Fundação Getúlio Vargas, 1962.

Macridis, Roy C., and Bernard E. Brown (eds.). *Comparative Politics:*

Notes and Readings. Homewood, Ill.: Dorsey Press, 1961. Gabriel A. Almond, "Interest Groups and the Political Process" and "Comparative Political Systems."

Maier, Joseph, and Richard W. Weatherhead (eds.). *Politics and Change in Latin America*. New York: Frederick A. Praeger, 1964. Charles Wagley, "Luso-Brazilian Kinship Patterns: The Persistence of a Cultural Tradition."

March, James G., and Herbert A. Simon. *Organizations*. New York: John Wiley & Sons, Inc., 1958.

Martin, Roscoe Coleman. *A Ambiência da Administração Pública*. Rio de Janeiro: Escola Brasileira de Administração Pública, Fundação Getúlio Vargas, 1955.

Mello Franco, Afonso Arinos de. *História e Teoria do Partido Política no Direito Constitucional Brasileiro*. Rio de Janeiro, 1948.

Menezes, Raimundo Xavier de. *Elementos de Técnica de Avaliação de Cargos*. Rio de Janeiro: Departamento Administrativo do Serviço Público, Serviço de Documentação, 1958.

Mering, Otto von. *A Grammar of Human Values*. Pittsburgh, Pa.: University of Pittsburgh Press, 1961.

Merton, Robert K., et al. (eds.). *Reader in Bureaucracy*. Glencoe, Ill.: The Free Press, 1952. Alvin W. Gouldner, "On Weber's Analysis of Bureaucratic Rules," and Philip Selznick, "A Theory of Organizational Commitments."

Morães Filho, Evaristo do. *Relações e Humanas na Indústria: Lições de Sociologia Industrial*. Rio de Janeiro: Serviço de Documentação, 1955.

Moojen, Guilherme. *Orçamento Público*. Rio de Janeiro: Edições Financeiras, 1959.

Morstein- Marx, Fritz. *The Administrative State: An Introduction to Bureaucracy*. Chicago, Ill.: University of Chicago Press, 1957.

Myrdal, Gunnar. *An American Dilemma*. 9th ed. New York: Harper & Bros., 1944.

Nascimento, Kleber. *Classificação de Cargos no Brasil*. Rio de Janeiro: Fundação Getúlio Vargas, 1962.

Needler, Martin C. (ed.). *Political Systems of Latin America*. Princeton, N.J.: D. Van Nostrand Co., 1964. Phyllis Peterson, "Brazil, Institutional Confusion."

Oliveira e Silva, Francisco (ed.). *O Funcionário e o Estado*. Rio de Janeiro: Editôra Nacional de Direito, 1957.

Oliveira Torres, João Camillo de. *A Democracia Coroada: Teoria Política do Império do Brasil*. Rio de Janeiro: Livraria José Olympio Editôra, 1957.

———. *A Formação do Federalismo no Brasil*. São Paulo: Companhia Editôra Nacional, 1961.

———. *O Presidencialismo no Brasil*. Rio de Janeiro: Edições O Cruzeiro, 1962.

Oliveira Viana, Francisco José de. *Instituições Políticas Brasileiras*. 2 vols. Rio de Janeiro: Livraria José Olympio Editôra, 1949.

Ouro Preto, Luiz Vicente Belfort de. *Responsabilidades dos Servidores do Estado: Da Ação Disciplinar*. Rio de Janeiro: Imprensa Nacional, 1943.

Paige, Glen D. *Proposition-building in the Study of Comparative Administration*. Papers in Comparative Administration, Special Series, No. 4. Chicago, Ill.: Comparative Administration Group, American Society for Public Administration, 1964.

Parsons, Talcott. *Structure and Process in Modern Societies*. Glencoe, Ill.: The Free Press, 1960.

————, and Edward Shils (eds.). *Toward A General Theory of Action*. Cambridge, Mass.: Harvard University Press, 1951.

Pereira, Armando. *Os Direitos e Vantagens dos Funcionários*. Rio de Janeiro: Fundação Getúlio Vargas, 1964.

Pereira, Joaquim Neves. *O Problema do Recrutamento*. Rio de Janeiro: Imprensa Nacional, 1950.

Pessoa Sobrinho, Eduardo Pinto. *Classificação de Cargos*. Rio de Janeiro: A. Coelho Branco Filho, 1962.

————. *Curso de Classificação de Cargos (Cursos de Administração)*. Rio de Janeiro: Departamento Administrativo de Serviço Público, Cursos do Administração, 1952.

————. *Manual dos Servidores do Estado*. 6th ed. Rio de Janeiro: A. Coelho Branco Filho, 1953.

————, and José de Nazaré Teixeira Dias. *Princípios de Administração de Pessoal*. Rio de Janeiro: Imprensa Nacional, 1949.

Pimental, Antônio Fonseca. *Alguns Aspectos do Treinamento*. Rio de Janeiro: Escola Brasileira de Administração Pública, Fundação Getúlio Vargas, 1954.

Pinto, Francisco Bilac Moreira. *Enriquecimento Elícito no Exercício de Cargos Públicos*. Rio de Janeiro: Revista Forense, 1960.

Pompêo de Barros, Gessner Pompílio. *Princípios de Administração Pública*. Rio de Janeiro: Gráfica Editôra Aurora, 1959.

Presthus, Robert. *The Organizational Society: An Analysis and a Theory*. New York: Alfred A. Knopf, Inc., 1962.

Ramos, Arlindo Vieira de Almeida. *Curso de Recrutamento de Pessoal (Cursos de Administração)*. Rio de Janeiro: Departamento Administrativo do Serviço Público, Divisão de Seleção e Aperfeiçoamento, 1949.

Ribeiro, Luiz Guilherme Ramos. *Do Elemento Pessoal no Serviço Público*. Rio de Janeiro: Imprensa Nacional, 1946.

Richardson, Ivan L. *Bibliografia Brasileira de Administração Pública*. Rio de Janeiro: Fundação Getúlio Vargas, 1954.

Riggs, Fred W. *Administration in Developing Countries: The Theory of Prismatic Society*. Boston, Mass.: Houghton Mifflin Co., 1964.

————. *Convergences in the Study of Comparative Public Administration and Local Government*. Gainesville, Fla.: Public Administration Clearing Service of the University of Florida, 1962.

————. *Models and Priorities in the Comparative Study of Public Administration*. Chicago, Ill.: Comparative Administration Group, American Society for Public Administration, 1963.

————. *The Ecology of Public Administration*. New York: Taplinger Publishing Co., 1962.

Rodrigues, José Honório. *Conciliação e Reforma no Brasil: Um Desafio Histórico-Político*. Rio de Janeiro: Editôra Civilização Brasileira, 1965.

Rodrigues Vidal, Valmiro. *Extranumerários União-Estados-Autarquias: Direitos e Vantagens.* Rio de Janeiro: Conquista, 1956.

Roethlisberger, Fritz J., and William J. Dickson. *Management and the Worker: An Account of a Research Program Conducted by the Western Electric Company, Hawthorne Works, Chicago.* Cambridge, Mass.: Harvard University Press, 1940.

Rose, Arnold M. (ed.). *The Institutions of Advanced Societies.* Minneapolis: University of Minnesota Press, 1958. Emílio Willems, "Brazil."

Rostow, W. W. *The Stages of Economic Growth: A Non-Communist Manifesto.* Cambridge, Mass.: Harvard University Press, 1962.

Russomano, Mozart Victor. *O Emprezado e o Emprezador do Direito Brasileiro.* Vol. I. Pôrto Alegre: Livraria Tabajará, 1950.

Seabrá Fagundes, Miguel. *O Contrôle dos Atos Administrativos pelo Poder Judiciário.* 3rd ed. Rio de Janeiro: Revista Forense, 1957.

Selznick, Philip. *TVA and the Grassroots: A Study in the Sociology of Formal Organization.* Berkeley, Calif.: University of California Press, 1949.

Sharp, Walter R. *The French Civil Service: Bureaucracy in Transition.* New York: Macmillan, 1931.

Sherif, Muzafer (ed.). *Intergroup Relations and Leadership: Approaches and Research in Industrial, Ethnic, Cultural, and Political Areas.* New York: John Wiley & Sons, Inc., 1962.

Silva, Benedicto. *A Era do Administrador Profissional.* Rio de Janeiro: Escola Brasileira de Administração Pública, Fundação Getúlio Vargas, 1955.

———. *Taylor e Fayol.* Rio de Janeiro: Fundação Getúlio Vargas, Serviço de Publicações, 1965.

———. *Uma Teoria Geral de Planejamento.* Rio de Janeiro: Fundação Getúlio Vargas, Serviço de Publicações, 1964.

Simon, Herbert A. *Administrative Behavior: A Study of Decision-making Processes in Administrative Organization.* New York: Macmillan, 1957.

———. *Models of Man, Social and Rational: Mathematical Essays on Rational Human Behavior in a Social Setting.* New York: John Wiley & Sons, Inc., 1957.

Smith, T. Lynn. *Brazil, People and Institutions.* Baton Rouge, La.: Louisiana State University Press, 1954.

Spiro, Herbert J. *Government by Constitution: The Political Systems of Democracy.* New York: Random House, 1959.

Stein, Harold. *Public Administration and Policy Development: A Case Book.* New York: Harcourt, Brace & Co., 1952.

Thompson, Victor A. *Modern Organization.* New York: Alfred A. Knopf, Inc., 1961.

Van Riper, Paul P. *History of the United States Civil Service.* Evanston, Ill.: Row, Peterson & Co., 1958.

Vasconcelos, Othon Sérvulo de. *A Classificação de Cargos como Problema de Organização.* Rio de Janeiro: Imprensa Nacional, 1950.

Viana, Arízio de. *Budget Making in Brazil.* Trans. Harvey Walker. Columbus, Ohio: The Ohio State University Press, 1947.

Vianna Moog, Clodomir. *An Interpretation of Brazilian Literature.* Rio de

Janeiro: Ministry of Foreign Relations, Cultural Division, Service of Publications, 1951.

Vieira, Astério Dardeau. *Como Classificar os Cargos.* Rio de Janeiro: Imprensa Nacional, 1943.

Vieira da Cunha, Mário Wagner. *O Sistema Administrativo Brasileiro, 1930–1950.* Rio de Janeiro: Instituto Nacional de Estudos Pedagógicos, Ministério de Educação e Cultura, 1963.

Visconde do Uruguay. *Ensaio sôbre o Direito Administrativo.* Rio de Janeiro: Typografia Nacional, 1862.

―――. *Estudos Práticos sôbre a Administração das Províncias no Brasil.* Part 1: *Ato Adicional.* 2 vols. Rio de Janeiro: Typografia Nacional, 1865.

Wagley, Charles. *An Introduction to Brazil.* New York: Columbia University Press, 1964.

Wahrlich, Beatriz Marqués de Souza. *Uma Análise das Teorias de Organização.* Rio de Janeiro: Escola Brasileira de Administração Pública, Fundação Getúlio Vargas, 1958.

―――. *Administração de Pessoal: Princípios e Técnicas.* Rio de Janeiro: Fundação Getúlio Vargas, Serviço de Publicações, 1964.

―――. *A Importância da Formação de Pessoal.* Rio de Janeiro: Serviço Social do Comércio, Departamento Nacional, 1960.

Waldo, Dwight. *The Administrative State: A Study of the Political Theory of American Public Administration.* New York: Ronald Press, 1948.

―――. *Comparative Public Administration: Prologue, Problems, and Promise.* Chicago, Ill.: Comparative Administration Group, American Society for Public Administration, 1964.

Warner, W. Lloyd, *et al. The American Federal Executive.* New Haven, Conn.: Yale University Press, 1963.

Weidner, Edward W. *Technical Assistance in Public Administration Overseas: The Case for Development Administration.* Chicago, Ill.: Public Administration Service, 1964.

White, Leonard D. *The Federalists: A Study in Administrative History.* New York: Macmillan Co., 1948.

―――. *The Jacksonians: A Study in Administrative History, 1829–1861.* New York: Macmillan Co., 1954.

―――. *The Jeffersonians: A Study in Administrative History, 1801–1829.* New York: Macmillan Co., 1959.

―――. *The Republican Era, 1869–1901: A Study in Administrative History.* New York: Macmillan Co., 1958.

Wildavsky, Aaron. *The Politics of the Budgetary Process.* Boston, Mass.: Little, Brown & Co., 1964.

Williams, Mary Wilhelmine. *Dom Pedro The Magnanimous: Second Emperor of Brazil.* Chapel Hill, N.C.: The University of North Carolina Press, 1937.

Willoughby, William Franklin. *Principles of Public Administration, With Special Reference to the National and State Governments of the United States.* Baltimore, Md.: The Johns Hopkins University Press, 1927.

Newspapers and Periodicals

Albuquerque, Urbano de. "Uma Política Segura na Administração do Pessoal," *Revista do Serviço Público,* I (January, 1954), 75–77.

Almeida, Fernando Henrique Mendes de. "Os Deveres de Obediência e Sigilo do Funcionário Público," *Revista da Faculdade de Direito, Universidade de São Paulo,* LIV: 1 (1959), 131–148.

Almond, Gabriel. "Political Systems and Political Change," *American Behavioral Scientist,* VI (June, 1963), 3–10.

Amaral, Azevedo. "Política e Serviço Público," *Revista do Serviço Público,* II (April, 1938), 13–15.

Amaral, José Wenceslau. "O Problema da Classificação de Cargos no Brasil," *Revista do Serviço Público,* IV (November, 1944), 49–57.

"Aprovado o Novo Regimento do Departamento Administrativo do Serviço Público," *Revista do Serviço Público,* I (March, 1946), 62–78.

Azevedo, Luiz Octávio Viotti de. "Evolução dos Partidos Políticos no Município de São João Evangelista," *Revista Brasileira de Estudos Políticos,* III (July, 1959), 183–194.

Barbosa Lima Sobrinho, Alexandre José. "A Constituição de 1946 e a Disposibilidade dos Funcionários Públicos," *Revista de Direito Administrativo,* XXIV (April–June, 1951), 11–21.

Barros Júnior, Carlos Schmidt de. "Direitos Adquiridos dos Funcionários Públicos," *Revista de Direito Administrativo,* LI (January–March, 1958), 19–28.

Berquó, Urbano C. "Eficiência Administrativa e Sabotagem Burocrática," *Revista do Serviço Público,* II (April, 1938), 5–9.

Blau, Peter M. "Critical Remarks on Weber's Theory of Authority," *American Political Science Review,* LVII (June, 1963), 305–317.

Braga, Murilo. "Problemas de Pessoal," *Revista do Serviço Público,* II (May, 1941), 102–113.

"Brazilian Civil Service Administrated by DASP," *Progress in Public Administration* (Brussels), III (February, 1954), 6–7.

Briggs, Moacyr Ribeiro. "Evolução da Administração Pública Federal," *Revista do Serviço Público,* III (August, 1938), 13–20.

———. "O Serviço Público Federal no Decênio Getúlio Vargas," *Revista do Serviço Público,* II (April, 1941), 217–225.

Brito, Mário Paulo de. "Seleção e Aperfeiçoamento do Pessoal do Serviço Público," *Revista do Serviço Público,* III (August, 1938), 11–12.

Campos, José Aloísio de. "Bases para um Novo Sistema de Remuneração," *Revista das Caixas Econômicas Federais,* XXXIV (January-February, 1955), 31–34.

Carneiro, Alaim de Almeida. "A Promoção nos Serviços Públicos," *Revista do Serviço Público,* I (February, 1945), 37–41.

Carneiro, Ennor de Almeida. "Avaliação de Cargos," *Revista do Serviço Público,* III (August, 1954), 28–37.

———. "O Plano de Remuneração: Fundamentos Teóricos e Técnica," *Revista do Serviço Público,* LXVII (May, 1955), 240–262.

———. "Política de Remuneração," *Revista do Serviço Público,* LXVII (April, 1955), 41–47.

————. "Salário e Relações Humanas no Trabalho," *Revista do Serviço Público*, LXVI (January, 1955), 14–23.

Carneiro, Palmyos Paixão. "Incapacidade e Doença no Serviço Público," *Revista do Serviço Público*, IV (October, 1952), 28–37.

Carvalho, Orlando M. "Os Partidos Nacionais e as Eleições Parlamentares de 1958," *Revista Brasileira de Estudos Políticos*, [no volume no.], No. 8 (April, 1960), 9–19.

————. "Os Partidos Políticos em Minas Gerais," *Revista Brasileira de Estudos Políticos*, I (July, 1957), 99–115.

Carvalho e Melo, José Augusto de. "Deveres e Responsabilidades," *Revista do Serviço Público*, I (February, 1943), 70–73.

————. "Estabilidade," *Revista do Serviço Público*, II (June, 1941), 54–61.

————. "O Estado e Seus Servidores," *Revista do Serviço Público*, I (March, 1949), 57–59.

————. "Funcionário e Extranumerário," *Revista do Serviço Público*, I (January–February, 1948), 38–45.

Cavalcanti, Themistocles Brandão. "Código do Processo Administrativo: A Unificação das Normas do Processo Administrativo," *Revista do Serviço Público*, III (August, 1938), 54–68.

————. "Direito Administrativo e a Ciência da Administração," *Revista do Serviço Público*, I (March, 1940), 73–74.

————. "Estatutos dos Funcionários Públicos," *Revista do Serviço Público*, IV (December, 1938), 84–89.

————. "A Função Pública e Seu Regime Jurídico," *Revista do Serviço Público*, IV (March, 1938), 35–43.

Cerqueira, Renato Bião de. "Os Antecedentes Teóricos da Reforma Administrativa no Brasil," *Revista do Serviço Público*, II (June, 1949), 9–16.

Correio da Manhã (Rio de Janeiro), September, 1945–December, 1949.

Cunningham, J. Lyle. "A Administração Pública no Brasil no Ano 2003," *Revista do Serviço Público*, XVI (May, 1953), 55–58.

Cysneiros, Pedro Augusto. "Administração Pública e Administração de Pessoal," *Revista do Serviço Público*, I (February, 1952), 139–145.

Delany, William. "The Development and Decline of Patrimonial and Bureaucratic Administration," *Administrative Science Quarterly*, VII (March, 1963), 458–501.

Diamant, A. "The Relevance of Comparative Politics to the Study of Comparative Administration," *Administrative Science Quarterly*, V (June, 1960), 87–112.

Dias, José de Nazaré Teixeira. "Devemos Incentivar o Ócio ou a Produtividade?" *Revista do Serviço Público*, LXVII (June, 1955), 423–427.

————. "O Elemento Humano em Administração de Pessoal," *Revista do Serviço Público*, III (September, 1942), 28–31.

————. "A Formação de Supervisores," *Revista do Serviço Público*, III (August, 1942), 27–29.

————. "A Formação e o Aperfeiçoamento dos Quadros Administrativos de Chefia," *Revista do Serviço Público*, LXVI (January, 1955), 11–13.

Dillon Soares, Gláucio Ary. "Alianças e Coligações Eleitorais: Notas para uma Teoria," *Revista Brasileira de Estudos Políticos*, XVII (July, 1964), 95–124.

———. "Participação Eleitoral e Separação de Poderes," *Revista de Direito Público e Ciência Política* (January–June, 1960), 36–66.

"Discussão a Mesa Redonda—Problemas de Pessoal no Serviço Público," *Revista do Serviço Público*, II (April, 1944), 130–136.

Dória, Herson de Faria. "A Seleção dos Servidores do Estado e a Diagnose das Contra-Indicações Profissionais," *Revista do Serviço Público*, II (April, 1954), 29–33, and II (June, 1954), 29–40.

Ericksson, Erik M. "The Federal Civil Service under President Jackson," *Mississippi Valley Historical Review*, XIII (March, 1927), 517–540.

Estelita Campos, Wagner. "Recuperação Moral na Administração Pública," *Revista do Serviço Público*, LXIX (December, 1955), 282–301.

Falcão, Amílcar de Araújo. "Extranumerário: Equiparação de Salários e Vencimentos; Princípios de Isonomia [Parecer]," *Revista Forense*, CLXXIV (November–December, 1957), 98–102.

Fellows, Erwin W. "Merit System Trends and Problems: Some Underlying Cultural Values," *Public Personnel Review*, XXV (October, 1964), 228–232.

Fernandes, Maria Joana de Almeida. "Aspectos da Política de Extranumerários," *Revista do Serviço Público*, II (May–June, 1947), 113–114.

———. "Pessoal," *Revista do Serviço Público*, II (July–August, 1948), 164–166.

Ferreira, Itagildo. "Legislação de Pessoal," *Revista do Serviço Público*, IV (November, 1950), 84–86.

Figueiredo, Paulo Poppe de. "O Moral no Serviço Público," *Revista do Serviço Público*, IV (December ,1949), 82–85.

———. "Pessoal das Emprêsas Concessionárias do Serviço Público," *Revista do Serviço Público*, I (March–April, 1948), 23–26.

———. "O Problema da Lotação," *Revista do Serviço Público*, III (September–October, 1947), 19–22; (November–December, 1947), 26–40.

Finer, S. E. "Patronage and the Public Service: Jeffersonian Bureaucracy and the British Tradition," *Public Administration*, XXX (Winter, 1952), 329–360.

Freire, Homero. "Competência Legislativa em Matéria de Funcionário," *Revista do Serviço Público*, LXVII (May, 1955), 343–347.

———. "O Problema de Classificação dos Cargos Públicos," *Revista do Serviço Público*, III (September, 1954), 24–28.

Furtado, Celso. "Obstáculos ao Desenvolvimento Econômico do Brasil," *Correio da Manhã* (Rio de Janeiro), February 24, 1965, p. 14, and February 25, 1965, p. 14 (the last two articles in a series of four derived from a lecture given by Furtado at the Institute of Foreign Affairs, Chatham House, London).

———. "Teoria do Departamento de Administração Geral," *Revista do Serviço Público*, II (May, 1946), 25–32.

Gandolfo, Orlando Carlos. "Impossibilidade de Acumulação de Funções de Dois entre os Três Podêres Constitucionais, Funcionário Público Vereador," *Administração Paulista*, II (July–December, 1959), 325–328.

Godoy Filho, Armando. "Experiência e Administração Científica," *Revista do Serviço Público*, III (July, 1954), 13–14.

Gonçalves de Oliveira, A. "Decentralização da Administração Pública Brasileira," *Revista Brasileira de Estudos Políticos*, III (January, 1959), 89–96.

Goulart, José Alípio. "Sociologia e Administração Pública no Brasil," *Revista do Serviço Público*, XVI (March, 1954), 38–41.

Gregoire, Roger. "The Civil Service in Western Europe," *Public Personnel Review*, XVII (October, 1956), 288–294.

Grodzins, Morton. "Administração Pública e Ciência das Relações Humanas" [trans. from English], *Revista do Serviço Público*, XV (February, 1952), 24–36.

Guerreiro Ramos, Alberto. "Fundamentos Sociológicos da Administração Pública," *Jornal do Brasil*, Part I: November 4, 1956, p. 8; Part II: November 11, 1956, p. 8.

Guimarães, Carlos Eloy de Carvalho. "A Vida Política e Administrativa de Dores de Indaiá," *Revista Brasileira de Estudos Políticos*, I (December, 1956), 170–179.

Gusmão, Paulo de. "Natureza da Relação Jurídica entre o Estado e o Funcionário," *Revista do Serviço Público*, III (July, 1946), 17–20.

Jaguaribe, Hélio. "Por uma Política Nacional de Desenvolvimento," *Cadernos de Nosso Tempo*, V (1956), 53–188.

Jones, Roger W. "The Merit System, Politics, and Political Maturity: A Federal View," *Public Personnel Review*, XXV (January, 1964), 28–34.

Jornal do Brasil (Rio de Janeiro), September, 1945–March, 1964.

Kammerer, Gladys M. "Kentucky's All-Pervasive Spoils Politics," *Good Government*, LXXV (July–August, 1958), 32–37.

LaOliva, Andrés. "La Reforma Administrativa en Brasil," *Documentación Administrativa* (Madrid), II (February, 1958), 53–56.

Lipson, Leslie. "Government in Contemporary Brazil," *Canadian Journal of Economics and Political Science*, XXII (May, 1956), 183–198.

Long, Norton E. "Party Government and the United States," *Journal of Politics*, XIII (May, 1951), 187–214.

Lopes, Tomás de Vilanova Monteiro. "Administração de Pessoal," *Revista do Serviço Público*, II (July, 1945), 50–57.

———. "História Política e Administrativa do Brasil: D. João VI e a Administração Pública Brasileira," *Revista do Serviço Público*, LXXXIV (July, 1957), 5–22.

———. "A Seleção de Pessoal para o Serviço Público Brasileiro," *Revista do Serviço Público*, IV (October, 1952), 19–23.

———, and Pedro Augusto Cysneiros. "Notas sôbre Legislação de Pessoal," *Revista do Serviço Público*, I (January, 1951), 80–82; I (February, 1951), 80–82; I (March, 1951), 57–59; II (April, 1951), 30–32; II (May, 1951), 48–51.

Maduro, Domingos. "Serviços de Escritório e Seu Pessoal," *Revista do Serviço Público*, I (February, 1946), 67–70.

Magalhães, Celso de. "O D.A.S.P.," *Revista do Serviço Público*, IV (October, 1951), 36–45.

———. "Ecologia Administrativa (O Papel do Técnico de Administração)", *Revista do Serviço Público*, LXVIII (July, 1955), 7–12.

Maya, Anibal. "Como Processar a Adaptação do Novo Servidor ao Ambiente de Trabalho," *Revista do Serviço Público*, IV (December, 1943), 96–99.

Medeiros, José. "Da Responsabilidade dos Servidores Públicos," *Revista do Serviço Público*, II (June, 1949), 46–47.

———. "Estabilidade de Extranumerário," *Revista do Serviço Público*, III (July, 1950), 56–58.

———. "Pessoal para Obra," *Revista do Serviço Público*, I (March, 1950), 39–41.

Medeiros Silva, Carlos. "Os Funcionários Públicos e a Constituição," *Revista do Serviço Público*, III (August, 1953), 193–215.

Meirelles, Hely Lopes. "Os Direitos, Deveres e Podêres do Administrador Público," *Revista de Direito da Procuradoria Geral*, VI (1957), 179–204.

———. "Os Podêres do Administrador Público," *Revista de Direito Administrativo*, II (January–March, 1958), 1–18.

Mello, Diogo Lordello de. "Técnicos em Administração Pública para o Brasil," *Revista do Serviço Público*, IV (October, 1953), 98–99.

Mello e Souza, Nelson, and Breno Genari. "Técnicas de Organização, Científica em Sectores Específicos para o Desenvolvimento da Administração Pública," *IDORT*, XXXI (November–December, 1962), 10–19.

Mendes Júnior, Manuel Alves. "O Sistema de Carreira e o Princípio da Profissionalização," *Revista do Serviço Público*, LXIX (November, 1955), 135–140.

Mesquita, Luciano. "Panorama da Administração Pública Brasileira," *Revista do Serviço Público*, XV (October, 1952), 43–47.

Miragaia Pitanga, Maria da Conceição. "Administração de Pessoal e Planejamento," *Revista do Serviço Público*, IV (December, 1946), 119–121.

Miranda, Hermínio de. "O Problema da Formação do Administrador," *O Observador Econômico e Financeiro*, CXL–CXLI (February–March, 1956), 57–59.

Modiano, Maria de Lourdes Lima. "Estímulo, Fator de Maior Eficiência no Serviço," *Revista do Serviço Público*, III (August, 1949), 39–41.

Moreira, Oscar Vitorino. "O Interino em Cargo de Carreira em Face da Constituição," *Revista do Serviço Público*, I (March, 1950), 14–16.

Morstein-Marx, Fritz. "The Brazilian Civil Service," *Inter-American Quarterly*, II (1940), 48.

———. "O Serviço Civil Brasileiro," *Revista do Serviço Público*, I (January, 1941), 31–33.

Moynihan, Daniel P., and James Q. Wilson. "Patronage in New York State, 1955–1959," *American Political Science Review*, LVIII (June, 1964), 286–301.

Nascimento e Silva, Geraldo Eulálio. "As Qualidades Diplomáticas e as Condições de Ingresso na Carreira," *Revista do Serviço Público*, LXXIX (April, 1958), 20–43.

Nigro, F. "Personnel Administration in Latin America," *Personnel Administration*, XX (1957), 33–39.

Nogueira, Oracy. "Os Movimentos e Partidos Políticos em Itapetininga," *Revista Brasileira de Estudos Políticos*, [no volume no.], No. 11 (June, 1961), 222–247.

"O D.A.S.P. e a Suprema Chefia Executiva" [editorial], *Revista do Serviço Público*, XCII (July, August, September, 1961), 3–6.

Pessoa Sobrinho, Eduardo Pinto. "Administração de Pessoal," *Revista do Serviço Público*, LXXXVI (March, 1960), 131–136.

———. "Classificação de Cargos no Brasil," *Revista do Serviço Público*, III (September–October, 1948), 91–100.

Phelan, J. L. "Authority and Flexibility in the Spanish Imperial Bureaucracy," *Administrative Science Quarterly*, V (June, 1960), 47–65.

Pimental, Antônio Fonseca. "O na Organização Homen do Trabalho," *Jornal do Brasil* (Rio de Janeiro), November 18, 1950, sec. 2, p. 8.

Pinto, Luiz. "Contribuição a Sociologia Administrativa do Brasil," *Revista do Serviço Público*, LXVI (January, 1955), 5–10.

Pondé, Lafayette. "A Responsabilidade dos Funcionários Públicos," *Revista de Direito Administrativo*, XXXV (January–February, 1954), 12–27.

Presthus, R. V. "Behavior and Bureaucracy in Many Cultures," *Public Administration Review*, XIX (Winter, 1959), 25–35.

———. "Weberian v. Welfare Bureaucracy in Traditional Society," *Administrative Science Quarterly*, VI (June, 1961), 1–24.

Price, Don K. "The Parliamentary and Presidential Systems," *Public Administration Review*, III (Autumn, 1943), 317–334.

Ramos, Arlindo Vieira de Almeida. "Base Científica da Administração do Pessoal," *Revista do Serviço Público*, IV (December, 1951), 39–46.

———. "Fundamento dos Princípios de Administração de Pessoal," *Revista do Serviço Público*, I (March, 1954), 33–37.

———. "A Moderna Administração de Pessoal e os Conselhos de Pessoal," *Revista do Serviço Público*, II (April, 1952), 41–55.

———. "Notas sôbre o Estudo da Personalidade em Administração," *Revista do Serviço Público*, I (March, 1943), 16–36.

Reid, Escott. "The Saskatchewan Liberal Machine before 1929," *Canadian Journal of Economics and Political Science*, II (February, 1936), 27–40.

Reining, Henry, Jr. "The Brazilian Program of Administrative Reform," *American Political Science Review*, XXXIX (June, 1945), 536–547.

Reis, Sebastião Alves do. "O Ilícito Disciplinar, na Administração Pública e o Ilícito Penal," *Revista da Faculdade de Ciências Econômicas da Universidade de Minas Gerais*, XI (January–June, 1957), 29–42.

"Reorganizado o Departamento Administrativo do Serviço Público (Decreto-lei No. 8.323-A)," *Revista do Serviço Público*, IX (January, 1946), 90–91.

"Reorganizado o Departamento Administrativo do Serviço Público: Novas Atribuições e Nova Estrutura Já Consubstanciados na Lei Orgânica e no Regimento," *Revista do Serviço Público*, I (February, 1946), 127–128.

Resende, Ernani da Mota. "As Carreiras Profissionais no Serviço Público," *Revista do Serviço Público*, I (January, 1941), 5–30.

Riggs, Fred W. "Relearning an Old Lesson: The Political Context of Development Administration," *Public Administration Review*, XXV (March, 1965), 70–79.

Robson, William A. "The Transplanting of Political Institutions and

Ideas," *Political Quarterly*, XXXV (October–December, 1964), 6–8.

Rodrigues, Nilo M. "A Iluminação Adequada como Fator da Organização do Trabalho," *Revista do Serviço Público*, III (September, 1942), 19–22.

Santos, Edilson Portela Santos. "Evolução da Vida Política no Município de Picos, Piauí," *Revista Brasileira de Estudos Políticos*, [no volume no.], No. 10 (January, 1961), 169–183.

Saraiva, Oscar. "A Crise da Administração," *Revista do Serviço Público*, XI (March–April, 1948), 5–14.

Silva, Benedicto. "O D.A.S.P. na Presidência da República," *Revista do Serviço Público*, XXIV (July–September, 1961), 7–16.

———. "A Moderna Administração de Pessoal," *Revista do Serviço Público*, LXVII (May, 1955), 216–239.

Simon, Herbert A. "The Decision-making Schema: A Reply," *Public Administration Review*, XVIII (Winter, 1958), 60–62.

Sorauf, Frank J. "Patronage and Party," *Midwest Journal of Political Science*, III (May, 1959), 115–126.

Strauch, Ottolmy. "Estabilidade e Demissão por Ineficiência," *Revista do Serviço Público*, III (August, 1941), 5–39.

Tácito, Caio. "O Abuso do Poder Administrativo no Brasil. Conceito e Remédios," *Revista de Direito Administrativo*, LVI (April–June, 1959), 1–28.

———. "O Extranumerário e a Perda da Estabilidade," *Revista do Serviço Público*, II (April, 1953), 7–9.

Távora, General Juarez. "Racionalização Administrativa do Brasil," *Revista do Serviço Público*, LXVII (April, 1955), 5–17.

"Technical Cooperation in Brazil," *Progress in Public Administration*, II (November, 1953), 2–3, 12.

Teixeira, Anísio A. "A Administração Pública Brasileira e a Educação, *Revista Brasileira de Estudos Políticos*, II (January, 1958), 155–180.

Teixeira, Ary. "O Treinamento como Atividade Meio no Serviço Público," *Revista do Serviço Público*, LXIX (October, 1955), 11–15.

Tejera-Paris, Enrique. "Observations on Personnel Management in Latin America," *Public Personnel Review*, XVII (October, 1956), 295–301.

Thompson, Victor A. "Objectives for Development Administration," *Administrative Science Quarterly*, IX (June, 1964), 91–108.

Urwick, Lyndall. "Public Administration and Business Management," *Public Administration Review*, XVII (Spring, 1957), 77–82.

Van Riper, Paul P. "The Constitution and the Patronage," *Personnel Administration*, XI (November, 1948), 1–6.

Viana, Arízio de. "Lo que es el D.A.S.P., *Revista de Ciências Jurídicas y Sociales*, XVII, Nos. 82–85 (1955), 213–218.

———, and Cavalcanti, Araújo. "Trabalho Integral de Estado Maior Administrativo," *Revista do Serviço Público*, XV (June, 1952), 59–72.

Vieira, Astério Dardeau. "Administração de Pessoal," *Revista do Serviço Público*, II (May, 1938), 5–10; II (June, 1938), 9–12; III (July, 1938), 5–8.

———. "O Interêsse Público e o Interêsse Privado na Administração de Pessoal: Estudo Comparativo dos Sistemas Brasileiro e Norte-Americano," *Revista do Serviço Público*, II (April, 1938), 9–12.

Vital, João Carlos. "A Seleção Profissional na Administração Pública do

Brasil," *Arquivos Brasileiros de Psicotécnica*, V (September, 1953), 7–15.

Wahrlich, Beatriz Marqués de Souza. "Administração Geral no Govêrno Brasileiro," *Revista do Serviço Público*, I (January, 1943), 124–129; (February, 1943), 142–151.

——. "O Ensino da Administração Pública e o Treinamento de Servidores Públicos no Brasil," *Revista Brasileira de Estudos Políticos*, XVIII (January, 1965), 57–80.

——. "O Sistema do Mérito na Administração Federal Brasileira," *Revista do Serviço Público*, XX (August, 1957), 237–254.

Waldo, Dwight. "The Administrative State Revisited," *Public Administration Review*, XXV (March, 1965), 5–30.

Walker, Harvey. "Aperfeiçoamento—Décima Reunião Mensal de 1943: Classificação de Cargos," *Revista do Serviço Público*, IV (December, 1943), 99–107.

——. "Public Administration Study in Brazil," *Revue Internationale des Sciences Administratives*, XIX, No. 2 (1953), 374–389.

Weil, Pierre G. "An Experience in Psychological Counseling and Training of Personnel in Brazil," *Training Directors Journal*, XVIII (February, 1964), 3–9.

Willems, Emílio. "Burocracia e Patrimonialismo," *Administração Pública*, III (September, 1945), 3–8.

——. "Problemas de uma Sociologia do Peneiramento," *Revista do Arquivo Municipal* (São Paulo), LXXV (April, 1941), 5–63.

Wilson, James G. "The Economy of Patronage," *Journal of Political Economy*, LXIX (August, 1961), 369–380.

Wohrle, Neusa Feital. "Recrutamento e Publicidade," *Revista do Serviço Público*, LXVI (January, 1955), 24–29.

Wood, Bryce, "A Administração Brasileira Analisada por um Especialista Americano: Uma Interessante Entrevista do Professor Bryce Wood, do Columbia University," *Revista do Serviço Público*, I (February, 1940), 57–58.

——. "O Serviço Civil Brasileiro." Part II. "O Serviço Federal," *Revista do Serviço Público*, II (June, 1941), 44–53.

Worthy, James. "The Problems of Patronage," *Good Government*, LXXII (March–April, 1955), 12–16.

Wyckoff, Theodore. "Brazilian Political Parties," *South Atlantic Quarterly*, LVI (Summer, 1957), 281–298.

Xavier, Rafael. "As Condições Materiais do Trabalho nos Serviços Públicos," *Revista do Serviço Público*, III (August, 1938), 21–24.

Government Documents (Brazil)

Anuário Estatístico do Brasil. Rio de Janeiro: Instituto Brasileiro de Geografia e Estatística, Conselho Nacional de Estatística. Vols. VI (1941–1945), VII (1946), X (1949), XII (1951), XV (1954), XVI (1955), XVII (1956), XVIII (1957), XXI (1960), XXII (1961), XXIII (1962).

Comissão de Estudos e Projetos Administrativos. *Estrutura Atual da Presidência da República*. Rio de Janeiro, 1945.

Comissão do Plano de Classificação de Cargos. *A Classificação de Cargos e a Revisão dos Níveis de Vencimentos do Funcionalismo Civil da*

União. Rio de Janeiro: Comissão do Plano de Classificação de Cargos, 1954.

——. *O Plano de Classificação de Cargos em Resumo.* Rio de Janeiro: D.A.S.P. Departamento Administrativo do Serviço Público, Serviço de Documentação, 1955.

Constitution of the United States of Brazil, 1946 (As Amended). Washington, D.C.: Pan American Union, 1963.

Departamento Administrativo do Serviço Público. *Relatório das Atividades do D.A.S.P., 1956.* Rio de Janeiro: Serviço de Documentação, 1957.

——. *Relatório das Atividades do D.A.S.P., 1957.* Serviço de Documentação, 1958.

——. *Relatório das Atividades do D.A.S.P., 1958.* Serviço de Documentação, 1959.

——. *Relatório das Atividades do D.A.S.P., 1959.* Serviço de Documentação, 1960.

——. *Relatório das Atividades do D.A.S.P., 1960.* Serviço de Documentação, 1961.

——. *Relatório das Atividades do D.A.S.P., 24 de Fevereiro a 10 de Outubro de 1961.* Serviço de Documentação, 1961.

"Lei Número 488—De 15 de Novembro de 1948. Dispõe sôbre o Pagamento de Vencimentos, Renumeração ou Salário de Pessoal Civil e Militário da União," in República dos Estados Unidos do Brasil, *Coleção das Leis de 1948, Atos do Poder Legislativo (Outubro a Dezembro),* Vol. VII, pp. 55–77.

Ministro Extraordinário para a Reforma Administrativa, Coordenador. (Eloah M. G. Barreto, Beatriz Wahrlich, Belmiro Siqueira, *rapporteurs*). "Normas para Preservação e Revigoramento do Sistema do Mérito." Rio de Janeiro: 1963 (mimeographed).

Presidência da República. Comissão de Estudo e Projetos Administrativos. *A Reforma Administrativa.* Vol I (1960): *Reorganização da Presidência da República;* Vol. II (1960): *Criação de Novos Minisérios;* Vol. III (1961): *Normas para Elaboração, Execução e Contrôle Orçamentários;* Vol. IV (1963): *Relatório Final.* Rio de Janeiro: Departamento de Imprensa Nacional.

Serviço Nacional de Recenseamento. *Brasil, Censo Demográfico: VI Recenseamento Geral do Brasil—1950,* Vol. I: Série Nacional. Rio de Janeiro: Instituto Brasileiro de Geografia e Estatística, Conselho Nacional de Estatística, 1956.

——. *Brasil, Sinopse Preliminar do Censo Demográfico: VII Recenseamento Geral do Brasil—1960.* Rio de Janeiro: Instituto Brasileiro de Geografia e Estatística and Serviço Nacional de Recenseamento, 1962.

Survey of the Brazilian Economy, 1959. Washington, D.C.: Brazilian Embassy, 1959.

Unpublished Material

Amaral, Carlos. "As Controvertidas Nomeações de Interinos para a Previdência Social em 1963." (MS to be published under the Fundação Getúlio Vargas case study program in public administration.)

Braibanti, Ralph. "Transnational Inducement of Administrative Reform: A Survey of Scope and Critique of Issues." Bloomington, Ind.: Comparative Administration Group, American Society for Public Administration, and International Development Research Center, Indiana University, 1964 (mimeographed).

Brown, David S. "Concepts and Strategies of Public Administration Technical Assistance: 1945–1963." Bloomington, Ind.: International Development Research Center, 1964 (April). Preliminary draft.

Diamant, Alfred. "Bureaucracy in Developmental Movement Regimes: A Bureaucratic Model for Developing Societies." Bloomington, Ind.: Comparative Administration Group, American Society for Public Administration, and International Development Research Center, Indiana University, 1964 (mimeographed).

————. "Political Development: Approaches to Theory and Strategy." Bloomington, Ind.: Comparative Administration Group, American Society for Public Administration, and International Development Research Center, Indiana University, 1963 (mimeographed).

Escritório do Govêrno Brasileiro para a Coordenação do Programa de Assistência Técnica (Ponto IV), "Folheto-Relatório sôbre o Programa Unificado do Ensino da Administração Pública e de Emprêsas." Mimeographed draft of a report, August, 1964.

Esman, Milton J. "The Politics of Development Administration." Bloomington, Ind.: Comparative Administration Group, American Society for Public Administration, and International Development Research Center, Indiana University, 1963 (mimeographed).

Ford Foundation. "Public Administration in an Ancient Society." Excerpt from a program specialist's report on his mission overseas.

Guerreiro Ramos, Alberto. "Desenvolvimento Tecnológico e Administração a Luz de Modelos Heurísticos." Rio de Janeiro: Centro de Pesquisas Administrativas, Escola Brasileira de Administração Pública, Fundação Getúlio Vargas, 1965 [?] (mimeographed).

Heaphey, James, and Philip Kronenberg. "Toward Theory-building in Comparative Public Administration." Bloomington, Ind.: Comparative Administration Group, American Society for Public Administration, 1966.

Jones, Edward J., Jr. "Brazilian School of Public Administration, Getúlio Vargas Foundation." Report, May 15, 1963 (mimeographed).

————. "End-of-Tour Report, July 12, 1961, to June 21, 1963" (mimeographed).

————. "The Ministry of Labor and Social Welfare." Typescript; n.d.

Keen, Harry. "Fact Book." A collection of materials on US/AID projects and contracts in public and business administration in Brazil.

Loew, Michael. "The Brazilian School of Public Administration, 1951–1956." Report prepared for the United Nations (mimeographed).

Machado, José Teixeira. "Comparative Study of National Budget in the United States and Brazil." Unpublished Master's thesis. Knoxville, Tenn.: University of Tennessee, June, 1957.

————. "The Rediscovery of Politics." Bloomington, Ind.: Comparative Administration Group, American Society for Public Administration, 1964[?], (mimeographed).

Presidência da República, IBGE (Conselho Nacional de Estatística), and Instituto de Previdência e Assistência dos Servidores do Estado, "Apurações do Censo do Servidor Público Federal. Realizado em 15–X–1958. Rio de Janeiro, July 31, 1959 (mimeographed).

Richardson, Ivan L. "Political Science in Brazil: A Selected Bibliography." Bloomington, Ind.: Comparative Administration Group, American Society for Public Administration, 1965 (mimeographed).

Siegel, Gilbert Byron. "The Vicissitudes of Governmental Reform in Brazil: A Study of the DASP." Unpublished Ph.D. dissertation, University of Pittsburgh, 1964.

Wahrlich, Beatriz Marqués de Souza. "An Analysis of DASP: A Contribution to the Study of Comparative Administration." Chicago, Ill.: Public Administration Clearing Service, February, 1955. (Unpublished paper.)

INDEX

Administrative Department of the Public Service (DASP): civil service reform through, 8; as agent of executive, 10, 130–131, 190; creation of, 28–29; functions of, 28–29, 126–127; and budget power, 34, 127; control of, over *extranumerários*, 35; administrative coordination by, during Estado Novo, 36; officials of, interviewed, 83, 85, 86, 89–91, 199; decline of, 125–127, 130–131, 142, 143, 189, 198; surveys civil service appointments, 129, 152; as guardian bureaucracy, 140, 184; opposes *extranumerário* interests, 141; revises *Tabelas Unicas*, 143–145; examinations by, for higher level *extranumerários*, 146; Kubitschek's attitude toward, 147; defends Kubitschek's *interinos* appointments, 148; IAPETC vacancies at disposal of, 154; IAPFESP employees examined by, 156; DNPS requests to, on candidate reports, 157; training program of, with U.S., 166–167; conflict with ministries during Estado Novo, 170; future of, 201; mentioned, 4, 27, 56
Alfonso, Almino: 156
Almond, Gabriel A.: on developing countries, 12; on politics, 14, 181
Amaral, Azevedo: on political goals of civil service, 30–31
Analysis of the Theories of Organization, An: 58
April Revolution: 122, 187
Argyris, Chris: rationalized systems model of, 49–50
Army, Brazilian: 21
Associação dos Servidores Civís do Brasil: protests appointment delays, 142
Association of Brazilian Civil Servants: protests appointment delays, 142
Ato Adicional: causes decentralization, 19
Australia: liberal tradition in, 195

Bahia (state): Canudos rebellion in, 21; administrative reform movement in, 82
Bahia, University of: 167
Banco de Lavoura de Minas Gerais: 199
Banco Nacional de Desenvolvimento Econômico: merit system maintained by, 129
Banks, Arthur S.: on civil service reform, 186; mentioned 14
Barnard, Chester I.: administrative management theory of, 41–42; Estelita Campos compared to, 56–57; Wahrlich on, 58; influence of, on Wahrlich, 77
Barros, Adhemar de: party of, 108
Belo Horizonte: 82, 83
Berquó, Urbano C.: on opposition to reforms, 33–34
Blau, Peter M.: on effective authority, 49; prime-beneficiary model of, 51; mentioned, 59
BNDE: merit system maintained by, 129
Bogotá, Colombia: 78
Bragança, House of: rules Brazil, 18, 162
Brasília: as capital, 82, 201
Brazilian Communist Party (PCB): illegality of, 109
Brazilian Democratic Movement (MOB): continues PSD-PTB alliance, 108
Brazilian Democratic Movement (MDB): continues PSD-PTB alliance, 108
Brazilian Great Tradition: Wagley on, 101
Brazilian Institute of Geography and Statistics (IBGE): patronage in, 156
Brazilian Labor Party (PTB): patronage pressures on, 92; populist style of, 95; use of civil service appointments by, 98; polyarchism of, 105; lack of tradition behind, 106–107; coalition